PATRICK,

THANK YOU FOR YOUR

FRIENDSHIP AND SUPPORT.

I HAVE LEARNED A LOT

FROM YOU.

What They're Saying

In the legal world, the highest form of respect is when another lawyer refers cases to you to handle. Especially when that lawyer is in the exact same specialty and the exact same state in which you practice.

That describes my relationship with John Fisher.

Like John, I am also a medical malpractice and personal injury attorney. I practice in the greater New York metropolitan area. I refer cases to John—cases involving improper medical care, cases involving patients who were injured upstate by careless doctors and hospital staff.

There's only one reason why I would entrust my clients to another attorney in the same state ...

It's because I trust John.

It's because of his integrity.

It's because of his systems.

It's because of how he communicates with our mutual clients.

It's because of his knowledge and experience.

It's because of how he communicates with me as the referring attorney.

It's because of his network of expert physicians who review cases for John in order to confirm whether there is or isn't a valid case to pursue.

Trust and experience are THE MOST IMPORTANT criteria for me as a referring attorney to consider when deciding which lawyer to send a new client to.

Over and over again, I have repeatedly made the choice to send people to John if their matter happened anywhere in upstate New York. This is a choice I intentionally make. You should know that I've been in practice for more than twenty-eight years in New York.

You should also know that John is an accomplished author who wrote a book called The Power of a System. *If you are an entrepreneur or work in any office, this is a MUST-READ. It will help you in understanding how systems run your business and how people run your systems.*

The question I have for you, as a potential client reading this and deciding which lawyer is best for you and your case, is: what are you waiting for? Pick up the phone and call John. I do, and encourage you to do the same.

—Gerry Oginski, Esq., Great Neck, New York

In 2016, someone recommended that I read John's book, The Power of a System. *That book gave me a confidence boost to go out on my own. More importantly, it motivated me to create systems and processes from the start. Fast forward to this November. My poor health forced me out of the office and I wasn't sure when I'd be able to get back to work. Because of the systems in place and my documentation, my team was able to step up and take on tasks I hadn't yet delegated. They kept things moving.*

If it wasn't for John, my entire firm would have been out of office for two weeks and my clients would have had no idea what was going on. John, your advice and your friendship mean more than you know. Thank you for helping me level up my firm. Thank you for this book.

—Joey Vitale, Esq., Chicago, Illinois

John Fisher is a hard-working, resourceful, relentless advocate who treats his clients like close family. Absolutely the "gold standard" among lawyers. To say he's trustworthy and honorable is an incredible understatement.

I've worked with hundreds of lawyers (being one myself), but very few are in John Fisher's league. I feel blessed to know him and reassured that he's a part of a profession that needs more folks like him.

—Ernie Svenson, Esq., New Orleans, Louisiana

Honest, caring, and generous. Those are three (of many) characteristics that set John Fisher apart from other lawyers.

In medical malpractice cases, you have to be prepared for a marathon, not a sprint. It is especially important you pick the right person to run with you; someone who will ensure you get the best results but who will also ensure you have a comfortable journey.

Hands down, John is that person.

—Ramesh Reddy, Esq., New Orleans, Louisiana

In my ongoing quest to improve and streamline my personal injury practice, I was looking for that special "book," which provided the blueprint to accomplish that. In particular, I wanted to establish a firm that would run itself, like big, fine-tuned businesses do. I desired to focus on the firm's strategic planning and marketing, delegate responsibility, and spend less time on depositions, drafting documents, and routine office tasks.

Finally, I found The Power of a System, *which I consider to be the Bible for a successful personal injury practice. Not only does it outline a structured plan on how to systematize all aspects of the practice, but it also gives you the roadmap to successfully meet your goals and make your practice shine. If you desire a prosperous and fine-tuned personal injury practice, I encourage you to read this book. It is a book like no other.*

—Albert Cohen, Esq., Forest Hills, New York

John Fisher is the smartest guy in the room. We worked together forming The Mastermind Experience for attorneys. He's a superb marketer, an excellent discussion leader, and a real human being. I highly recommend his book, The Power of a System.

—Larry Bodine, Esq., Tucson, Arizona

While not a client, I am a fellow lawyer, and I've heard John Fisher speak several times. I don't know that I've met an attorney who is so committed and dedicated to helping injured clients. That, coupled with his organization, knowledge of medical malpractice law, and reputation nationwide is truly amazing.

—Jason Kohlmeyer, Esq., Mankato, Minnesota

John Fisher is the epitome of a trusted advisor and legal authority. He has an incredible wealth of knowledge and is truly generous with his time. His diligence and dedication to the legal profession is unmatched.

—Dayne Phillips, Esq., Lexington, South Carolina

I can honestly say I'm light years ahead in my law practice as a result of John's book, The Power of a System. *In my opinion, this should be added to the required reading.*

—Keith Magness, Esq., New Orleans, Louisiana

John Fisher was a big hit with our attendees. John received rave reviews on the feedback questionnaire—it was very plain to see that he was easily one of the top speakers at our event.

My staff repeatedly kept hearing John's name come up in conversations between attendees, and a great deal of the remarks were comments expressing just how impressed they were with the knowledge he demonstrated of The Secrets of Referral Based Marketing, and his overall exposition of the material.

Once again, thank you for contributing to the success of our PILMMA Super Summit. It is our hope to bring you back next year!

—Ken Hardison, Esq., president and founder of PILMMA, North Myrtle Beach, South Carolina

John Fisher's The Power of a System *is exactly what I have been looking for in my four years of poring through business systems and law practice management books.*

It not only serves as a step-by-step guide to creating the law firm business that you always dreamed of, but could also serve as an operations manual without much customization.

It's an incredible gift to the legal community.

—Will Norman, Esq., Cleveland, Ohio

The mere fact that John Fisher puts, at the disposal of the public, a book that discloses any and everything related to his success means a lot.

I have read John Fisher's The Power of a System *from beginning to end. Even as a foreign lawyer working in a different field, I found John Fisher's book to be invaluable. It generously gives the ingredients for accurate and precise business development for any lawyer anywhere.*

—Bertrand Mariaux, Esq., Luxembourg

I've been practicing law for thirty years. It took me the first ten of those years to "figure things out" and start having control over my practice and life. I believe that if I had John's book back when I started, the exciting and often unpredictable learning curve I experienced during those first ten years would have been reduced down to one or two months.

For that reason, my recommendation is, if you're going to build the practice of your dreams, read John's book! His advice will accelerate the success process and save years of time!

—Mitch Jackson, Esq., Laguna Hills, California (2013 California Litigation Lawyer of the Year)

John Fisher is incredible. He's smart, eloquent, and caring. John is also incredibly generous, especially with his time and knowledge.

I live 1,443 miles from John, yet I'm not the only lawyer in my neck of the woods that idolizes John. His influence is that widespread and deep. Attorneys and clients across the country admire his skill. He is a rock star!

—Parker Layrisson, Esq., Ponchatoula, Louisiana

The Power of a System *is a must read for personal injury lawyers looking to build a better law firm. Written along the lines of John Morgan's book,* You Can't Teach Hungry, *and the classic* E-Myth *books, this book provides practical steps and gives valuable lessons.*

For personal injury lawyers looking to increase their book of business, improve their staff and procedures, manage their practice like a well-oiled machine, and to have time for the lawyer to do the things for the clients that matter most—this book is a ten.

—Rich Newsome, Esq., Orlando, Florida (former president of the Florida Justice System)

The Power of a System *is an indispensable tool for any lawyer who wants to build a successful practice. So much of what lawyers learn in law school has zero to do with the practice of law, much less running a law practice. I highly recommend this book for any lawyer in any type of practice.*

Its principles can be applied from the solo practitioner to an associate at a large law firm. In the weeks since reading The Power of a System, *I have revamped the way my staff interacts with me and my clients and the results have been fantastic. Follow this simple guide and watch your practice get better overnight.*

—John W. Dill, Esq., Orlando, Florida

The Power of a System *simulates sitting down with a mentor and hearing how they put together a successful contingency based practice. From operations to marketing to practicing law, John Fisher lays out his system for success.*

Whether you are just starting out or have a successful practice The Power of a System *will have plenty for you. I highly recommend it.*

—Seth Price, Esq., Washington, DC

For John Fisher who opened my eyes to a world of staying committed to your principles and vision in the practice and business of law!

—William "The Law Man" Umansky, Esq., Orlando, Florida (dedication from the book, *Tiger Tactics*)

The Law Firm of Your Dreams

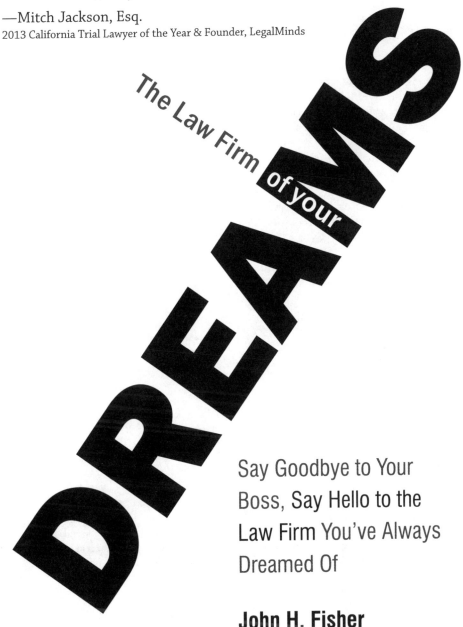

"This is the stuff they don't teach in law school."
—Mitch Jackson, Esq.
2013 California Trial Lawyer of the Year & Founder, LegalMinds

The Law Firm of your DREAMS

Say Goodbye to Your Boss, Say Hello to the Law Firm You've Always Dreamed Of

John H. Fisher

Advantage®

Published by Advantage, Charleston, South Carolina.
Member of Advantage Media Group.

ADVANTAGE is a registered trademark, and the Advantage colophon is a trademark of Advantage Media Group, Inc.

Printed in the United States of America.

10 9 8 7 6 5 4 3 2 1

ISBN: 978-1-59932-864-5
LCCN: 2019906681

Cover design by Katie Biondo.
Layout design by Megan Elger.

This publication is designed to provide accurate and authoritative information in regard to the subject matter covered. It is sold with the understanding that the publisher is not engaged in rendering legal, accounting, or other professional services. If legal advice or other expert assistance is required, the services of a competent professional person should be sought.

Advantage Media Group is proud to be a part of the Tree Neutral® program. Tree Neutral offsets the number of trees consumed in the production and printing of this book by taking proactive steps such as planting trees in direct proportion to the number of trees used to print books. To learn more about Tree Neutral, please visit **www.treeneutral.com**.

Advantage Media Group is a publisher of business, self-improvement, and professional development books and online learning. We help entrepreneurs, business leaders, and professionals share their Stories, Passion, and Knowledge to help others Learn & Grow. Do you have a manuscript or book idea that you would like us to consider for publishing? Please visit **advantagefamily.com** or call **1.866.775.1696**.

For being the best role model a lawyer could have,
James H. Fisher, Esq.

"Victory is always possible for the person who refuses to stop fighting."

—Napoleon Hill

Table of Contents

Part 1: The Power of Mind-set

Part 2: The Manager

MANAGEMENT OF YOUR TEAM

CASE MANAGEMENT

GOAL SETTING AND FINANCIAL MANAGEMENT

Part 3: The Entrepreneur

NON-DIGITAL MARKETING

INTERNET MARKETING

SOCIAL MEDIA MARKETING

THE ENTREPRENEURIAL LAWYER'S SECRET WEAPONS

Part 4: The Trial Lawyer

TRIAL PREPARATION

JURY SELECTION, TRIAL SKILLS & NEGOTIATION

Foreword

Most law firm practice management books are so general and non-specific that they come to be worthless. Many are written by those who have never run a successful law firm, so there is no good reason to trust the advice. Follow what you read in those books and you'll find yourself right back in the middle of the pack. It's fine to be there, if by deliberate choice, but it's not *really* what most of us want.

The Law Firm of Your Dreams is different. John Fisher is a real lawyer slugging it out in the competitive medical malpractice area in New York's very competitive jurisdiction. Within these pages you'll find not only John's advice, but his actual checklists and forms for creating the law firm of your dreams.

Importantly, John Fisher gives you the "why" behind each piece of advice he gives. The firm you build will be different—because you'll build it to suit your goals and ambitions—but if you follow John's blueprint, you'll likely avoid many of the mistakes he's made, which he reveals throughout the book. This will free up your creative self to be the very best lawyer you can be for your clients.

In the end, isn't this what we all want? A practice built so that our very best talents are used in the service of those we represent.

Ben Glass, Esq., Fairfax, Virginia
BenGlassLaw.com
GreatLegalMarketing.com

Introduction

A STORY OF REDEMPTION

In the fall of 1993, a thirty-year-old African-American man, Michael, came to my office for a consultation. Michael had sustained a brain injury when he was struck by a motorcycle after exiting a bus at an unsafe and dangerous location in a busy intersection. I knew nothing about personal injury law, but I was convinced that Michael's case had merit and promised to help.

After immersing myself in the procedures of personal injury law and the medical and legal aspects of proving a traumatic brain injury, Michael's case settled for a modest sum after one week of trial. I was disappointed in the result and disgusted by my discovery of a racist juror, but I had found my calling. There was nothing that would ever be as fascinating and gratifying as catastrophic injury law, and I made a decision to devote the rest of my career to the most seriously injured.

My Big Chance

In 1996, I got my big chance. An associate's position opened at a nationally prominent catastrophic injury law firm, and I jumped at the chance. I was thrown into the fire with complex injury and medical malpractice cases. There was no partner looking over my shoulder at the trials—I was the one and only lawyer for the injury victim in court, and everything rested on my novice trial skills. Somehow I survived.

Truth be told, I had more than my share of defense verdicts. I found that juries are unpredictable, have little attention span, and often render verdicts that have nothing to do with the evidence (or logic). Discouraged, but not beaten, I fought on.

In 1999, I became a non-equity partner in the law firm, and I thought my future was bright. In hindsight, I was extraordinarily naive.

A Big Wake-Up Call

In the summer of 2007, I handled a complex case involving an extremely dangerous railroad grade crossing. The grade crossing had been the site of way too many collisions between trains and tractor trailers, and I was determined to do what I could to prevent another wreck. I was facing the best railroad defense lawyer in the business, and the case involved complicated and novel issues of law and fact. Worse yet, I was learning railroad law on the fly.

The case settled after a week of trial, and I was happy with the result ... but my bosses weren't. Shortly after the trial, I was asked to meet with the senior partners, and I was told that I was "incompetent." The assessment made by the senior partners was tough to swallow after years as a partner, but it prompted a radical change in my mind-set.

I realized that working for someone else had no security—I could be fired at any time, even as a partner with a history of multi-million-dollar results. I had to begin planning for my departure from the firm. To be ready for that day, I needed one thing more than anything else: clients.

A Long-Overdue Epiphany

I realized—perhaps for the first time—that the practice of law involved a lot more than technical proficiency. Even the most gifted trial lawyers can struggle to make a living, and it finally dawned on me why: being a great trial lawyer means nothing without clients.

I realized what few lawyers ever admit: getting clients is the most important thing lawyers do. While lawyers will begrudgingly admit that marketing is important, few ever do anything to improve their systems for getting clients. I was determined to avoid this mistake.

I began devoting my time and spare money to building marketing systems, both online and offline. I immersed myself in books and seminars about marketing and learned everything I could. Slowly, things began to change. New clients and referring lawyers began calling me from across the country. A little at a time, my marketing efforts were paying off.

The Best Thing that Ever Happened

On June 2, 2010, I was called into a meeting with the senior partners. At first we made small talk, and then one of the senior partners dropped a bomb: "John, it's time we part ways." I knew eventually the day would come where I would have to fend for myself, but I was the guy bringing the clients to the firm. As that guy, I thought I had job security. I was wrong. I had no idea at the time that this would be the best thing that would ever happen for my career.

I had little to work with: no secretary, computer, or office equipment. But I had one thing that counted more than anything else: clients. Four months after being fired, I settled a case for $2 million, and I was off to the races—still making tons of mistakes and learning about law firm management on the fly, but also having fun and kicking some butt.

Only You Can Control Your Future

Fast forward to the summer of 2019. Following a deposition, a long-time adversary/defense lawyer pulled me aside and volunteered, "I must say, you're happier than I've ever seen you." Wow, didn't expect that. But the defense lawyer was spot on. I was never really happy working for someone else. My life was comfortable, and I paid my bills, but that isn't what life is really about.

Life is about taking a chance (sometimes an extreme risk) to live the life of your dreams. There are many more ups and downs in solo law practice than I ever could have imagined, but with small, incremental improvements made on a daily basis, anything is possible. Taking a risk is not really risking anything at all—*failing to take the chance is the real risk.*

> *"Playing it safe is the most dangerous thing you can do."*
> —**Grant Cardone,** *Be Obsessed or Be Average*

No law firm will take care of you—you can't expect your boss to look out for you. Even if you are an equity partner at a prominent law firm, one day you will eventually be on your own, without a safety net. The sooner you confront this reality and begin taking steps to build the law firm of your dreams, the better off you will be.

Learn from My Mistakes and Failures

I wrote this book, *The Law Firm of Your Dreams*, to help show you the mistakes I've made and the policies and systems that have made a big difference. I hope you can implement some of them to build the law firm of your dreams. You may not agree with everything, but take what you can and start building the systems and policies that will give you the law firm—and life—that you've always dreamed of.

And maybe, one day, you'll thank your lucky stars that your bosses fired you.

Your Takeaway from My Story

Without this backstory, you would not be able to relate to me. I'd just be another lawyer. You share your backstory because you want prospective clients to know about your weaknesses and vulnerabilities. If they can relate to where you came from, they will follow you. This is how you become a leader.

Redemption stories are powerful because they show the benefits of going through hardship and meeting challenges. Most lawyers never use this tool.

> *"The degree of success you achieve in life is directly proportional to the amount of pain you can tolerate."*
> **—Jon Morrow**

No one wants to hear about the perfect lawyer, yet most of us try to put on a facade of perfection and end up alienating the prospective clients we are trying to reach. Once your clients know you're not perfect—that you have flaws—they will empathize with you, because you are just like them: imperfect.

A Lawyer's Brilliant Backstory

Florida injury lawyer, Craig Goldenfarb, Esq., uses his backstory in his TV ads. Craig's most effective TV ad tells the story of his mother's background as a lawyer and how her story inspired him to become a lawyer.

The story does not scream, "Hire me. I'm the best lawyer on the planet." The story mentions nothing about settlements, verdicts, or Craig's skills, but instead tells his backstory—namely, why he became a lawyer. This is powerful stuff and, it turns out, is very effective in attracting new clients. Why? Because no other lawyers are doing this, and the prospective clients can empathize with Craig's story.

Does this tactic work? Craig has fifty-five employees and is one of the premier injury lawyers in the ultra-competitive market of South Florida. You can be the judge.

Beyond *The Power of a System*

This book goes deeper into the policies and systems for a multimillion-dollar personal injury law firm than my first book, *The Power of a System*. If you have not read *The Power of a System*, I suggest that you read it first. *The Power of a System* is, in essence, our law firm's office manual, and lays out every detail of our systems and policies.

You will find that this book incorporates more detailed versions of our firm's policies and systems—I just ran out of space in *The Power of a System*.

What This Book Is About

The Law Firm of Your Dreams has four basic parts:
1.   The Power of Mind-set

2.   The Manager

3.   The Entrepreneur

4.   The Trial Lawyer

Mind-set is the most important. Without the right mind-set, the best policies and systems won't do you much good—that's why I put "The Power of Mind-set" first. Controlling your thoughts—both positive and negative—is the most important thing you do.

"The Manager" delves deep into specific management policies. I did not create this management style—it is derived from great books such as Verne Harnish's *Mastering the Rockefeller Habits*, Matthew Kelly's *The Dream Manager*, and Brian Moran's and Michael Lennington's *The 12 Week Year*. "The Manager" has three categories, namely, management of your team, case management, and goal setting and financial management.

"The Entrepreneur" is a more advanced look at marketing than is found in *The Power of a System*. "The Entrepreneur" has four parts consisting of non-digital marketing, internet marketing, social media marketing, and the entrepreneurial lawyer's secret weapons. I give you everything I've got.

"The Trial Lawyer" gives you my best tips for jury selection, trial techniques, and getting the best settlement.

Throughout the book, I refer at times to laws in New York State, where I practice. For those practicing law outside of New York, I hope you can apply these policies to the law in your state.

My Gratitude for You

Most of all, a humble "Thank you" for picking up this book. Just by reading this book, you've shown that an average life is not good enough. You want something more. To the extent that you can leverage my failures, mistakes, and few successes, I congratulate you for taking action.

Now, let's get started building the law firm of your dreams.

Part 1

THE POWER OF MIND-SET

I'd tell men and women in their mid-twenties not to settle for a job or a profession or even a career. Seek a calling.

If you're following your calling, the fatigue will be easier to bear, the disappointments will be fuel, the highs will be like nothing you've ever felt.

—Phil Knight, "Shoe Dog"

1

THE BEST ADVICE
I EVER GOT

At the time, it seemed like a rude thing to say.

I was fresh out of law school and trying to figure out what to do with the rest of my life. I was taking any new client I could get my hands on and was struggling, but I was starting to make some inroads at my father's law practice in upstate New York. My dad was referring new cases on occasion, and I was starting to grow a client base by accepting almost any new client who walked through the door. I was beginning to think I knew what I was doing and was starting to build confidence.

Then, seemingly out of nowhere, one of my father's real estate clients said something to me that seemed strange (and a bit rude) at the time. As this forty-something-year-old man was waiting around in the reception of my dad's law office, he stopped me as I was walking by and said, "You need to get out of here."

At first, this seemed more than a little rude, and I had no idea what he meant, until he explained, "If you stay here at [my father's law practice in upstate New York], you will always be in the shadow of your father. You might become the best lawyer in town, but you will always be judged as someone who simply rode your dad's coattails." He went on, "You should leave and prove yourself somewhere else for five or ten years, and if you're good, you can always come back … after you've proven yourself."

Deep down, I knew my dad thought the same thing—he just wanted me to figure it out on my own. So, I left that small town in upstate New York in August, 1992, to stake my own claim in the world.

Three Secrets to Success that Will Change Your Career

In hindsight, I realize that I was clueless as a young lawyer in the early to mid-nineties. Like almost everyone else, I had no clear sense of what I wanted to do after law school. I accepted what everyone told me: work hard, and you will have all the clients you want, lots of money, and a good life. What a bunch of crap!

There are secrets to building a great law practice, and like everyone else, I had to learn through trial and error. But if I could get in a time machine and go back to my father's law office in the early nineties to have a chat with myself, I wouldn't say, "Work hard and everything will be fine." Instead, I'd have a much different conversation about three secrets that will make all the difference in my (and your) law career.

#1: Become a Specialist

First, I'd tell the young me that you have to specialize in something. Find what you love to do and then *say "no"* to everything else. I know, lawyers are not supposed to say we are "specialists" in anything—

our ethical rules say this is a "no-no." *But if you don't specialize in something, you will be marginal in everything.*

The days of the general practitioner are long gone. Perhaps thirty or forty years ago, you could be all things for all clients, but now, you'd be a lawyer who's bad at just about everything. Even worse, as a general practitioner, you will be viewed as "just another lawyer," and consumers will view you as a commodity that they can buy for the lowest fee.

A specialist limits their practice to a very narrow area of the law and becomes an expert in it. Your website, letterhead, and all of your marketing materials are designed to send a single message: you only do one thing, and you're damn good at it. A specialist commands respect from consumers, injury victims, and other members of the bar.

When a new injury client is interviewing lawyers and sees that you limit your practice to a single, very specific area of the law while your competitors are the quintessential "jacks of all trades and masters of none," who do you think that client is going to hire? You make it much easier for prospective clients to hire you by promoting yourself as a specialist.

But even better, by limiting your practice to a very specific area of law, you become a master of it. You're damn proud of this, and you'll put yourself up against anyone. But this is only the first piece of advice I'd give to the young, inexperienced version of me.

#2: Delegate Almost Everything

Your career (and life) will be chaos if you answer every phone call or email during your workday. You will never get home in time for dinner or attend your kids' ball games if you insist on being everything for your clients. That's why you have to delegate everything you can and do only those things that you cannot delegate.

Before you do anything, think: can this task be delegated to your secretary or paralegal? If so (and I'm guessing the answer is "yes" for almost all of your tasks), you have to delegate that task.

Now, I know what you're thinking. "Okay, but I can do this task faster and better than anyone else." This is exactly the type of thinking that will ruin you. Granted, there are certain things that only I can do. I can't delegate depositions and trials, for example, because our paralegal doesn't have a law degree. But I can delegate almost everything else.

But don't stop with your law practice. Try delegating the menial, time-consuming tasks in your personal life. Hire someone in your town on Craigslist for a few bucks an hour to do your grocery shopping and get your dry cleaning. Guess what—you saved three or four hours a week and can spend more time building your law practice and attending your kids' ball games.

#3: Getting Clients is Your Most Important Job

This is one thing law schools get wrong. Sure, they teach you everything you need to know about torts, contracts, and constitutional law, but that's only a small piece of what you need for success.

There should be mandatory classes on marketing in every law school in America, but they don't offer a single class or even an hour of instruction on owning and operating your law firm. Perhaps our erudite law professors expect us to learn practice-building through osmosis.

The best thing you can do for your career is to devote as much time and energy as you can to marketing and growing your law practice. Now, this is a taboo subject among most lawyers—I know,

I know, you're a lawyer not a marketer. But this is precisely the type of thinking that can prevent you from having the career and life you work so hard for.

If you are not marketing and growing your law practice every day, it doesn't matter if you're the greatest lawyer in the world. You will be sitting around, waiting for the phone to ring with your next case. If there's only one thing I could tell the young, naive me back in 1992, it's that learning and implementing marketing in your law practice is the single most important thing you can do.

Action Is Everything

Yes, specializing, delegating, and marketing are the three cornerstones for a successful law practice. But these concepts are meaningless without one final ingredient: ACTION!

> *"In the real world, you have to take real 'action' to succeed."*
> —T. Harv Eker, *Secrets of the Millionaire Mind*

It's easy to stay in your comfort zone and keep doing things the way you have. But taking action and implementing specific policies in your practice are what separates the winners from the wannabes.

My final words of advice for the young, naive me are to take action every single day, even if it's a small baby step toward your goals. You will not see any concrete changes in a few weeks or even two to three months, but you will begin to see changes in six months if you take small steps toward your goals every day. And after a year or so, you will be stunned at the changes in your law practice (and your life), and your professional and personal worlds will never be the same.

2

HOW TO DEFINE YOUR LAW FIRM'S CORE VALUES

Most elite law firms recognize the importance of having a basic set of core values that dictate how the firm and its employees behave. A law firm's core values are akin to its constitution: bedrock principles that will be around for the life of your law firm. When questions are raised, the employees can refer to the firm's core values for answers. With core values, your employees have guidance and a clear sense of right and wrong.

Let's put this in a real-world setting. Following a settlement, the defense lawyer calls your paralegal to request confidentiality of the terms and amount of the settlement. Your paralegal doesn't ask you what to do, because they already know one of your core values is, "We never agree to confidentiality." Your paralegal tells the defense lawyer that there is no settlement if confidentiality is a condition of the settlement, and the defense lawyer quickly backs off. Problem solved, and you didn't have to do a damn thing.

This is the beauty of having a set of core values—your staff knows what to do when you're not in the office. You're not confronted with a barrage of questions from your staff, because they already know what to do. Your core values are reinforced at daily and weekly meetings, and you post a framed picture of your core values in your conference room.

Most law firms, however, make the mistake of creating core values that are aspirational—for example, "We do the right thing"— that could be copied and used as the core values for any law firm or business. Aspirational values are what you want the values of the law firm to be, such as integrity, compassion, and service. But your staff will know if your core values aren't real, and they'll become cynical if you're not living what you preach. Aspirational core values can actually hurt your law firm.

> *"Some values are desirable, but not true. We call these 'aspirational values' because they are worthy of our aspirations."*
> —Patrick Lencioni, *The Three Big Questions for a Frantic Family*

The problem is that when lawyers sit down to agree upon their core values, they ask, "What should our core values be?" rather than, "What are our core values?" And what they come up with is a list of aspirational values that look nothing like the actual values of the law firm.

How to Create Your Law Firm's Core Values

You should create your law firm's core values by focusing on your law firm's current, actual values. What are the values that guide your law firm *right now*? These values should be completely unique to your law firm so that you cannot imagine any other law firm having the same values. It doesn't really matter what your values are, just that you have them and that you are living by them *right now*.

> *"Those are traits or qualities that are fundamental parts*
> *of an organization's culture. You don't make them up, you*
> *just look around and describe what's already true."*
> —Patrick Lencioni, *The Three Big Questions for a Frantic Family*

Begin by looking at the traits of your best secretary, paralegal, or lawyer. What values do they actually live by? If a Martian came down from outer space to watch your law firm, what would it think are your core values? Write them down, and ask your staff whether the values are real. If they are, you're on the road to creating your law firm's core values.

Our Practice: The Difference between Aspirational Values and Actual Values

We made the same mistake made by most businesses when we created aspirational values that weren't real. In 2013, our core values began like this:

Our Aspirational (and Forgettable) Ten Core Values in 2013

1. We limit our practice to catastrophic injury law for injury victims.

2. We do NOT accept cases that have questionable merit.

3. We accept very few cases.

4. We always put our clients' interests first.

5.   We treat our clients like family.

6.   We do the right thing.

7.   We do what we say we'll do.

8.   We practice open, real communication.

9.   We check our egos at the door.

10.   We invest in continuous improvement.

These core values are aspirational, forgettable, and for the most part, *not real*. Sure, they sound good, and we could impress our friends and family with them, but they're not *real*. I sensed that our team was not completely committed to these values, and more importantly, they didn't live by them.

> *"No culture book is worth much unless it reflects cultures and values that are already in place."*
> —Tony Hsieh, *Delivering Happiness*

We shifted focus to the core values we were actually using at that moment in time, and here's what we came up with:

Our Four Core Values (2020)

1.   We only handle catastrophic injury cases.

2.   We never agree to confidential settlements.

3.   We do NOT accept cases that have questionable merit.

4.   We are brutally honest with our clients.

This set of four core values is simple, basic, and *real*. If facing a lie detector test, any member of our team could truthfully answer that these core values are real and currently practiced by our law firm.

And here's another nice thing about simplifying your core values: they are so basic that they're tough to forget.

It's easy to come up with ten core values for your law firm, but when it comes to core values, fewer is better. Your staff won't remember ten core values, and those values will become aspirational, poster-board fluff that will not guide the actions of your team. Try to keep your core values to three to five simple, basic principles that everyone agrees upon.

But you're just getting started. Share your core values with your staff, and ask them to critique the values—no fluff allowed. You want your team to assault your core values: "That's crap, we don't actually do that!" By letting your staff help create your core values, they will buy into your values.

How to Instill Your Core Values in Your Team

Core values are meaningless if your staff doesn't know what they are. Once you've identified core values for your law firm, you must instill them in your staff. Begin by posting your core values everywhere. Some businesses post a framed picture of their core values in the copy room or in their lobby. Perhaps you put the core values in your email signature or monthly newsletter, or on a large infographic at the front door of your office.

At Zappos, when new employees join the company, they are required to sign a document stating that they have read the core values document and understand that living up to the core values is part of their job expectation.

"When you walk with purpose, you collide with destiny."
—Beatrice Berry

But whatever you do, you don't want to just *have* a set of core values—you want to make sure your team knows what they are and has reminders that continually reinforce them. Once you have a set of core values, you will have a shared belief system that will guide everyday decisions of your team for as long as your law firm is in business. Talk about a specific core value at weekly and daily meetings with your team, and celebrate moments when a team member applies a core value to a real-world problem.

Every day I tell our prospective clients that even with the best case in the world, there is a fifty-fifty chance they will lose their malpractice case. Why do I do this? One of our core values is brutal honesty with our clients. Almost without fail, our clients appreciate our brutal honesty, and it strengthens our relationship.

Before long, your secretary and paralegal will share examples of how they applied one of your core values. During a daily team meeting, your paralegal will share that they were "brutally honest" in telling a prospective client that they don't have a case. This is when you know your core values are actually being used for guidance. When this happens, politely excuse yourself from the room, go outside, and shout at the top of your lungs, "Hell yeah!"

How to Instill Your Core Values with Your Book of the Month

Core values can be quickly forgotten in the hectic workday. You have a whole lot on your plate from trials, depositions, and paperwork, and let's face it: instilling core values at your law firm might not be your first priority. But if you're not focused on reinforcing your law firm's core values, your team will forget them in the grind of the workday.

A book reading program at your law firm is a simple and effective way to reinforce your core values. Here's how it works: pick one book a month that illustrates your firm's core values—let's say the core value is "excellent client service." Pick a book that breathes life into this value, such as *Fish!* or *The Fred Factor* (both must reads for any business).

> *"There is power in reading good books and sharing ideas as a team."*
> —Mark Sanborn, *Fred 2.0*

Buy extra copies of the book and hand them out to your team members with a read-by date. Give your team members one month to read the book, and at the end of the month, meet to discuss the book. Your employees will answer questions about the book and highlight points that were interesting to them.

For employees who want to read more, you should create a library of your recommended books (check out my list of recommended books at the end of this book) and take your employees to lunch whenever they read a new book.

> *"The endeavor encourages the exchange of ideas and creative thinking, and it acknowledges everyone's thoughts and experience."*
> —Mark Sanborn, *Fred 2.0*

Reading books creates a common bond that includes everyone on your team, whether they are an associate, paralegal, secretary, or janitor. But more important, it shows your team that you care about their growth and personal development, and ultimately, you will be the beneficiary of a team that cares about learning and shares your values.

3

WHY LAW FIRMS DIE

The question at first seemed simple enough. A business owner asks the executive officers of Infusionsoft (now known as Keap), "What separates those who succeed from those who fail?" Infusionsoft's chief technology officer quickly responds in a matter-of-fact way, "That's easy. Those who schedule firm dates for quarterly strategic meetings *right now* will succeed—everyone else will struggle."

The executive leaders of Infusionsoft nod in unison. It's almost as if the executive team at Infusionsoft is surprised the question was even asked, and meanwhile, I'm convinced that I've just discovered the holy grail for the success of my law firm. It sounds simple and pretty basic—you'd think all lawyers have strategic planning days with their leadership team at least once in a while, right?

The truth is that virtually no lawyers plan their future with strategic planning. Lawyers run around putting out fires and doing the "lawyer work" that we all must do (depositions, paperwork, and trials), and *maybe* they set aside a day every once in a while to discuss big plans for their law firm. But how many of you plan your future

with quarterly meetings with your team? Well, let's be straight—
pretty close to no one does this.

> *"If you frequently defer the strategic work to accomplish the urgent,*
> *lower-value activities, you will never accomplish great things."*
>
> —Brian P. Moran and Michael Lennington, *The 12 Week Year*

Working *on your business* (strategic thinking) rather than *in your
business* (technical work) is the biggest mind-set difference between
great law firms and those that struggle. You need to set aside a day
with your team to think about where you're going and how you'll get
there—this is the power of strategic planning for lawyers. If you have
no vision for your law firm, you'll spend your career letting others
dictate your future.

The Power of Strategic Planning: Alignment of Your Team around a Specific Goal

Do you think great American companies, like Infusionsoft, just run
around from one task to the next without a clear vision of where
they're going? Of course not. And like great companies, successful
law firms have a plan for their future; their quarterly planning gives
them clear goals and creates alignment among their team.

> *"Unless a company has the ability to determine where it*
> *is today and project where it's going to be this week, this*
> *month, this quarter, and this year, it's not on a trajectory*
> *for growth. It might not even be on track for survival."*
>
> —Verne Harnish, *Mastering the Rockefeller Habits*

Your quarterly meeting might focus on reducing the time it takes to get a case to trial. You should track the time it takes to serve discovery responses, complete depositions, and between the filing of the lawsuit and the trial. Now you're tracking every step of a lawsuit and discovering why some of your "A" cases are taking too long to get to trial.

With strategic quarterly planning, you're identifying what works and what doesn't. But you're not just fixing the glitches in the systems of your law firm; you're communicating with your key team members and making sure they're "buying in" to the solutions.

Three Simple Rules for Your Quarterly Strategic Meeting

So, you've finally agreed to set aside a day for a quarterly strategic planning meeting with your team. Kudos—you're ahead of the 98 percent of lawyers who refuse to set aside time to think strategically about the future of their law firm. You won't get anywhere without a vision for your future, and there is nothing better than a day committed to crafting the vision.

Rule One: Meet at an Off-Site Location

Do not bother scheduling a quarterly meeting without following rule 1: Your quarterly strategic meeting *cannot* be held in your office. It's easy to promise you'll shut the doors of your office and refuse to let anyone interrupt you, but little "emergencies" will pop up, and inevitably you'll be pulled away from your meeting.

With an off-site location, you force yourself to spend the day focused on the biggest problem facing your law firm—you can't wander off to take an urgent phone call or respond to emails. All of the little emergencies (phone calls, emails, client visits) must be put on hold for the day, or the quarterly meeting will be a waste of time.

The off-site location should be somewhere that no one can find you. This might be the jury deliberation room at the courthouse or a conference room at a hotel—it really doesn't matter where, only that you are guaranteed a day of total solitude.

Rule Two: Eliminate All Interruptions and BS

Ask your staff to clear your schedule for the day—no appointments, no phone calls, etc. It's tempting to squeeze in a phone call or meeting with a new client for later in the day, but this will get in the way of your commitment to focusing on the single most important problem facing your law firm.

> *"What most often keeps you from being exceptional is not a lack of time, but the way you allocate the time you have."*
> —Brian P. Moran and Michael Lennington, *The 12 Week Year*

Set three simple ground rules for the meeting:
- Turn off cell phones.
- No web surfing or text messages during breaks.
- No BS!

If your ideas suck, tell your team that you want them to tell you. Your team understands the biggest problems facing your law firm, and you want to pick their minds for solutions. Perhaps *you* are the biggest problem facing your firm, if you're not responding to your team when they need your feedback. You want to confront the issue, discuss specific ideas for fixing it, and make a concrete plan.

Rule Three: Post Your "Rallying Cry"

What exactly do you do at a quarterly strategic planning meeting? Begin by setting an agenda. Your agenda might consist of the biggest management or marketing problem facing your law firm. Ask for your team's input about the number-one problem facing your firm, and get their help setting the agenda.

The agenda should be super simple and measurable—avoid the temptation to bite off too much. When it comes to the scope of quarterly strategic meetings, *less is more*. The agenda (a.k.a. "rallying cry") for your quarterly strategic meeting might look like this:

- Getting trial dates for your best lawsuits within ninety days.

- Measuring smart numbers (a.k.a. key performance indicators) on a monthly basis for case management, income, marketing, and website.

- Creating a five-year strategic plan for your law firm (i.e., what your perfect law firm looks like).

Be as specific as possible in drafting the agenda, and give the agenda to your staff before the meeting. Ask your team to think about ways of fixing the problem and bring specific ideas to the meeting. The quarterly meeting should be a collaboration and exchange of ideas, and the best input will come from your team, because they understand the problems facing your firm better than you.

> *"The key is to rally the entire leadership team—and thus, everyone else in the organization—around a single purpose for a given period of time."*
>
> —Patrick Lencioni, *Silos, Politics, and Turf Wars*

This is the magic ingredient for a successful quarterly meeting: post your rallying cry on a poster board in your conference room. The rallying cry will be the number-one goal of you and your staff for the next ninety days, and the poster board will remind you to keep your goal "top of mind" at your daily and weekly meetings.

Celebrate moments of progress when you reach important milestones. The rallying cry from our law firm's last quarterly strategic meeting was simple: we wanted to get a confirmed trial date for our top lawsuits within the next ninety days. Challenging? Yes, but not impossible. Over the next ninety days, we celebrated when we were given each new trial date, and with seven days to spare for our ninety-day rallying cry, we had eleven confirmed trial dates over the next nine months.

> "Every organization needs a top priority. When a company is tempted—and most always are—to throw in one or two extra top priorities, they defeat the purpose of the thematic goal, which is to provide clarity around whatever is truly most important."
> —Patrick Lencioni, *Silos, Politics, and Turf Wars*

These kinds of results are only possible when you have a rallying cry that is in writing, posted in your conference room, and discussed at your daily and weekly meetings. Ask your team at every meeting, "What will you do today to help us toward our rallying cry?"

Focus on the Number-One Thing that Needs to be Fixed

Okay, great, you say, but you're really busy, and there's a ton of stuff you need to fix with your firm. You have loads of things that need fixing—maybe your lawsuits are not getting to trial, your website isn't bringing in new cases, or your clients aren't happy—forget all of that stuff.

You'll go nuts if you worry about everything that needs to be fixed, so focus on only one thing during your strategic planning. Take one step at a time by focusing on a specific goal—set a ninety-day finish line and get your team focused on a specific task. It's okay to have more than one quarterly theme, but you want to have one overriding goal for every quarter.

> *"Quarterly themes are powerful goal motivators. They focus the entire workforce on that single, overriding quarterly target in a way that people can not only understand, but get excited about."*
> —**Verne Harnish**, *Mastering the Rockefeller Habits*

Your team isn't worrying about ten things—there's just one thing that must be fixed, and you have a specific, ninety-day deadline to fix it. This is the power of a focused strategy. You probably already have a good idea about something at your law firm that you want to fix, but your staff might know better than you. You should always ask your team leaders, "What should we start, stop, or keep doing?"

Step One: The One-Page Strategic Plan

You want to make your strategy so simple that you can write it on the back of a napkin. The one-page strategic plan pinpoints exactly what you need to accomplish. Now, you and your team know what you are going to be doing and are in alignment with a single goal.

Step Two: Your Accountability Chart

It's great to have a plan, but a plan is worthless if there's no account-ability. You need to establish which members of your team will be responsible for specific tasks. At your quarterly meeting, keep a log of who said what they would do and when.

Let's say your strategic goal for the next ninety days is a content creation plan for your website. You want to name the people respon-sible for each task:

- Your paralegal will write two new blog posts a week.

- Your receptionist will add two updates to Facebook every week.

- A lawyer will add three new FAQs and articles to your website every week.

Now you have a plan for roughly thirty new pieces of content for your website every month (which should be the goal for your website), and everyone on your staff has specific tasks. It's great when everyone knows what everyone else is doing and is aligned around a common goal.

Step Three: It's Time to Measure Your Success

Let's say that your quarterly goal is to build the next great lawyer website. Using Google Analytics, the metrics (your key performance indicators) for your quarterly priority might be the following:

- Number of new website visitors per month

- Number of website visitors who contacted your law firm via the intake form, email, or phone

- Number of website visitors converted into clients

You should take your quarterly theme and align it with a specific goal—the one key measurable that you want your team to focus on. Perhaps you want to increase the number of visitors to your website to seven thousand per month. Okay, now you have your critical number—a number that you and your team can focus on.

Avoiding the Push Back

It's just a matter of time until new "emergencies" get in the way of your plans for a quarterly strategic meeting. Perhaps a judge calls to order depositions to be held on the day of your quarterly strategic meeting, or your trusty secretary is too busy for the meeting. This is when you need to avoid the push back to your quarterly meeting.

The best way of avoiding this push back is to schedule quarterly meetings on four dates over the next twelve months that are locked in granite. Barring a death in the family, these dates for your quarterly meeting will not be postponed—you need to treat the date as if it is the same as a trial date. If you don't take quarterly meetings seriously, neither will your team.

And when push comes to shove, remember that you are responsible for setting the vision for your law firm. The vision for your law firm depends on *you*—if others are not on board, you need to tactfully and delicately tell them why the quarterly meeting is the most important thing for the future of your law firm.

4

YOUR FIVE-YEAR STRATEGIC PLAN

You are consumed by the grind of the workday. With depositions, needy clients, and trials, you can't find time to come up for air. You're moving cases and paying bills, but are you getting ahead? Unless you take some time to plot your future, you'll be in exactly the same place five years from now.

> *"The future you are going to live is the one you are creating right now at this very moment."*
> **—Brian P. Moran and Michael Lennington, *The 12 Week Year***

But where do you begin mapping out your strategic five-year plan? Block out an afternoon for five solid hours of uninterrupted thought about your future. No phone calls, emails, or text messages— just you and a pad of paper. Describe in as much detail as possible what a great personal and professional life would look like five years from today. Be as specific as possible.

Establish Your Vision

What would your perfect law firm look like? Begin by writing down the basics:

- Number of employees

- Number of practice areas

- Number of active cases and trials every twelve months

- Desired income

This is the law firm you deeply desire—*the law firm of your dreams.* Creating a vision for the future of your law firm takes time—keep working on it until you have something that is perfect for you. Dream big! Perhaps you want to transition from smaller injury cases to catastrophic cases. Write the vision for your practice in five years: for example, twenty active lawsuits with a minimum case value of $500,000 for each case, and refer small cases to outside counsel.

The Big Question: Your Perfect Average Workday

Take the next step of creating a vision for your perfect workday. The big question you must ask: If there were no limitations, what would your perfect average day look like? Be as specific as possible.

- What would you spend the first half of your workday doing?

- What would you actually do at work?

- What are your clients like?

- What time will you leave the office?

- Will you work weekends?

Focus on creating a vision for your perfect workday that focuses on the best use of your time. For most CEO/entrepreneur lawyers, the best use of your time is creating systems and policies for running your firm, such as policies for client communication, case management, and quarterly strategic planning.

> *"Nothing great is ever accomplished without first being preceded by a big vision."*

—**Brian P. Moran and Michael Lennington, *The 12 Week Year***

Begin by eliminating the stuff that wastes your time: eliminate unscheduled phone calls, have your secretary respond to your email and letters, and have your team draft the discovery demands and responses. Weeding out the busywork will allow you to focus on the work that constitutes the best use of your time.

Sharing Your Vision with Your Staff

It's not enough to have a big vision for your law firm—you must print it out, share it with your team, and keep it with you. Once you've created your vision, you must ask, who have you shared your vision with? How often have you looked at your vision since you wrote it?

Make sure your team knows your vision, and create an action plan for achieving it. Put your vision in a framed picture in your conference room, and remind your team about your vision at your weekly meetings. Sharing your vision creates alignment around a common goal.

"Sharing your vision increases your commitment to it."
—Brian P. Moran and Michael Lennington, *The 12 Week Year*

Even better, laminate your vision on an index card, keep it with you in your wallet or purse, and look at the vision card once a day. There is no better way of creating "top of mind" awareness of your vision.

What Does Your Perfect Law Firm Look Like?

Do you have a vision for your perfect law firm? The perfect law firm is where you're not spending time on crappy cases and you get to focus only on the "A" cases. Your clients are grateful when they hire you, you have a steady pipeline of high-quality cases, and you're getting home in time for dinner.

The first step is to describe your perfect law firm. Take a couple of hours to envision your perfect law firm, and don't hesitate to dream big. Keep things simple with three categories:

- Marketing

- Case management

- Income

For example, the dreams for our perfect law firm are:

Marketing Goals

- 1,000 referral partners

- 25,000 website visitors per month (www. ProtectingPatientRights.com)

- 10,000 email subscribers (www.UltimateInjuryLaw.com)

Case Management Goals

- Twenty active lawsuits

- Minimum settlement value of $500,000 for each active lawsuit

- Twelve new lawsuits per year

- Twelve trials per year

Income Goal

- Annual income: $2.5 million

Take Baby Steps at First

Begin by setting base camps for each goal that you can use to measure your success. We set a four-year marketing goal of 500 referral partners on October 19, 2013. A *referral partner* is a lawyer or someone in the legal field who has referred at least one new case to our law firm in the last five years. There was just one problem: we only had 124 referral partners on October 19, 2013.

We set base camps for the number of referral partners in each year:

2014: 185

2015: 265

2016: 365

2017: 500

Our marketing blitz consisted of:

- Sending our monthly print newsletter, *Lawyer Alert*.

- Sending our weekly email newsletters.

- Launching a website, UltimateInjuryLaw.com, with our best marketing and management tips for lawyers.

- Speaking at seminars for local, state, and national trial lawyer organizations, e.g., PILMMA, Great Legal Marketing, and the National Trial Lawyers.

- Publishing articles for trial lawyer organizations, e.g., American Association for Justice and the New York Law Journal.

- Updating a referral partner at least once a day about the status of a referred case.

- Hosting self-funded seminars and parties for lawyers.

- Creating a mastermind (Mastermind Experience) with high-achieving lawyers across the country.

- Publishing our second book for lawyers, *The Law Firm of Your Dreams*, with our best advice for marketing and managing a law firm.

Our firm celebrates whenever we receive a referral from a new referral partner and we send a shock and awe package to new referral partners with our best marketing and management materials. Every new referral partner is added to our mailing list for our monthly print newsletter, *Lawyer Alert*, and weekly email newsletter, so we stay top of mind with them.

An Experiment Gone Awry ... Kind of

More than six years later, we have 388 referral partners. Since we began the marketing campaign, we acquired 264 new referral partners, but came nowhere close to our mission of 500 referral partners.

Did we fall flat on our face? The number of our referral partners is three times more than what it was and increased at the rate of forty-three new referral partners per year. Over the period of six years, the average value of our cases has increased, our net income is much higher, and our marketing budget is the same. The goal: low overhead, high profit.

> *"The team that makes the most mistakes usually*
> *wins, because doers make mistakes."*
> —John Wooden

Among marketing principles, I like this one the most: show up like no one else. I am not aware of any other lawyer who has focused the bulk of their marketing budget on acquiring lawyer referrals. This marketing strategy is our attempt to be different.

If You're Not Growing, You're Dying

We are increasing our mission from 500 to 1,000 referral partners over the next four years. These are the annual goals (a.k.a. base camps) for our mission year by year: 2020: 475; 2021: 600; 2022: 750; 2023: 1,000. This is our "Road to 1,000 Referral Partners." Our mission is to have 1,000 referral partners by October 19, 2023.

To accomplish this, we will keep doing what we're doing and add some new marketing tactics. Here's our plan:

- Become a certified provider of continuing legal education (CLE) credits by the New York State Bar Association.

- Publish a weekly column for the New York Law Journal.

- Have lunch dates with current and prospective referral partners at least once a week.

- Speak for the American Association for Justice at their annual convention.

- Expand the Mastermind Experience to Maui and London.

Will we reach our mission of 1,000 referral partners by October 19, 2023? We'll let you know in 2023, but one thing is for sure, our team will be aligned around a common mission.

5

LIFESTYLES OF THE RICH AND FAMOUS LAWYERS

Success (or the lack thereof) is determined by one thing: habits. The most successful lawyers have good habits, and the mediocre don't. Luck has nothing to do with it. If you have bad habits (e.g., mindless TV watching and web surfing), you will be destined for a life of mediocrity. If you have good habits, you will have a serious advantage over every other lawyer, and over the long haul, success will be almost inevitable.

Habits are customary responses that you repeat the same way over and over. Once you establish a habit, they become virtually self-executing and require almost no conscious thought. With habits, your workday is on automatic pilot.

> *"Becoming a successful person is more a matter of choice than circumstance."*
> —Rory Vaden, *Take the Stairs*

Here are a few thoughts on the habits of the "rich and famous" lawyers.

Daily Habits of Uber-Successful Lawyers

No Email before Noon: Avoid the temptation of email by turning off the email notification window on your computer.

Filter Email: Have an assistant read your email, respond to as much as possible, and only bother you with email that requires your personal response, e.g., an email from the judge.

No Unscheduled Phone Calls: Never accept unscheduled phone calls or clients who drop by your office for a "second" of your time. These thoughtless time grabs distract you from your goals for the day.

Block Off Time for Phone Calls: Block off one hour for phone calls, ideally at the end of the day, between 4:00 p.m. and 5:00 p.m. To make the calls productive, ask your clients to send an email specifying the purpose of the call.

No Web Surfing: If you're screwing around on the internet, you can't expect better from your staff. A study of 10,000 US employees found that the average worker admitted to wasting 2.09 hours each day on non-job-related activities.

> *"Self-discipline is the simplest and fastest way to make life as easy as possible."*
> —Rory Vaden, *Take the Stairs*

No Internet, Facebook, or Email at Home: When you get home from work, be present with your family. Thank you to Mike

Campbell, Esq., an excellent injury lawyer in Missouri, for this simple but extraordinary tip.

Daily Meeting with Staff: Meet with your staff for a daily huddle at 9:15 a.m. to discuss each employee's top three goals for the day. The daily huddle is very brief (fifteen minutes), creates alignment around common goals, improves communication, and gives your staff daily access to you to resolve obstacles. The daily huddle may be the number-one habit of the "rich and famous."

Begin with a Positive Focus: Begin every daily huddle by stating one thing—personal or professional—that you are grateful for. When you begin with gratitude, you focus on the positive things in your life.

Crazy, Unorthodox Motivational Habits

Dream Manager Program: Money does not inspire or motivate. The best way to motivate your staff is to show that you care about them. Show your staff that you care about their dreams by investing time and money in the Dream Manager program (discussed later in chapter 15 this book). This alone will set you head and shoulders above every other law firm.

Treat Your Employees Like Gold: This is far more important than client satisfaction. Focus on employee satisfaction, and they will treat your clients with the same respect. Ultimately, you will be the beneficiary, with great results. Ask your superstar employees, "What can I do to make work easier for you?" Hire an executive assistant for your superstar paralegal, or take an employee to lunch every week (thank you to South Florida plantiffs' lawyer, Craig Goldenfarb, Esq. for this golden tip).

Never Accept Mediocrity: Demand complete compliance with your policies. Policies and systems aren't worth squat if you don't enforce them.

Fire Whiners: Weed out whiners. The mind-set of "My life sucks" must be ruthlessly gutted from your law firm.

> *"A life of average comes from having an average attitude."*
> —Rory Vaden, *Take the Stairs*

Document Systems: When you face a question or issue that is likely to recur, write a policy. With written policies, you won't have to revisit the same question more than once. Documented systems are essential if you want your law practice to function when you're not there.

Distraction-Free Work Environment: The ultimate work environment has zero distractions and is free of internet, email, and phone calls. Go to a quiet place with no distractions like a public library, turn off your cell phone and internet access, and you will be crazy productive.

> *"Distraction is a dangerously deceptive saboteur of our goals."*
> —Rory Vaden, *Take the Stairs*

Mind-Set Habits of the Successful

"We," not "I": Never underestimate the impact of your words. Give credit to and focus on the team with your language: "We," not "I." Pass along the credit for great results to your team.

Purpose, Values, and Mission: There is nothing more important than core values—for any business. What are the basic values that govern the conduct of your law firm (e.g., your Core Values)?

> *"It's a shame that we spend years of our life doing activities we think we're supposed to do, and we spend only minutes figuring out what we really want."*
>
> —Rory Vaden, *Take the Stairs*

Embrace Culture: What makes your superstar employees great? This is how you define the culture of your law firm. Our law firm's culture is based upon *humility* and *hunger*: employees who are humble, down-to-earth, and highly motivated (hungry) to get the job done at all costs. A group of highly motivated and humble staff will be ultra-committed to your success.

Walk through Fire: Successful people form the habit of doing things that failures don't like doing.

> *"Success comes from being tested in the fire, being pushed to your limits, and having your character and confidence shaped by challenging circumstances."*
>
> —Rory Vaden, *Take the Stairs*

The Power of a Mastermind: Join a mastermind group. Surround yourself with high-achieving, elite lawyers at a mastermind group, and have them dissect your marketing and management practices. Expose yourself to the best practices, and avoid mistakes. There is nothing more powerful than a small group of like-minded individuals working toward a common purpose.

Financial Habits of the Best Lawyers

Know Your Numbers: Review your profit/loss statement and balance sheet every month at a face-to-face meeting with your bookkeeper and accountant. Know your overhead to the penny, and trim the fat. Break down the expenses by marketing, case management, and operating overhead.

Project income based upon trial dates over the next twelve months. Make sure your projected income is realistic, and then fight to make it happen.

Be Frugal: Invest heavily in marketing, and for everything else, watch every penny. If marketing pays for itself, invest more. Your best investment will always be in yourself.

> *"Every dollar you spend today is worth at least five dollars in ten years and ten dollars in thirty years."*
> —Rory Vaden, *Take the Stairs*

Habits of Gratitude

Birthday Cards/Phone Calls to Clients: Shock your clients with a phone call on their birthday. Just say "hi" and let them know you're thinking of them. Your clients will never forget your personal touch.

Weekly Lunch with Employee: Show your team that you care by taking them to lunch once a week. Avoid talking shop, and find out what they do in their spare time. You will be amazed that they too have lives outside of work.

Monthly Meals with Clients: Take a client to lunch once a month with your team. Your clients will appreciate the friendly gesture, and your staff will see how their work has improved your clients' lives.

Book Gift for Holidays: Make your holiday card unique by offering to send copies of your book to the friends of your referral partners. Gift wrap your book and send it as a gift.

Buy Lunch for a Referral Partner's Law Firm: Don't just mail the referral fee check to your referral partner. Buy lunch for your referral partner's law firm, and hand-deliver the check when lunch is delivered.

Daily Handwritten Notes: Write a daily handwritten note to one of your referral partners just to say "hi." Handwritten notes are treasured.

Habits for Managing a Lawsuit

No Adjournments: *Never* adjourn trial dates or depositions. For a plaintiff's lawyer, adjournments are a deadly enemy that will screw up your income projections.

Don't be a Minimum-Wage Worker: What is the most effective thing you can be doing, right now, with the time you have available? Not all the things you *can* be doing—all the things you *should* be doing. If someone else can do the task, you have to delegate.

Case Debriefing: Evaluate your successes and failures with your team at the end of each case. Review your goals for the settlement/judgment, legal-fee-to-disbursement ratio, and length of the lawsuit. Always search for ways to make small, incremental improvements in your systems.

Go Paperless: Go 100 percent paperless! You will have instant access to your files wherever you have an internet connection, specific documents will be easy to locate electronically, and you will eliminate the hassle of storing paper documents.

Case Budgets: Establish a written case budget for every phase of a lawsuit (discovery, pre-trial, and trial), and estimate the costs as precisely as possible. The budget will show you whether the costs of litigation justify the projected legal fee. Ideally, your legal fee will exceed the disbursements by a ratio of ten to one.

Budgets for Experts: Put expert witnesses on a written budget. Tell your experts that they cannot exceed the budget without prior written approval from you. You can create a case budget that is precise and the costs won't be a surprise.

The Power of Mind-Set

Ninety-eight percent of lawyers race through their workday with little thought or planning as to the best use of their time. That doesn't have to be you. Once you begin thinking strategically about each decision that you make in every moment of the day, you instantly raise your game to a higher level.

Part 2
THE MANAGER

When I die and I'm standing in front of God, I want to be able to say,
"God, I don't have any talents left. I used everything you gave me."

—Caylin Moore, Rhodes Scholar from Compton, CA

Part 2

Management of Your Team

6

HOW TO CHART THE FUTURE OF YOUR LAW FIRM

It's easy to think that you don't need an organizational chart for the growth of your law firm. You're not a mega-corporation and an organizational chart is nothing more than a fancy corporate document that the employees ignore. Think again.

A few years ago, I spent a day at a mastermind at Infusionsoft, where we focused on defining the roles and duties of the members of our small law firm (three employees). The co-founders of Infusionsoft, Clate Mask and Scott Martineau, explained how they went from a tiny business run by two guys to one of the leading technology companies in the country, at least in part, by implementing a growth/

organizational chart. Clate emphasized that an organizational chart *"instills clarity and confidence from chaos and confusion."*

Now they had my attention. An organizational chart (a.k.a. growth chart) creates a plan for growth based upon defined roles and expectations. The team members know what is expected of them and have specific metrics (the Big Three) that define their success for every quarter.

Begin with the End in Mind

What are your goals in three years? Be as specific as possible, including the number of employees, annual revenue/income, number of cases, and what your ideal workday looks like.

What would your law firm need to look like to achieve those goals? Write titles and write in the names of the people serving those functions (your name may be in every box at first).

> *"If you don't make a conscious effort to visualize who you are and what you want in life, then you empower other people and circumstances to shape you and your life by default."*
>
> —**Stephen R. Covey,** *The 7 Habits of Highly Effective People*

Once you know what you want your law firm to look like in three years, create a growth chart that will get you there.

The Entrepreneurial Growth Chart for Lawyers

A growth chart gives you a roadmap. Lay out the functional areas of your law firm in a simple manner—do not follow the typical organizational chart. Think of how you can align existing talent with this roadmap and structure your law firm around the value you provide. Keep it simple and be unique.

The growth chart of John H. Fisher, PC has three departments: finance, operations, and marketing.

Chief Executive Officer

Objective: Goal setting, define purpose, values, and mission, and strategic planning for improvement.

> *"Vision is the number one responsibility of every great leader."*
> —Clate Mask, CEO of Infusionsoft

Finance

Objective: Track revenue/income, track cash flow, and create budgets for marketing and operations.

Positions:

- Vice president of finance
- Controller
- Bookkeeper

Vice President of Finance: Manage accounting and ensure adequate working capital.

Controller: Maintain financials and keep firm's expenses within a budget.

Bookkeeper: Keep books, reduce expenses and pay vendors, and respond to billing inquiries.

Operations

Objective: Hiring and onboarding of employees, manage lawsuits, and track our firm's progress.

> *"Vision without execution is just hallucination."*
> —Thomas Edison

Positions:

- Chief operating officer
- Human relations manager
- Case manager
- Executive assistant to the case manager
- Client care advocate
- Dream manager

Chief Operating Officer: Ensure compliance with office policies.

Human Relations Manager: Hiring and onboarding of employees.

Case Manager: Manage all phases of a lawsuit, including filing lawsuits, drafting discovery demands and responses, and meeting discovery deadlines.

Executive Assistant to the Case Manager: Acquire medical records and schedule depositions.

Client Care Advocate: Ensure fanatical "WOW" support of clients and referral partners.

Dream Manager: Help team members achieve their dreams by meeting with them to formulate specific plans for dream fulfillment.

Marketing

Objective: Attract new clients, keep clients for life, and attract new referral partners.

> *"Look for opportunities to be uncomfortable because that means you're growing."*
>
> **—Clate Mask, CEO of Infusionsoft**

Positions:

- Vice president of marketing

- Copywriter

- Internet marketing expert

- Customer relationship management ("CRM") expert

- Community relations leader

Vice President of Marketing: Identify target markets, find new clients, expand relationships with new referral partners, expand list-building capabilities, and decrease costs of acquiring new clients.

Copywriter: Write sales letters and create information products.

Internet Marketing Expert: Online lead generation of clients and referral partners.

Customer Relationship Management (CRM) Expert: Maintain database of clients and referral partners, apply CRM to lead generation and client communication, and integrate CRM with case management software.

Community Relations Leader: Launch community marketing programs and establish relationships with members of the media.

Your growth chart is a fluid document that will change over time as your firm grows. Share the growth chart with your team members, get their feedback and make sure you're not missing anything. Once your team members agree to the assigned duties and job descriptions, create a graph of your growth chart and post it in your conference room.

Employee Evaluations Using the Big Three

Every position on your growth chart should have a Big Three for evaluating their performance on a quarterly basis. Identify the core three responsibilities for each of the defined positions on your growth chart and change the Big Three as the need arises. Each team member should score themselves on the Big Three.

> *"When performance is measured, performance improves.*
>
> *When performance is reported, performance improves dramatically.*
>
> *When performance is reported publicly,*
> *performance improves exponentially."*
> —Thomas S. Monson

Do quarterly reviews of each employee based upon the Big Three metrics for their position. Create a Quarterly Review Form for the Big Three metrics and measure performance based on these criteria.

Each of the Big Three metrics is graded based upon the following:

- "E": Consistently EXCEEDS expectations as measured by three metrics.

- "M": Consistently MEETS expectations as measured by three metrics.

- "I": IMPROVEMENT needed; does not consistently meet expectations.

On the Quarterly Review of our law firm, the first metric for a case manager is getting at least three confirmed trial dates every three months. Make the Quarterly Review Form simple and easy to understand and celebrate when a team member achieves her Big Three.

Quarterly Review Form of John H. Fisher, PC

Employee name: Jane Doe

Role: Case Manager

Quarter: 1st Quarter

Metric #1: Confirm one new trial date per month

Description: A trial date must be scheduled and confirmed by the court

Expected Result: Three new trial dates per quarter

Actual Result: Confirmed two new trial dates

Rating: IMPROVEMENT needed

Comments about Performance: The discovery phase of the lawsuit has taken more than nine months (14 ½ months) and does not meet our goals for the completion of discovery.

Some of the delays were beyond our control, but we need to focus on completing discovery within nine months and implementing our twelve-step Litigation Checklist as each step of discovery is completed.

Vision: Purpose, values and mission memorized?

Yes <u>X</u>   No __

Our four core values: Knows what they are AND what they mean?

Yes <u>X</u>   No __

At the end of the year, you won't be guessing about your employees' performance, you'll have quarterly evaluations for your review.

Measure Your Success at Monthly Progress Meetings

Try measuring the key metrics in financial, marketing and internet marketing. If you get too bogged down in numbers, they become meaningless. Less is more. Pick three to five important metrics and track them every month.

Start with these metrics for your financial, marketing, and internet marketing goals.

Financial

- Current revenue/profitability (year to date)

- Projected annual revenue/profitability

- Marketing costs

- Operating costs

Marketing

- Total number of active cases

- Total number of leads acquired

- Total number of potential cases

- Total number of referral partners

Internet Marketing

- Total number of website visitors to ProtectingPatientRights. com

- Total number of inbound links (ProtectingPatientRights. com)

- Total number of website visitors to UltimateInjuryLaw. com

- Total number of inbound links (UltimateInjuryLaw.com)

Have your chief operating officer (a.k.a. officer manager) provide these metrics on a flow chart for all team members at a monthly progress meeting. The metrics will be easier to understand and you'll have numbers to measure your progress. Better yet, post your goals on a whiteboard in your conference room, so they stay top of mind.

Are You Up for a Challenge?

With a growth chart, quarterly performance evaluations, and monthly progress reports, you're not praying for success—you're virtually guaranteeing it. And in the process, you're charting a clear path for your law firm's future. And hey, if these business practices were the foundation for the success of one of the nation's top technology companies (Infusionsoft), maybe you should give them a shot too.

7

WHY LAWYERS
HATE MEETINGS

It's no wonder lawyers hate meetings.

From the minute you step into a meeting at your law firm, there is meaningless chit-chat and gossip, some members of your staff (maybe you) show up ten minutes late, and by the time everyone's there, you've wasted fifteen minutes of your best work time. Most meetings at law firms are disjointed and unorganized—the subjects are random and bounce around among your staff. And making things worse, the meetings last an hour and a half and destroy the middle of your workday.

You're right, this kind of meeting is a complete waste of time and is unproductive for you and your staff. Here's the problem: no one ever taught you how to run a productive meeting. This is why meetings suck!

What if your next meeting had a specific agenda as well as a start and stop time? No random chit-chat allowed—only laser-focused conversation on a specific agenda, and once the meeting is supposed to end, you leave the room. You keep a written log of the goal to be achieved and exactly who is going to do what and when, and the log is reviewed at the next meeting. Everyone is held accountable to a specific goal. Wow, this is not your same old lawyer meeting. You just accomplished a ton in only fifteen minutes.

The Power of Focus and Alignment

In meetings without a clear agenda, the meeting has no purpose or direction. Yes, your staff is working hard, and they appear very busy, but are they doing what you want them to do? Who knows! Your top paralegal might be working on the worthless slip-and-fall case while you're losing sleep about all the things that need to be done in your huge, upcoming trial.

But without regular meetings (daily and weekly), you have no clue what your staff is doing. Do you want to keep winging it and just hope for the best? What if, instead, you scheduled daily and weekly meetings to make sure your staff is working on the "A" cases that will pay your bills? This is the power of daily and weekly meetings: you know what your staff is doing, you set goals for their work, and everyone is held accountable.

Sharing the Collective Wisdom with Your Staff

Most law firms do a crappy job at sharing the collective wisdom of the lawyers and staff. A law firm with four to six lawyers has a ton of wisdom and knowledge about the law—you are a virtual walking dictionary. You know just about everything about the law, and if there is a stumbling point in a case, there's a good chance you know how to fix it. But your vast knowledge is worthless unless it's shared with your staff.

The benefit of regular meetings is that you share your knowledge among the lawyers and staff within your firm. When there's a choke-point in an upcoming trial, you troubleshoot the issue at your regular meetings, and you might pick up tips for handling the problem in a way that you never thought of. This is the power of regular meetings— you are tapping into the collective wisdom of your partners, associates, paralegals, and yes, secretaries, and receptionists.

The Secret Ingredient to a Successful Daily Meeting

Still don't see the benefit of regular meetings? I know, you've tried this before, and it didn't work. Before giving up, try one thing: schedule a fifteen-minute meeting at a specific time, say 9:15 a.m., and limit the meeting to fifteen minutes. Show up on time, start on time, and use a stopwatch to end the meeting after fifteen minutes.

At this daily meeting, you discuss your top three goals for the day and write them down on an index card (your "Top Three Meeting"). You say, "Today, I'm going to accomplish X, Y, and Z," write them down, and have your paralegal and secretary do the same. Now you know exactly what your staff is doing with their time, and you have specific tasks that you must accomplish. No matter what, stop the meeting after fifteen minutes, even if there's more to discuss.

> *"The rhythmic pulsing of daily and weekly meetings constitutes the real heartbeat of a growing company."*
> —**Verne Harnish,** *Mastering the Rockefeller Habits*

But don't stop there: throughout your workday, remind yourself of your Top Three for the day by holding the index card of your Top Three goals in front of your face every hour. It is crazy how this will keep you focused on your goals for the day. This is a great way to avoid the distractions and little "emergencies" that always seem to get in the way of a productive day.

How to Get Stuff Done at Weekly Meetings

On Monday morning, meet with your staff for forty-five minutes to set the goals for that week. Similar to your daily meetings, set a "Top Five" for your week and a "Top One of Five." These are the Top Five things you must get done this week and the Top One of Five is the most important goal of your Top Five. You write down these goals on a large poster board for you and your staff and make sure their goals are aligned with your goals. Now, your staff is doing the work you want them to do.

Each task gets a number assigned to it: number one is the Top One of Five of your goals and you work from there to define your Top Five goals for the week. Yes, there will always be more than five things you need to do and that's fine. You should call the extra stuff your "*should-do*" list—things you should be doing but are not crucial and can wait if you don't get them done this week.

How to Make Sure Your Staff Gets Stuff Done

At the next weekly "Goal Meeting," check with your staff and keep a written log of who's accomplished their Top Five goals. You will be amazed at how productive your staff became—they're not only achieving their Top Five, they're doing their "should-do" list too. Hell, your staff is out-working you!

"It's just easier to get the job done than to have to face the team each day, each week, and make the same excuses for having failed to get it done."

—**Verne Harnish,** *Mastering the Rockefeller Habits*

And here's the great thing: when your staff (and you) know they will be held accountable for their weekly goals, they know they will "face the music" if they're not getting their work done. Did your paralegal serve the expert response and file the note of issue? If not, they have to face the music at your next meeting.

8

HOW TO HIRE YOUR NEXT SUPERSTAR

When it comes to hiring, lawyers suck! You hate the process of hiring, so avoid it at all costs and let someone else do it. You don't want to waste your time reviewing resumes and interviewing job candidates when you'd rather be doing the "real" work of trying cases and meeting new clients.

Hiring should be just as important to you as marketing or preparing a case for trial. Your team is the most important thing your law firm has. If you don't put in the time and effort to find and retain a team of superstars, your law firm will always be second-rate. It's time to change this with a hiring system that is documented, consistent, and systematic.

Step #1: Defining Your Ideal Candidate

Begin by defining the ideal qualities of the candidate. If you could hire the perfect employee, what qualities and abilities would they have? Put this in writing, as this will be the backbone of your job advertisement.

Here's a snippet of our advertisement for a litigation paralegal:

A positive, enthusiastic self-starter who does not work by the clock and can prepare discovery demands, responses, and bills of particulars in a medical malpractice lawsuit with almost no guidance.

The candidate should be willing to stay at work until the job is done, including weekends and working nights when necessary. They don't need to be told what to do and are not afraid of making mistakes. They don't wait for the next job assignment—they know what to do.

The candidate should be willing to travel to remote locations to attend two-week trials and assist with witnesses and technology during trials.

The candidate should absolutely love technology and marketing.

The candidate should exude a positive attitude and be grateful for the opportunity to transform the lives of the severely injured. They accept responsibility for their mistakes and love what they do. They are committed to our purpose of stopping medical injustice.

If this describes you, you are a perfect fit for our law firm.

Be as specific as possible in writing the job description and avoid vague requirements, e.g., "good attitude." If you need a litigation paralegal who is self-sufficient and needs almost no supervision, put that in the job advertisement. Your advertisement for a litigation paralegal might state that candidates should not apply unless they can draft a complete set of discovery responses and demands including

- a bill of particulars from beginning to end with little to no supervision,

- discovery demands for a medical malpractice lawsuit with little to no supervision, and

- a proposed jury charge and verdict sheet for a medical malpractice lawsuit with little to no supervision.

By specifying the requirements of the position, you will scare off those who are not serious candidates. And if you're going to ask the candidate these questions at their interview anyway, why not ask them at the outset?

Step #2: Creating a Big List of Candidates

Once you've defined the qualities of the ideal candidate, you need to expand the pool of applicants as wide as possible. Your job advertisement should sell the candidate on the almost unlimited opportunities and benefits at your law firm.

Make an Irresistible Offer: Make the job advertisement so enticing that candidates will be jumping over each other to apply. Here's a sample of the benefits offered in our job advertisement:

Do You Like Having Fun at Work?

You will get challenges, responsibility, and the best money and benefits in the market. We have an exciting and fun workplace, and you will get to play an important role improving the lives of severely disabled people. We offer plenty of opportunities for your professional and personal development.

You will receive the following:

- Medical insurance (individual and spouse premiums 100 percent covered)

- Twenty-three paid days off in your first year

- 401(k) and profit-sharing retirement plans

- Inclusion into our Healthy Lifestyle Program with a personal trainer, a nutritionist, and a life coach at your disposal

- Complimentary membership to Weight Watchers

- $5,000 allowance every year for personal development programs

- Inclusion into our Dream Manager Program with a Dream Manager at your disposal (let us help make your craziest dreams come true!)

Does your website describe the growth potential for a new employee? Does it tell the story of what you stand for?

Build Your Employment Brand: Candidates want to work for a cause that has a bigger purpose than making money. Incorporate your firm's purpose and core values into your job advertisement and show the candidates that your law firm is different. Our firm's core values and purpose are listed in the job listing.

> *"Great people want to work for great companies."*
> —**Adam Robinson,** *The Best Team Wins*

We've formally defined the culture of John H. Fisher, PC, in terms of four core values:

1. We only practice catastrophic injury law.

2. We never agree to confidential settlements.

3. We do NOT accept cases having questionable merit.

4. We are brutally honest with our clients.

Our purpose, stopping medical injustice, and core values are the framework from which we make all of our decisions. Our four core values are reflected in everything we do, including how we interact with each other and how we interact with our clients and our referral partners.

Post Advertisement on Job Sites: Post your job advertisement on the leading online sites for legal jobs, such as Indeed, Craigslist, ZipRecruiter, Monster, CareerBuilder, iHireLegal, LawCrossing, and LawJobs.

Review Resume Databases: Most of the job sites offer access to a resume database which you can review once you post an ad. Using the resume database, you can specify the criteria for the position, e.g., candidate must live within thirty minutes of your law office.

Leverage Social Media and Pay-Per-Click: You might spend a few bucks on pay-per-click ads to promote your job advertisement within a specific geographic region. Send out a post to your Facebook friends about your open position and include a link where candidates can apply. This doesn't cost a penny.

Step #3: Narrowing the List of Candidates

In the job advertisement, you should require that the candidates follow a very specific procedure to apply. Candidates who cannot follow instructions should be eliminated from consideration. Our job advertisement has five distinct requirements for applying. The applicant must

1. send their resume through UPS;

2. address it John H. Fisher;

3. include a cover letter that contains the subject line, "I am the perfect candidate for your litigation paralegal";

4. include a list of three references from direct supervisors at past employers where the candidate has worked in the past ten years; and

5. adhere to our policy of no emails or phone calls.

Did the candidate send the resume via UPS and personalize the letter to you with the correct subject line? Look for typographical and grammatical errors on the cover letter and resume. If the candidate's resume has errors, the candidate will be even more careless on the job. Eliminate these candidates from consideration.

> *"Who you put on your payroll is the only thing you have 100% control over in your business."*
> —Adam Robinson, *The Best Team Wins*

If the candidate calls our office or contacts us through an online job site, they did not follow the instructions and should not be considered. The candidate's failure to follow instructions reveals a lack of attention to detail.

If the candidate follows your instructions for applying, and the cover letter expresses some specific knowledge about your law firm, the candidate has done their research and knows how to follow directions.

Step #4: The Telephone Interview

Don't bother scheduling interviews until you've spoken to the candidate first via phone or videoconference. The telephone interview weeds out 75 percent of the candidates and will save a lot of time. The goal is to interview the top 25 percent of the candidates.

> *"If you skip the telephone interview and go straight to the in-person interview, you're going to end up spending a lot of time talking to people who will demonstrate in the first few minutes that they are not the right fit."*
> —Adam Robinson, *The Best Team Wins*

The purpose of the telephone interview is to determine whether the candidate should get a personal interview. With a five-minute phone interview, you might discover that the candidate's salary requirements are double what you are offering or they are only interested in temporary employment.

Step #5: Interviewing the Applicant

Make sure the candidate is appropriately dressed, smiles, and makes eye contact. If the candidate is inappropriately dressed, e.g., wears flip flops or casual clothes, eliminate them from consideration. If the candidate has a drab personality, mumbles, or cannot maintain eye contact, they do not have the personality to work for your world-class law firm.

> *"Great companies don't hire skilled people and motivate them.*
> *They hire already motivated people and inspire them."*
>
> —Simon Sinek, *Start with Why*

Be prepared for the interview with specific questions. Create a list of questions that you can use for every interview.

Preparation for the Interview: "What did you do to prepare for this interview?"

The candidate's answer reveals their preparedness and ingenuity. If the candidate did no homework about your law firm, they are not resourceful or prepared, and they will be no different while working at your law firm.

If the candidate read your books and has researched your law firm, they will show the same ingenuity and preparedness when they come to work for you.

Ideal Workday: Ask them what they are best at, what they love doing, and what type of work they don't like doing. If the candidate "hates doing paperwork," you know they're not a good fit to be your litigation paralegal.

Gaps in Employment: Look for gaps in employment. Ask why the candidate left their employment. Ask, "What would your past employer say are your strengths and weaknesses?" If the law firm dissolved, ask "Why did the law firm fail? What would you have done differently?"

Goals and Vision: Ask the candidate about their twenty-year, five-year and one-year professional goals. Ask the candidate about the last time they set a goal for themselves that they failed to achieve. Ask, "What is your ideal vision of the perfect job? Where do you see yourself in five to ten years?"

> *"When the process is thought out, documented and meticulously followed, the results are consistent and produce actionable outcomes."*
> —**Adam Robinson**, *The Best Team Wins*

You want highly motivated, goal-driven employees. If the candidate has no clear vision for their future, look elsewhere.

Self-Development: Ask the candidate, "What books are you reading?" Most people do not read a single book in a year. Does the candidate read trashy novels or self-development books like Dale Carnegie's classic, *How to Win Friends and Influence People*?

Organizational Skills: For a personal assistant or office manager, you might want an employee who is exceptionally well organized. Ask, "How do you organize your closet?" (thanks to South Florida injury lawyer, Craig Goldenfarb, Esq., for this question). If the candidate has a system for organizing their closet, they are a type-A person who will bring the same organizational skills to your law firm.

Attitude: Attitude is the candidate's disposition toward work. Employees who have a positive attitude are more productive, helpful, and likely to stay at their jobs. If the candidate complains about past employers, they will almost certainly complain about you.

"The most valuable asset in your business is your people."
—Adam Robinson, *The Best Team Wins*

Ask the candidate to describe the most frustrating aspect of their prior job and what makes it harder for them to do their job, e.g., "My boss is a jerk." If the candidate bad mouths their prior boss, they have a bad attitude. Steer clear of candidates with a bad attitude—it will only get worse.

Character: Ask the candidate to name four people whose careers they've fundamentally changed. Did the candidate change the life of a person above or below them?

"You can easily judge the character of a man by how
he treats those who can do nothing for him."
—Simon Sinek, *Leaders Eat Last*

If the candidate changed the life of a person who could do nothing to advance their career, they are a generous person. You want go-givers in your law firm.

Vulnerability and Honesty: Ask the candidate about their biggest weakness or failure. This reveals the candidate's willingness to be vulnerable, e.g., "I have trouble being on time." This candidate is honest and open. Ask what they think they need to do to improve as a paralegal.

Caring too much or working too hard are not weaknesses—that candidate has difficulty with transparency and being vulnerable. If the candidate responds, "I can't think of anything," they have difficulty being honest and open. Everyone needs improvement.

Performance: Ask the candidate about a job where their success was measured. If the candidate does not like having their work measured, they are not a good fit for a system-driven law firm.

Step #6: Trust, But Verify

The reference check is the final and most important part of the interview process. Only accept references from people who directly supervised the candidate over the last five to ten years, i.e., no friends or coworkers. Every direct supervisor should be spoken to. If the candidate is unwilling to give you the names of their direct supervisors, disqualify them.

Ask the candidate's former supervisor the following questions:

- How do you think the candidate might perform in the role they are applying for?

- What would you consider the candidate's biggest areas for improvement?

- On a scale of one to ten with ten being outstanding, how would you rate the candidate's performance?

- If given the opportunity to hire the candidate again, would you do so enthusiastically?

Google the candidate and learn all you can about them. Check out the candidate's social media profiles, e.g., Facebook, Instagram, and LinkedIn. You might be surprised at what you find on their public social media profiles, e.g., "I hate my boss."

Step #7: Criteria for Hiring

The goal is to have three to five viable candidates. Assuming the candidates have the necessary skills and a good personality, make the hiring decision based on their stability of employment, their passion for your practice area, and their recommendations from past employers.

"[S]tart with the mindset that a candidate cannot work in your business and affect your life unless they prove to you to be absolutely stellar."
—Jay Henderson, *The Ultimate Small Business Guide to Hiring Super-Stars*

Stability of Employment: If the candidate has worked for the same employer for at least five years, they must have had some level of success. The average job tenure for an early- to mid-career employee is under three years. If the candidate jumps from job to job, they will not be a long-term employee for your law firm.

Passion for Your Practice Area: If the candidate has worked for a plaintiff's personal injury law firm, they have already shown a commitment to the rights of the disabled. You don't have to guess whether the candidate has a passion for your line of work—they've already shown it.

A Known Commodity: The easiest hire is a known commodity. Specifically, someone recommended by a person you trust and even better, someone whose work you've seen first-hand. You don't need to interview this candidate, because you already know they're perfect.

The Ultimate Red Flag

The ultimate red flag is whether the candidate wants the job. If you have to sell the job to the candidate, you should look elsewhere. Ask, "If you were offered the job, and the pay and benefits were acceptable, would you take it right now?"

Unless the candidate gives an emphatic, "Hell, yes!" take a pass and keep looking. Be patient, take your time and follow the process. There are no guarantees, but a meticulously scripted process for hiring might result in your next superstar employee.

And if you have any doubts at all, don't hire.

* * *

HOW TO MAKE SURE PROSPECTIVE EMPLOYEES CAN DO THE WORK

Most hiring decisions are subjective. For the most part, you base hiring decisions upon your gut instinct and intuition, but your subjective assessments are rarely accurate (check out Malcolm Gladwell's book *Talking to Strangers* if you don't believe me). You have to do more than rely on your instincts. You have to test the prospective candidate to make sure they can do the job.

The Power of a Shadow Day

What can you do to ensure that the prospective employee *really* has the skills that you need? Don't accept the word of the prospective employee that they can do the job—test their skills and make them show you. Tell the prospective employee that you will pay for one day to work at your office and explain you want to make sure your firm is a good fit for them.

"Spend an inordinate amount of time on the front end."
—**Michael Smith**, *SBC & Associates, Inc.*

What are the core competencies for a litigation paralegal? Identify the skills and create a test to check the candidate's core competencies. Write three specific assignments and ask the prospective employee to do the work. Answering written questions (like a bar exam) is not enough—you need the prospective employee to show you what they can do.

Task #1: Draft a Supplemental Verified Bill of Particulars

You are asked to prepare a supplemental bill of particulars for a disabled client who continues to treat for their injuries with eight doctors, two hospitals, and two therapists and the first day of trial is forty days away. Our client's medical treatment has been extensive with many new dates of treatment since the date that the plaintiff's amended verified bill of particulars was served six months earlier.

List the top three activities that you would do to prepare the supplemental verified bill of particulars. Tell us precisely how you would prepare the supplemental verified bill of particulars and what information you would need.

Next, we would like you to draft the supplemental verified bill of particulars. Instructions for drafting the supplemental verified bill of particulars are set forth in Fisherpedia.com. If you cannot prepare the supplemental verified bill of particulars, tell us why and what information you are missing.

Task #2: Prepare a Settlement Statement

One of our cases settles four days before trial and you have been asked to prepare a settlement statement in a medical malpractice case. A form for the settlement statement is contained in the Miscellaneous tab in Trialworks. The Costs tab in Trialworks contains an itemized list of our disbursements and our bookkeeper also has a list of disbursements.

The case settled for $1M and we have experts in neurological surgery, radiology, and an economist and have sent subpoenas to a process server to obtain medical records. Additionally, travel arrangements were previously made for the transportation and hotel accommodations of our expert witnesses.

You are on your own, as there is no one to assist you. What is the first thing you would do? Is there any information that you are missing? Please prepare a settlement statement for our review and approval. Be as precise as possible.

Task #3: Schedule a Deposition of a Non-Party Witness

We need to depose a non-party witness, Robert Smith, MD, during discovery. We videotape all depositions, except for the plaintiff's.

What is the first task that you would do to schedule the non-party deposition? Identify specifically the tasks that you would do and tell us what documents are necessary to schedule the non-party deposition. Next, prepare every document that is necessary to schedule the non-party deposition.

HOW TO TEST KNOWLEDGE WITH BEHAVIORALLY ANCHORED QUESTIONS

Ask about specific situations that the prospective candidate will encounter and how they would handle it.

For example: "Let's say a defense attorney calls you to adjourn a court-ordered deposition of the defendant at 4 p.m. on the day before the deposition and an attorney is not available in our office to respond. The defense lawyer does not ask for your consent and simply tells you that they are adjourning the deposition."

- Have you ever experienced that?

- How would you handle that?

- Would you consent to adjourn the deposition?

Checking with the attorney is not the answer. Find out if the prospective employee can function independently.

HOW TO TEST BASIC COMPUTER SKILLS

Prior to an in-person interview, ask the prospective employee to complete a test that evaluates their basic computer skills. This will eliminate candidates who do not have basic computer skills.

This is the computer skills test, courtesy of Michael McCready, Esq., an excellent plaintiff's lawyer in Chicago. Ask the prospective employee to follow these instructions:

1. First, open a new Word document. Create a letterhead with your name and address, using different fonts.

2. Create a business letter addressed to John H. Fisher, Esq. at the Kingston office.

3. In the body of the letter, include three facts about the firm and two facts about this position.

4. Include a signature block.

5. Save the Word file to your desktop.

6. Convert the Word file to a .pdf.

7. Take a screen shot of the Word document from your desktop and insert the image into the .pdf, anywhere in the document is fine, and re-save it.

8. Create an Excel sheet that includes two formulas and save it.

9. Convert the Excel sheet to a .pdf.

10. Combine the two saved .pdfs into one document.

11. Email the Word document, the Excel document and the combined .pdf document to Jfisher@ fishermalpracticelaw.com.

12. The exercise will be complete when I receive the email.

According to Michael McCready, Esq., prospective employees with good computer skills should be able to complete these tasks within ten minutes, those with less ability will take fifteen minutes, and some will never finish. If the prospective candidate is unable to complete the test, you can find out where they had difficulty and how they attempted to work through it. This will help show the prospective employee's ability to navigate difficult work assignments.

PERSONALITY TESTING & GROUP INTERVIEWS

Assess Personality & Reliability: Kolbe's "RightFit ™" tests the prospective employee's reliability, personality, and capabilities.

Multiple, Group Interviews: Get two or three other people with you to conduct the interview. Make this a group process. Interview candidates at least two to three times in different settings, e.g., office, dinner at a restaurant with their spouse, etc. Is the person that you interviewed the first time the same as the second interview? Is it getting better or worse?

Memorize and Recite Your Purpose, Values, and Mission: Ask the prospective candidate to memorize your law firm's purpose, values, and mission.

At the interview or shadow day, ask the prospective employee to recite your law firm's purpose, values, and mission. If the prospective employee cannot recite your purpose, values, and mission, they are not a good fit for your value-driven law firm. This is a major red flag.

HAVING UNCOMFORTABLE CONVERSATIONS WITH YOUR "C" EMPLOYEE

Let's say the prospective employee passes the shadow day and computer skills test with flying colors and you hire them. In your offer letter, make sure the new employee is on notice that the first ninety days are a probationary period.

> *"When you hire you want to be giddy, but six months later you want to be ecstatic."*
> —Michael Smith, *SBC & Associates, Inc.*

During the ninety-day probationary period, be radically candid and have uncomfortable conversations with your employee. If you expected the secretary/paralegal would be able to do more, tell them. It's not about judging. Give kind and caring counseling. Ask your employee:

- "Is this really a good fit for you?"

- "Are you aware that a few people have said you have a problem with body odor?"

Is this C employee ever going to be a B? How do you coach someone out of your law firm? If you can help someone move out of your law firm, you are helping them and your firm.

THE SOLE CRITERIA FOR TERMINATING EMPLOYMENT

Once you reach the ninety-day probationary period, make a decision based on one criteria: *Would you enthusiastically rehire the employee if you could do this again?* If not, you have to be ready to terminate their employment.

> *"You are the lion, but sometimes you don't want to do lion's shit because it's hard. Do the lion's shit—this way of thinking has transformed our business."*
> —John Morgan, *Esq., Morgan & Morgan*

There are some people who just cannot stay on your team. If you don't part ways with them, you're hurting your clients. Surround yourself with people who you appreciate and value.

THE MISSING INGREDIENT TO A GREAT HIRE

Relying on interviews and reference checks is not enough when hiring. You need to verify that the prospective employee can do the work. When you make the prospective employee show that they can do the work, there will be fewer surprises once they enter the workplace. And only then, my friend, have you made a great hire.

9

HOW TO SET EXPECTATIONS FOR YOUR TEAM

Your new employees should know exactly what you expect from them. A "position contract" defines what you expect and leaves little to the imagination. With a position contract, your employee will never say, "I didn't know I was supposed to do that."

Have your new employee review and sign the position contract before they begin. Here's the position contract for a receptionist (a.k.a. problem solver and happiness maker):

POSITION CONTRACT

We are very excited to begin working with you. We believe you will make an excellent addition to our team.

Why Your Position Contract Exists

In order to give you guidance and help you succeed, we prepared this position contract to describe the basic duties and tasks you will have as our receptionist.

More than anything, your position contract is your roadmap for success. We want you to know exactly what it will take to succeed with our law firm as well as the high expectations that we set.

Ultimately, our goal is for you to move on to bigger and better things than our law firm. And we are here to help you achieve your goals and ambitions. Strive to continue your personal development every day—attend seminars and workshops, go to a personal trainer and nutritionist, start jogging, participate in our Dream Manager Program, etc. Let us know what we can do to help you get to the next step in your career, even if that means leaving our law firm.

With this position contract, we are giving you two books: *The Fred Factor* and *Fish!* These books illustrate the "wow" client service that we expect from you. We strongly recommend that you read the books and re-read them from time to time as a reminder of our commitment to a "wow" service.

OUR PROTOCOLS

Weekly Goal Meeting

We meet every Monday at 10 a.m. for our "goal meeting." At the goal meeting, you should be prepared to do two things:

1. Your "Positive Focus": Tell us something in your life—personal or professional—that you are grateful for.

2. Your "Top Five Goals": Tell us your Top Five goals for the week and your "Top One of Five" (i.e., your most important goal for the week).

The Top Five goals set the agenda for your work week. We suggest that you make your Top Five goals for the week realistic, but not too easy—you want to stretch and accomplish more than you expect.

On the following Monday's goal meeting, we will review the prior week's goals and give you a score for each of the five goals, ranging from one (nothing done) to five (goal was achieved). Scores of two, three, and four reflect that you were partially successful but did not complete a goal. A top score for the week is twenty-five.

In addition to your Top Five goals, you may have other goals that you'd like to accomplish—you will call this your "should-do" list. You will receive three points for each goal that you accomplish from your "should-do" list.

Our Daily Huddle

At 9:15 a.m. on Tuesday through Friday, we meet to discuss your top three goals for the day. Similar to the weekly goal meeting, be prepared with a positive focus and the top three goals that you want to accomplish for the day.

At our Daily Huddle, there will be time for you to raise any questions or problems that you're having (e.g., defense counsel is refusing to cooperate in scheduling depositions). We will do our best to answer your question.

Arrive on time for the Daily Huddle no later than 9:15 a.m.— we do not want to have to wait for you. Don't hesitate to speak up if there is a process or system in our office that we can do better. You will likely have insights that we never thought of.

Show Up on Time

We expect that you will be at your desk and ready to work **no later than 8:45 a.m.** and **leave no earlier than 5:00 p.m.** on workdays. Showing up a few minutes late or leaving early is not alright. While there will be the occasional family emergency, this should be a rare occurrence.

Unfortunately, we have had to end the employment of employees who were unable to show up on time. We don't want this to happen to you.

How to Succeed at Our Law Firm

Your job is to provide our clients and referral partners with an amazing "WOW!!!" experience that they've never had at any other law firm. We want our clients to love you and tell us how wonderful you are. Take the initiative to call our clients and referral partners.

Our best advice for you is to make yourself indispensable. Give ten times more value than you receive. Think of ways to reduce our costs or refer new clients to our firm.

Make a decision, be proactive, and don't ask for permission. **We are giving you permission to make mistakes.** As long as you work hard and are completely committed to our clients, mistakes are acceptable.

No gossip or drama. We are brutally honest with each other and expect the same from you.

Our Culture

Our culture is *hungry* and *humble*. We are highly motivated (hungry) and treat each other as equals (humble), and we hope you will embrace our culture. If a specific task or goal isn't done by 5:00 p.m., it's okay to stay until the job is done.

Our Core Values

Our core values are the equivalent of the Constitution that governs our conduct. You should become intimately familiar with our four core values:

- We only practice catastrophic injury law.

- We never agree to confidential settlements.

- We do NOT accept cases having questionable merit.

- We are brutally honest with our clients.

We ask that you memorize our core values and when asked, be ready to recite them to us.

At our Daily Huddle, we encourage you to tell us how you've implemented one of our firm's core values. Core values mean nothing unless they are discussed and continually reinforced—we want you to show us how you have implemented our values.

Our purpose, which governs every decision that we make, is "Stopping Medical Injustice."

Raises, Promotions, and Probation

You will never be given a raise because of how long you work here. If you want a raise or bonus, earn it. Don't just do your job—we already pay you fairly to do that. Produce more than we pay you to do, exceed our expectations, and work to "wow" our clients and referral partners. The responsibility to earn more money is on you.

The first six months will be a probationary period. In six months, **we hope you will be doing more for our law firm than just the job we hired you to do.**

YOUR THREE MAJOR RESPONSIBILITIES

Your three major responsibilities are

1. answering the phone,

2. getting medical records, and

3. opening, scanning, and emailing correspondence.

In this position contract, we've set forth your responsibilities in detail so you have a clear understanding of what we expect from you. Our office manual (*Our Team's Playbook*), which is attached to this position contract, provides a complete set of our law firm's policies and procedures. You should keep *Our Team's Playbook* by your desk and refer to it whenever you are not sure what to do.

RESPONSIBILITY ONE: ANSWERING THE PHONE

You will be the front line for answering our phones and scheduling appointments. The phone calls to our law firm generally consist of three types of phone calls:

1. **Calls from New Clients:** New clients are people calling about a new case or attorneys referring a new case.

2. **Calls from Existing Clients:** Existing clients are our clients who have an active or potential case with us.

3. **Scheduling Depositions:** These are phone calls to schedule a deposition.

Phone Calls from New Clients

There are two kinds of new case calls:

1. New cases that are *not* referred by an attorney.

2. New cases that *are* referred by an attorney.

The handling of the new case call will vary depending on whether the case is referred by an attorney. When a new client calls our law firm, the first question you should ask is, "How were you referred to us?"

If the new client was not referred by a lawyer, then follow the steps set forth in the category, "New Cases That Are NOT Referred by Attorneys." If the new client was referred by a lawyer, then follow the steps set forth in the category called, "New Cases That Are Referred by Attorneys."

Cases That Are NOT Referred by Attorneys

When a new client calls with a potential case, the phone call should be transferred to our intake specialist. On the right-hand side of your phone, there is a button labeled "Intake" that you can press to send the new client to our intake specialist.

Once you determine that the client is calling with a new case and was *not* referred by a lawyer, you should explain to the new client: "Will you mind holding for a moment while I transfer you to our intake specialist?" You should then press the button on your phone to transfer the client to our intake specialist.

New Cases That Are Referred by Attorneys

When a case is referred by an attorney (our "referral partners"), the call should be transferred to me. If I am not available to take the phone call, you should transfer the call to our paralegal. **We place the highest value on new cases referred by lawyers, and I always want to speak directly with the lawyer when a new case is referred to us.**

If I am not available and our paralegal is not available, then you should schedule a time for me to speak with our client by phone. I prefer to schedule phone appointments between 4:00 p.m. and 5:00 p.m.

There is no need to ask for my permission to schedule an appointment. If the calendar has an opening for me, this means that I'm free and you can schedule the appointment.

When you schedule an appointment, please send me an email confirming that you scheduled an appointment.

If our paralegal and I are not available to speak with the client, you should enter all of the client's contact information in Lead Docket, our lead intake software.

Phone Calls from Existing Clients

When existing clients call to ask for information about the status of their case, you should try to answer their question. At first, this will be impossible, since you are not familiar with our cases, but as you get familiar with the cases and our civil case management software program, you will be able to answer most of their questions.

The typical questions asked by clients may include: "What is the date of my deposition? When can I meet with John to prepare for my deposition? Have you received my settlement check?"

Our clients are typically severely disabled or handicapped. The most important thing is to express compassion and understanding.

Our clients are sometimes difficult to handle and may be unreasonable, but you should treat them as though they are "always right." By the time our clients' cases are over, you should have a strong, lasting friendship with them.

If you can't answer the clients' questions, you should feel free to transfer the call to our paralegal. However, keep in mind that you should try to answer questions whenever you can so that our paralegal is not interrupted by phone calls.

Scheduling Depositions

The procedure for scheduling depositions is contained in *Our Team's Playbook*. Please don't hesitate to ask questions of our paralegal or me about these procedures.

Our paralegal will give you a list of cases where you will be asked to schedule dates for depositions.

We place the highest priority on our "A" cases, since they will have the highest monetary value. Every case has a "Priority Code" of either an "A," "B," "C," or "D" case, and you can find the Priority Code in the Case/Retainer tab of Trialworks for every client with an active case (an "active case" is a case in which the lawsuit has been filed).

- "A" cases: A settlement value over $1 million (our highest-value cases that make the most money for us).

- "B" cases: A settlement value between $500,000 and $1 million.

- "C" cases: A settlement value between $300,000 and $500,000.

- "D" cases: A settlement value less than $300,000.

Of all of the duties you will have at our law firm, the scheduling of depositions is the top priority. Our cases will not progress to trial until the depositions have been scheduled and completed and hence, we want to avoid delays and adjournments of depositions.

You must confirm dates for depositions with a letter to the defense counsel (e.g., "Per our telephone conversation, the deposition of our client, Ms. Jones, will be held on June 15, 2019 at 10:00 a.m. at Valley Reporting Service in Kingston.").

Unscheduled Phone Calls for John H. Fisher

Unless the caller is on my "VIP List," **I do *not* accept unscheduled phone calls**.

My VIP List includes

- lawyers referring a new case (our "referral partners"),

- claims adjusters with whom I am discussing a settlement,

- judges, and

- my family.

If the caller is not on my VIP List and does not want to schedule an appointment to speak with me, you can refer their call to our paralegal. However, I will not accept the phone call.

RESPONSIBILITY TWO: GETTING MEDICAL RECORDS

You will be responsible for requesting medical records.

Requesting Medical Records

In all of our cases, our clients sign a power of attorney that allows me to sign a release authorization on their behalf. A copy of the power of attorney is located in the Miscellaneous tab in Trialworks.

When I request medical records, I will send you an email that reads, "Please get Mr. Jones's updated medical records from Dr. Smith from February 1, 2018, to the present." It will be your job to prepare the release authorization for my signature and to send the release authorization with the power of attorney to the physician or hospital. The request for the medical records should be mailed **within twenty-four hours** of the time that we ask you to get the medical records.

Follow Up with Doctors and Hospitals

Most importantly, it will be your job to make sure that we receive the requested medical records. It is not unusual that *the doctor or hospital will ignore our request for medical records.*

Under section 18 of New York's Public Health Law, the physician or hospital has ten days to send the medical records to us. You should follow up with phone calls and letters to the physician or hospital if we have not received the medical records within ten days of our request.

We suggest that you follow up with the physician or hospital about the medical records within the following timeframes from the date of our initial request:

- Ten days

- Twenty-one days

- Thirty-one days

If we do not have the medical records within thirty-one days of our initial request to the physician or hospital, please notify our paralegal and me by email (e.g., "It has been more than thirty-one days since our request for Dr. Smith's updated medical records and he has not responded.").

When we receive new medical records, you should scan them into the Medical Records tab in Trialworks.

RESPONSIBILITY THREE: OPENING AND SCANNING MAIL

When you get the mail from the mailbox (mail arrives between 12:30 and 2:00 p.m.), your top priority should be to do the following:

- Sort mail before opening.

- All non-client-related mail goes to our paralegal.

- Open the mail.

- All invoices go to our office manager.

- Date-stamp when appropriate (items that are not stamped: original documents such as wills, death certificates, official court documents, original documents signed by clients, like POAs).

- Scan the mail to the appropriate tab in Trialworks.

- Email the correspondence to the intended recipient.

- No original mail goes to John.

This procedure for mail has the highest priority. It is never acceptable to postpone the opening and scanning of new mail because you are busy doing something else. Mail should *never* be left sitting on your desk after it is received.

When we receive a fax, scan the fax to the appropriate tab in Trialworks and email the correspondence to the intended recipient.

We are a paperless office. If a document is not scanned into Trialworks *as soon as it is received*, our paperless office will not function.

All outgoing mail must be delivered to the post office by 4:30 p.m.

Final Tips for Your Success

Random Acts of Kindness

Wowing our clients and referral partners is the number-one priority for you.

Our clients and prospective referral partners will get their first impression of our law firm from you. A friendly smile and a nice personal touch (e.g., "It's great to hear from you.") make all the difference. You should smile every time you answer the phone—a warm smile ensures that you're happy to speak with our clients.

You should do at least one "random act of kindness" every day that will convey a warm, personal touch. The warm touch might be a handwritten "thank-you" letter or a box of chocolates or flowers, but it can be anything—use your imagination and be creative. You have my complete permission to perform "random acts of kindness" whenever you see a chance to "wow" our clients and referral partners.

John's Email Policy

I only review email twice a day—once at noon and again at 4:00 p.m. (some days I do not open Microsoft Outlook at all). I cannot be effective unless I have large blocks of uninterrupted work time, and responding to email is not a productive use of my time.

If you have an urgent matter that requires my immediate attention (e.g., the judge wants to speak with me), you should buzz my phone or come back to my office to tell me. *Email is not an effective way to communicate urgent information.*

Read Before You Sign

Read this position contract, and let us know if you have any questions or disagreements. Please initial each page of this position contract, sign the last page, return one original to us, and keep one original.

_____ Dated:

New Team Member

_____ Dated:

John H. Fisher

10

TIME MANAGEMENT FOR MANIACS

Manage your day by saying "no" to almost everything. Everyone is competing for your time and trying to force their way into your workday. Every time you say "yes" to something, you are simultaneously saying "no" to something else. It's damn hard to say "no," because you want to be liked, but you'll be more respected by your peers when you say "no."

Eliminating Distractions with Your Rules of Communication

Write a list of the things that you can eliminate from your schedule. Let's start with the basics—if you want to be productive, you have to eliminate the time-vampires:

- Web surfing

- Email

- Texts

- Unscheduled phone calls

Create **Rules of Communication** with your clients, and make sure your staff follows your system for client communication. There will be no unscheduled phone calls. If you don't enforce your rules, you can't expect your clients to follow them.

"Sometimes what you don't do is just as important as what you do."
—Greg McKeown, *Essentialism: The Disciplined Pursuit of Less*

Ask your clients to sign your Rules of Communication at your first meeting, and remind them of your communication rules with email auto-responders. Whenever a client sends you an email, the auto-responder sends a gentle reminder, "Our Rules of Communication are attached as a friendly reminder."

John's Rules of Communication

Rule 1: I do NOT take unplanned phone calls.

Rule 2: You should never come to our office without an appointment.

Putting Your Law Firm on Autopilot with Automation

With your Rules of Communication, you've eliminated the busywork of answering phone calls and responding to emails. You're focused on working on your priorities instead of someone else's. But you still need to communicate with your clients and let them know that you're working on their case. This is where you automate everything you can.

When a new client contacts you, you should have an automated sequence of emails that explain the process for evaluating their case. The introductory email contains a video explaining your three-step process for (a) getting the medical records, (b) reviewing the medical records with an expert, and (c) making a decision to accept or decline the case.

> *"Automation is to your time what compounding interest is to your money."*
> —**Rory Vaden**, *Procrastinate on Purpose*

Your email explains the time that it takes to complete each part of the case evaluation. You're giving your clients instant feedback as soon as they send their first email or call your office. And even after the initial contact, you can automate the client communication as your case evaluation progresses.

Automating your law practice with CRM software is a game-changer. Infusionsoft is a software that combines email marketing, CRM, and e-commerce, all in one place. We use Infusionsoft for almost every aspect of our law firm:

- New client inquiries (our "365-day nurture campaign")

- Status updates to current clients for potential and active files

- Book sales

- Email newsletters

- My wife's judicial campaign

After the initial client contact, you can automate the follow-up with a sequence of emails relevant to the initial inquiry. If a new client calls about a delay in diagnosing cancer, you can send a series of emails through your CRM that set forth the factors in evaluating the case.

Become a Master Delegator

You have to get over the idea that you have to do everything. Your paralegal or secretary should be responding to your email and mail, and you should never answer the phone unless your client has a scheduled appointment.

> *"You are always paying someone to complete a task.*
> *You are either paying someone else at their rate of*
> *pay, or you are paying yourself at yours."*
> —Rory Vaden, *Procrastinate on Purpose*

What are the things in your office that only you can do? Write that list, and delegate everything else. For starters, you should delegate these tasks:

- Drafting discovery responses and demands.

- Responding to mail and email.

- Answering phone calls from opposing counsel.

- Speaking with clients about the status of their case.

You know you can do the work faster and better than anyone, but that's the type of thinking that will get you in trouble. Perfection is the enemy—"good enough" is your friend. Just think of all the free time you'll have once you've eliminated, automated, and delegated your work.

Building for Tomorrow (and Multiplying Your Time)

Don't get caught up putting out the wildfires that pop up. You must *always* be thinking long term by creating policies and systems that will give you more free time.

> *"Anything you create a process for today saves you time tomorrow."*
> —Rory Vaden, *Procrastinate on Purpose*

What can you do right now that will create more free time? Here's some food for thought:

- An office manual setting forth your policies.

- Position contracts spelling out what is expected of each employee.

- An organizational chart assigning individual roles.

- Creating forms for your pleadings, discovery responses, and release authorizations.

Just think about how much time you spend every day answering the same questions. With policies, your staff has answers for almost every issue, and your office operates on autopilot while you're on vacation or in trial.

Your Highest-Impact Activities

What can you do right now that will have the biggest impact on your law practice? It's not returning phone calls or responding to emails. The best use of your time is business development (e.g., getting more of the "A" cases). Everything falls into place when you have an inventory of "A" cases.

What is the best use of your time for business development? It's different for everyone, but it might be one of these:

- Creating a content creation strategy for your website.

- Nurturing relationships with your referral partners through newsletters (print and email), books, and speaking events.

- Updating referral partners about the status of a referral.

Once you've defined the activities that are the best use of your time, you know what to focus on.

11

THE ULTIMATE SYSTEM BUILDER

Have you ever wondered why it seems that you answer the same questions over and over again? When new employees begin, don't you hate telling them the same thing that you told the last employee … five years ago?

Sure, you have great systems, but if they aren't documented and shared with your staff, they are essentially worthless. There are few things more important than documenting the core processes of your law firm—ranging from your processes for hiring and firing, case management, and even ordering a replacement for the water cooler.

It's as simple as watching what you do and writing down the systems, i.e., documenting the knowledge that you have. But documenting your core processes is only the start—you have to share the core processes with your staff and get their help creating the policies.

Why Documenting Your Core Processes Is Critical

If you die, what will happen to your firm? For most of us, the answer is chaos. Your staff would have no idea what to do and eventually, your law firm would die. But it doesn't have to be this way.

> *"It puts me in the position where I can spend less time in the business and more time on the business."*
>
> —Jay Ruane, Esq., Shelton, Connecticut

By documenting and sharing your core processes, you create a system that can survive your death. If you want to spend the winter in Hawaii, the system is in place that will let you do that. And if the time comes that you want to stop practicing law, you will have a real business that lawyers will want to buy.

The System for Creating Systems

Ruane Attorneys, the largest criminal defense law firm in Connecticut, has an ingenuous tool for documenting their core processes. With a password-protected website, "Ruanepedia" (modeled after the collaborative website, Wikipedia), the firm creates new policies for their firm on an almost daily basis. When a new issue comes up, the employees check the firm's online website and if a policy doesn't exist, they create one.

> *"If I have to explain it more than once, it's certainly a system that needs to be in our Wikipedia."*
>
> —Jay Ruane, Esq., Shelton, Connecticut

Here's how it works. Let's say an employee wants to add a new policy providing directions to the courthouse. The associate takes a few photographs showing where to park and where the courtroom is, adds a link to the court's website and voila! The photos are uploaded to Ruanepedia from the employee's smart phone. With this simple step, no one has to get lost.

With our firm's Fisherpedia, every office policy is described in detail and has an explanation why it exists, including

- what this is,

- how we do it, and

- why we do it this way.

Ruanepedia has a search bar at the top that allows employees to find the policies. You can also embed a private YouTube video into the website. Jay uses Ruanepedia to promote his firm to new employees, e.g., "Here's how we do everything." Ruanepedia has a side bar that identifies the employee responsible for each task, similar to an organizational chart.

The website's dashboard lists the latest and most popular policies, e.g., "How to Create a pdf from a Microsoft Word document." When Jay and his marketing director attend marketing seminars, they share their insights on Ruanepedia in the marketing folder.

A Training Tool Unlike Any Other

Before a new employee begins their employment, have them read the first forty entries on your firm's wiki-style website. The online operations manual can be a resource for new employees with specific instructions for every policy. Your offer of employment might read:

"Welcome to the team. Please read these forty entries before you come to work on Monday and you'll know more about our firm than anyone else."

When you need to hire a new intake specialist, your team knows how to do it, e.g., "Hiring Paralegal, Intake, Legal Assistant." The process for posting an ad for a paralegal is on your website, so if you're not around, a staff member can post the online advertisement.

As you open new offices and expand your staff, you will have an online operations manual that will help new employees get up to speed quickly. You can outsource work to virtual assistants—just ask the VA to follow the directions on your wiki-style website. All of your employees are working based on the same, shared collective knowledge base.

Everything Your Team Needs in One Place

The website has everything your staff needs to know with pictures and video, e.g., "How to copy a CD or DVD of Medical, Legal or Other Documents." Once you create the system, you don't have to explain this to anyone. You can give associates examples by uploading motions filed in other cases to the website.

There is no limit to what your policies can be:

- How to Electronically File a Summons and Complaint in Supreme Court

- How to Schedule the Deposition of a Non-Party Witness

- How to Subpoena Medical Records for Trial

Bottom line, if you're gone from the office (e.g., death or extended illness), you staff will know exactly what to do. You have all of your core processes in a single place and there will be a wealth of information for new employees to learn about your core processes.

Incentivizing Your Team to Document Core Processes

Jay has a point system for associates, where points are rewarded when employees create new systems. The staff is rewarded for their work based upon their point total and the firm is rewarded with an online office manual that is one-of-a-kind.

If the associate earns one hundred points by the end of each quarter, they receive a bonus. For creating a new system (e.g., "How to negotiate a traffic ticket"), the associate earns thirty points.

> *"The core functions of my office can happen*
> *without me actually being there."*
> —Jay Ruane, Esq., Shelton, Connecticut

The firm's employees are constantly adding to the policies. New policies go live on Ruanepedia almost every day and Jay reviews the policies once a week. The firm's online website has 245 systems created by Jay and 1,158 systems created by the firm's employees.

Getting Your Staff to Document Systems

First, create a how-to system for documenting core processes and make sure your staff is aware of it. Ask your staff to document the mechanics of what they do on a daily basis. To get started, offer a $50 bonus. It becomes a rite of passage for new employees to celebrate the first time they create a new system, e.g., "Hey, I've built my first system!"

Remind your staff that there will be less work for them if they don't have to train new employees. Jay gave each of his employees a bonus of one hundred dollars when their firm reached 1,000 systems. You might offer to buy lunch for your employees if they create ten new systems by the end of the week.

> *"If I am the only person who knows how to do something and something happens to me, this whole business fails."*
> —Jay Ruane, Esq., Shelton, Connecticut

Constantly remind your staff to create new systems, like a mother telling her kids to brush their teeth. Make a game out of it by celebrating new policies with your team, e.g., "Someone just completed this system—that's phenomenal!"

The Do-It-Yourself Style of Documenting Core Processes

To get started, your new employee should read the entry, "How to Add a New Entry." The template for new entries provides an explanation of the process, so they understand the importance of the task. The initial entries for new employees might take them through "How to Add a Photo to a Client's File" or "How to Add a Screenshot to a New Entry."

If you want to do it yourself, pay attention to what you do and write down the steps for everything. Every time you do an administrative or marketing task, ask: "Do I have a system for this yet?" You might already have systems in your office manual or sitting around on a yellow legal pad.

*"It's one less thing I have to be responsible for in the future,
so I can turn to the things that really matter."*

—Jay Ruane, Esq., Shelton, Connecticut

You might hire a temporary employee (or high school student) to document the most basic core processes. The temporary worker will have a unique view of your systems that might not be obvious to you.

Ensuring Compliance with Your Online Operations Manual

Review the systems at the end of the week to make sure your staff is complying with them., e.g., "Are they following the systems for creating systems?" Every Friday afternoon, Jay reviews the new entries and might add an image or tweak them.

You might schedule a "training day" on Friday afternoons to review new systems and discuss how they can be improved and implemented. Because let's face it, if you're not implementing the systems, your systems aren't worth diddly.

Creating a Website that will be the Envy of Your Peers

It's not expensive to create a website for documenting core processes. You can get started with a knowledge-based website through HeroThemes.com. Even better, call Jay's brother, Brendan Ruane (LightswitchAdvisors.com), who is the web guru who created Ruane-pedia. Brendan can create the same website for you.

For a one-time fee, you will have a made-for-you, wiki-style website that will be the envy of your peers and an investment in your future. And with this system for documenting your core processes, one day you might be able to tell another lawyer, "I'm selling my firm and here's how you do everything."

When that day comes, I want you to call Jay Ruane, Esq. to say thanks. And you might want to tell Jay that his "system for creating systems" was a game-changer for you.

12

THE INTAKE SYSTEM THAT WORKS WHEN YOU SLEEP

When you speak with a new client, everything's copacetic. The client is happy, you're excited to have the new case and everything seems wonderful. Then, with time, things start to change. Your client doesn't hear from your staff and they have no idea what you're doing. A few phone messages aren't returned and before long, your client starts calling other lawyers.

This is a problem. Your marketing dollars are a waste of money if your intake system is not tracking and following up with new leads. You have to fix your intake system before you spend more money on marketing. But where do you begin?

Your Unique Process for Converting Leads into Clients

Document the step-by-step process to accomplish the key processes of your intake system. What is the value that your clients get from each step in the process? List all of the activities that you do to create value for your clients—breakdown your process and label each stage.

Your goal? A defined intake system that is easy to use and implemented by staff. With a defined intake process, the metrics for your intake process will be accessible on a daily basis:

- Metrics for new leads, e.g., number of leads, source of leads and conversion ratio of leads into clients

- Customized questions for new clients that are relevant to the nature of their inquiry

- A system for following up with new clients and keeping them informed of the status of your case evaluation

Explain each step of the process of case evaluation. Define what occurs in the process, who's responsible for each step and how you can make it better. For each step, describe the value that is given to your clients.

This is our five-step process for new case evaluations.

Our Five-Step Process for Evaluating Your Claim

Step #1: Intake Phone Call

How it Creates Value: Creates relationship with new client, determines the specific nature of their claim and whether the claim is still viable under the applicable statute of limitations. This educates our clients about our procedures for evaluating their claim.

Action Item: New case is created in Lead Docket by our intake specialist.

Who's Involved: Intake Specialist

Step #2: Get the Medical Records & Send to Medical Expert/Surgeon

How it Creates Value: Determines whether our clients' claims of substandard medical treatment are substantiated by the medical records.

Action Item: Written request for medical records is mailed to medical provider.

Upon receipt, the medical records are reviewed by our medical records custodian to determine whether we received the medical records that were requested.

Our medical records custodian forwards the medical records to the attorney and our medical expert/surgeon.

Who's Involved: Medical records custodian

Step #3: Meet or Speak with Expert to Discuss their Opinions

How it Creates Value: Standard of care is defined by a board-certified surgeon based upon their review of the medical records.

Action Item: Meet or speak with the expert/surgeon

Who's Involved: Lawyer/litigation paralegal

Step #4: Follow Up Phone Call with Client about Expert's Opinions

How it Creates Value: Keeps client informed about our case evaluation.

Action Item: Speak with our client about our evaluation of their claim.

Who's Involved: Lawyer/litigation paralegal

Step #5: Make Decision to Accept or Decline

How it Creates Value: Provides resolution for client and when appropriate, client is referred to another lawyer.

Action Item: Letter sent to client informing them of our decision to accept or decline and a copy of the letter is mailed to our referral partner. Send thank you letter to our referral partner.

Who's Involved: Office manager

Why You Should Have a Defined Intake Process

With a defined intake system, clients know what to expect. Your intake process can explain your core values for new clients, e.g., brutal honesty with clients.

With a defined intake process, you will be able to

- track deadlines for each step of the process,

- notify clients when each step is completed, and

- give clients access to their file through a website portal, so they can check on the status of your case evaluation.

Create a checklist for every new case call and document whether the steps are being performed. Create a Slack channel for your law firm and require daily updates from your intake specialist, e.g., # of calls or new referral partners.

How to Create More Value for Your Clients

Think of ways that you can provide more value to your clients on the front stage (the front stage is your communication system with clients). You might send new clients a sequence of informative emails and video through your CRM, including:

- Giving your clients electronic access to the client welcome package (e.g., "What to Expect in Your Lawsuit")

- Personalized welcome video explaining your process for case evaluation

- Send e-book, e.g., *The 7 Deadly Mistakes of Malpractice Victims*

- Automate the follow up email campaign with Customer Relationship software (CRM)

- Hire an in-house intake specialist

- Use lead intake software, such as Lead Docket, for a centralized database of new leads and customize the questions for the different types of cases

- Use artificial intelligence to prequalify online leads for merit with Ngage Live Chat

Create an infographic (99Designs.com) that explains each step of the process for evaluating a claim., e.g., "Our 5-Step Process for Evaluating Your Claim." Explain the duration of every step by providing a range, e.g., two to four weeks to get the medical records.

You Don't Know What You Don't Know

If you don't think you're losing clients right now, you're kidding yourself. Clients won't hesitate to leave you for another lawyer if you're not providing value, educating them, following up, and nurturing your relationship.

So, before you spend another penny on marketing, define your intake system, spot the holes in your process and implement the system. Nothing is more important.

13

FOUR STEPS FOR AN INCREDIBLY PRODUCTIVE DAY

There is only one thing that is irreplaceable: TIME. And everyone has the same twenty-four hours in a day, 168 hours in a week. It's what we choose to do with our time that makes a difference.

You excel when you focus on work that only you can do—your "Unique Ability*." You are passionate, focused and "in the zone" when you do the work that no one can do quite like you.

#1: What Do You Want to Do Less of?

Begin by writing your "Not-To-Do" List—the work that you can't stand. What do you want to do less of?

Here's my top three on the Not-To-Do List.

1. **Paperwork**: I *hate* paperwork, including expert responses, discovery responses, responding to mail, etc. I'd much rather let our paralegals do the paperwork.

2. **Less Client Communication**: I don't like speaking with clients to inform them about the status of their case. I'd much rather let other team members update our clients on a weekly basis.

3. **Accountability**: I don't like checking to make sure team members are doing what they are supposed to do. Drives me crazy when I have to ask more than once for something, and ideally, our team members know what do to without being asked.

What are the payoffs of delegating this work? More time for strategic planning and less time checking the work of our team members. In essence, this creates more time to create and implement systems and policies for the growth and *self-management* of our law firm.

#2: What are You Going to Delegate?

How can you delegate the activities on your Not-To-Do List? Create a top three list of activities you want to delegate. Each of your top three delegations should address the activities on your Not-To-Do List.

Your top three delegations might be:

1. **Implement the Pre-Litigation and Litigation Checklists**: Ensure cases are completed within eighteen months with specific timeframes for each phase of discovery.

2. **Client Communication**: Create a system for ensuring frequent communication (a.k.a. touchpoints) with clients and referral partners. Have multiple touchpoints that are checked at various milestones in the lawsuit.

3. **Quarterly Evaluations of Team Members**: Evaluate team members based upon three key metrics (Big Three) for every position on our firm's growth/organizational chart. Don't wait to the end of the year evaluations to evaluate your team.

Once you've identified the activities you don't want to do, and the top three delegations, it's time to focus on the activities that you love.

#3: What Do You Want to do More of?

Once you've created the activities that you don't want to do, it's time to create the list of the activities that you want to do.

My unique ability consists of five activities:

1. **I Love Writing!**: This includes books, articles, newsletters, and updates to referral partners about the status of a referred case.

2. **Spending Time with Wife and Kids**: I enjoy building stronger relationships and carefree timelessness with Lisa and the kids (and our pooch, Patch).

3. **Strategic Planning for Law Firm**: Creating and implementing systems and policies for every aspect of marketing, case management, and law firm operations including quarterly strategic planning with team members.

4.   **Mentoring Lawyers**: Building relationships with referral sources is something I get a kick out of.

5.   **Evaluating New Cases**: Analyzing medical records and reviewing the strengths and weaknesses of a new case. I enjoy updating referral partners about our evaluation of a referred case—this is the one thing I do (almost) every day.

#4: What Have You Learned About Yourself?

You live for a higher purpose than pushing papers. For many of us, our unique ability is to do creative, visionary, and strategic work. If your unique ability is anything like mine, you've discovered a few things about yourself:

1.   **I Love Creative Work!**: I enjoy forming strategic and visionary plans and goals that are one-of-a-kind. Love creating something from scratch (e.g., Mastermind Experience) and watching it grow.

2.   **I Hate the Grind**: The day-to-day grind sucks. Don't bother me with details—just let me know when the work is done.

3.   **I Love a Self-Managed Law Firm**: I'm totally into creating policies and systems for marketing and management of a law firm and not having to check to make sure the work gets done.

A self-managed law firm frees you up to do the creative, fun work that you want to do, but haven't given yourself permission to do.

A Harsh Reality that Few Lawyers Will Ever Admit

A few years ago, I met with one of the nation's top marketing gurus. No topic was off limits as we brainstormed the best marketing ideas for growing a law firm. I can't say I learned much, except for one take-away: the marketing guru told me that the highest earning entrepreneurs spend more than 50 percent of their time on marketing and business development.

I did not completely accept the guru's advice, at least not at first. But time and again some of the leading plaintiffs' lawyers would tell me the same thing: marketing is your business. Without marketing, you don't have clients, without clients, you don't have money, and without money, you don't have a business.

This is the reality you face. Once you accept this reality, you will be head and shoulders above all of the other lawyers in your community.

* * *

THE MAGIC FORMULA FOR GETTING STUFF DONE

The Quick Launch Challenge is a thirty-day program for getting stuff done. Think of the one thing you want to get done more than anything else, but keep putting off. It's time for a change.

You will work with a "coach" (a.k.a, a peer or member of your mastermind) and every day, you must call the coach at 9:00 p.m. to report the level of effort you gave that day toward your goal. If you forget to call, you must at least text or email your coach.

The Quick Launch Challenge consists of three simple steps:

Step One: The Daily Question

The question you ask every day is simply: Did I do my best to ...

- Eat healthy?

- Exercise?

- Make my spouse happy?

- Finish the edits of my book manuscript?

You're not being asked how you performed, but rather your level of effort. If you gave no effort, your score is one, your best effort is a ten, and other levels of effort should be scored according to your honest judgment.

Step Two: Daily Accountability

You won't get better without follow up. You and your coach will track the scores on an Excel spreadsheet so you can see the trends. Your coach reminds you what you are supposed to be doing.

"The act of self-questioning ... changes everything."
—**Marshall Goldsmith**, *Triggers*

By tracking your effort on a daily basis, you have structure, commitment, and top of mind awareness for your goals. You'd hate to call your coach to report that you gave no effort and making at least some effort on a daily basis will be on your mind. With daily questions and nightly follow up, there's no turning back.

Step Three: Sharing Your Results

Every week, you and your coach will post your Excel spreadsheet among your peers, e.g., a mastermind group.

> *"The only essential element is that the scores are reported somewhere."*
> —Marshall Goldsmith, *Triggers*

Reporting your scores to a peer group increases your accountability. With peer group accountability, you're not only reporting to your coach, your friends and peers will also remind you what you are supposed to be doing.

The Results Will Shock You

More than a year ago I finished the manuscript for my new book, *The Law Firm of Your Dreams* and the book was scheduled to be available from my publisher in November, 2019. There was only one problem: the publisher (Advantage Media Group) needed my final approval of the manuscript. I procrastinated and put this off.

> *"A coach reminds the fragile doer what he's supposed to do."*
> —Marshall Goldsmith, *Triggers*

Houston injury lawyer, Don McClure, Esq., reminded me that the book is not helping anyone until it is printed and delivered. So, I started the Quick Launch Challenge, and guess what?

As result of daily accountability phone calls and a renewed commitment, the edits of the manuscript were approved and submitted to my publisher in ten days. In ten days, I finished the edits as a result of daily accountability check-ins.

And there's no reason you can't do the same thing. If you have a goal that can be accomplished in thirty days, let me know (jfisher@fishermalpractice.com) and I'll be your coach and join you in the Quick Launch Challenge.

* "Unique Ability is a registered trademark, protected by copyright and an integral concept of the Strategic Coach, Inc. All rights reserved. Used with written permission.

www.strategiccoach.com

14

CREATING A CULTURE OF "WOW" FOR YOUR CLIENTS

Doing a great job for your client is par for the course. Your clients expect a great result and assume they can get the same result from any other lawyer. A great result for your client doesn't really differentiate your law practice from other lawyers.

So, what can you do to deliver a "wow" experience to your clients? You want to deliver an experience that is so unique that your clients will rave about you—not just during their lawsuit but long after it's over. Your goal should be to create loyal fans for life who will refer new cases to you over the rest of your career.

A Powerful Welcome Package Unlike Any Others

You've heard this a million times: the first impression means everything. When a new client hires you, you can start with a nice "welcome" card that contains a brief biography and a photograph of your paralegal and legal secretary. A few personal quips about your staff adds a nice touch, and you can humanize your staff by showing what they do in their spare time (e.g., working in their garden). Now your clients can put a face to the person they are dealing with. You and your staff should hand-sign the "welcome" card.

> *"Reasonable quality and service are an expectation, not a tiebreaker."*
> —Jack Trout, *Differentiate or Die*

Barry D. Kowitt, Esq., a premier traffic defense lawyer in Plantation, Florida, sends an email to new clients with a cool video that answers their "top ten" most frequently asked questions. Just think, with this simple step you answered most of the questions posed by new clients, and you didn't even have to speak with them. And the beauty of creating a "welcome" video for new clients is that once you've created the video, you have a powerful "wow" package for your career.

Grassroots "Wow" That Your Clients Will Never Forget

Here's something that no lawyer does (which is precisely why you should): a *client appreciation party*. Once a year, invite your current and former clients to a dinner party, and wine and dine them (the more casual, the better). You will be amazed at the gratitude of your clients, and as an added bonus, they will be reminded to refer new cases. Try this one time, and you'll swear it was the best thing you've ever done.

Don't have a few extra bucks for a client appreciation party? Try this: block out one day a month from your calendar to call your clients to say "hi" and update them on their case. Even if there is nothing to report about their case, your clients will love hearing from you. This random act of kindness always works—your clients will be effusive in their gratitude for your phone call, and it builds a stronger bond.

Don't have money in your budget for a monthly print newsletter? Then send a letter to your clients once every three months with an update about you and your law firm—a kind of "here's what we're up to" letter about things like speaking engagements, trials, settlements, things you're crossing off on your bucket list, and personal stuff (e.g., your vacation to Disney World). Your clients and friends will love hearing what you're up to.

Making "Wow" a Part of Your Firm's Culture

Touch base with your clients at important milestones in their case. Start by identifying a number of touch points with your client (e.g., the filing of the lawsuit, scheduling of a trial date, etc.), and then contact your client when you reach these milestones. You might even automate the process through email updates (chapter 10 of *The Power of a System* has our nurture campaign for following up with clients).

Taking this one step further, the website for Finkelstein & Partners, LLP has a client portal that allows their clients to access parts of their case file and sends updates to clients via email when there are new developments. It's a fantastic way to automate follow-up.

You're one person, and you can't build a culture of "wow" alone. So, give your paralegal and secretary permission to send handwritten notes and special "thank-you" cards to your clients. Even a small gift like a box of cookies won't soon be forgotten by your clients.

One Lawyer Delivering a Wow Experience

Joe O'Connor, Esq., an excellent injury lawyer in Kingston, NY, bought eight summer golf passes for college students who could not afford to golf at the country club. Joe didn't get an immediate payback for his magnanimous gesture, but guess who's been talking about his generosity? Eight college students talk about Joe every time they hit the links, and their friends are spreading the word. Joe didn't advertise his good deed, but his fan base is growing ... and who will these students recommend when their friends need a personal injury lawyer?

Instilling the Wow Culture in Your Law Firm

That sounds great, but you're crazy busy and don't have two minutes in your workday for this "wow" stuff. Fair enough, but you can get started by buying the books *Fish!* and *The Fred Factor*. Ask your staff to read these books by a certain date, and then meet to discuss the books and the ways you can implement the "wow" experience into your law firm's culture.

> *"Make WOW a verb that is part of your
> company's everyday vocabulary."*
> —Tony Hsieh, *Delivering Happiness*

Whenever a member of your staff delivers a wow experience, have them report it to your team, and then celebrate. You might write down the random acts of kindness on a whiteboard in your conference room for all to see, or give the staff member a fifty-dollar gift card for their favorite restaurant. Find some way to celebrate each "wow" experience.

Nine Basic Rules for Answering the Phone

To help instill a "wow" experience for our clients, we have nine basic rules at our law firm for answering the phone. We laminate our rules and ask that our receptionist keep them facing them at their desk. These rules are a constant reminder of how we expect our receptionist to answer the phone. If you do not have simple rules for answering the phone, your receptionist will create their own rules.

We see our clients as guests invited to a party, and we are the hosts. It's our job to make every part of our clients' experience a little better.

#1: Answer the Phone in Less Than Three Rings

Why it's done this way: If it takes three rings or more to answer the phone, the caller will hang up and call the next lawyer.

#2: Greet the Caller

Example: "Thank you for calling the law firm of John H. Fisher, PC, How can I help you?"

Why it's done this way: You are doing two things at the moment you answer the phone—you are showing appreciation for the phone call and you are extending an offer to help.

#3: Use the Caller's Name

Example: "Thank you, **Mary**, for calling us … **Mary**, do you have any other questions?"

Why it's done this way: Everyone loves the sound of their name. You should use the caller's name at the beginning of the phone call, at the end of the phone call, and as often as you can.

#4: Be Empathetic

Example: In a death case, "I am very sorry for your loss." In injury cases, you might express compassion by saying, "I am very sorry to hear this. We'll do our best to help you."

Why it's done this way: We care about our clients, and our commitment to caring should be conveyed as soon as you learn about the caller's loss (especially in death cases).

#5: Smile!

Example: Put a mirror next on your desk, and look at the mirror every time you answer the phone. Make sure you smile every time you answer the phone.

Why it's done this way: Yes, this is strange at first, but this almost forces you to have a positive, happy mind-set for every phone call.

#6: Listen Without Interruption

Example: Do not speak until the caller stops speaking.

Why it's done this way: Everyone hates being interrupted while they're speaking—not to mention, it's rude. Be patient with clients and let them finish what they are saying.

#7: Confirm Satisfaction

Example: "Is there anything else we can help you with?"

Why it's done this way: You want to confirm that you've answered all of the client's questions.

#8: Take Ownership

Example: If the caller complains, take ownership by acknowledging our mistake and assuring them we will do better (e.g., "I am so sorry we did not get back to you sooner.").

Why it's done this way: If the caller is unhappy, you should apologize and offer to make things right. Callers are not always right, but you should treat them as if they can do no wrong.

9: Say "Thank You" and Invite Them Back

Example: "It was my pleasure speaking with you, Mary. Please don't hesitate to call us if you think of any other questions."

Why it's done this way: You should always end the phone call by showing appreciation for the phone call and making a final offer to help. This ends the call on a positive note.

15

GETTING MORE FROM YOUR STAFF THAN YOU COULD EVER DREAM POSSIBLE

It's a problem that's a constant struggle for you: your employees come late, leave early, and surf the web at work. You want your staff to have an ownership mentality, but you can't give them an equity stake in your firm. You decide you have to pay your staff more money.

You raise their salary or give them a fat bonus. Your staff is effusive with their appreciation, but you quickly realize that the pay raise and bonuses don't change a damn thing. Your staff is doing the same things they were doing before the bump in pay, and you're ready to give up.

An Irrefutable Truth that Lawyers Ignore

You come to the same conclusion that all lawyers inevitably reach: *money doesn't motivate*. Rewards and penalties may motivate in the short term, but they won't do squat for your law practice over the long haul. If you're not a believer, read Daniel Pink's *Drive*, about the futility of motivating with rewards and penalties (a.k.a. "carrots" and "sticks").

Perhaps you're ready to give up and accept your lot or fire your lazy, unmotivated staff. You think there's no way that you can motivate your staff—either they're hardworking and committed to your clients, or they only show up for a paycheck. But you're ignoring the one thing that your staff wants more than anything else: a strong, unequivocal sign that you care about them, personally and professionally.

You're thinking, "This guy Fisher is nuts—of course I care about my team." No doubt you compliment your team when a big case settles, and perhaps you take them to lunch or throw a birthday party. But what you're doing is the bare minimum—your team still won't work harder or become more invested in your practice.

The Power of Dreams for Your Staff

Everything you do is motivated by dreams. Your dreams are why you work weekends and stay at work long after everyone else has gone home—you're trying to build a better life for your family. Your dream might be to retire early, take a month-long vacation to Europe, or send your kids to an Ivy League school, but did you ever bother to think that *your team has dreams too?*

The dreams of your staff might be as simple as owning their own home or taking a trip to Disney World. These dreams may seem simple and easily attainable, but your staff's dreams are the reason they're living. Once you tap into your staff's dreams, you discover what motivates them and why they come to work.

If you can find out what your staff's dreams are and help them achieve those dreams, you will have discovered the key to unlocking the power of dreams. Your staff will know that you're not just using them to get rich; you care about their future, and you have a specific strategy to make their dreams come true. Once your staff knows that you care about their dreams, they will walk through walls for you.

Step One: The Dream Book

Begin by asking your staff to list their dreams in a journal that you give them (the "Dream Book"). Explain that your staff's participation in the Dream Manager Program is completely optional, but for those willing to take a chance, you will take the leap with them. Show your Dream Book to your staff, and tell them about the biggest dreams that you have—not just for your practice, but your personal goals too.

Ask them to set aside a couple of hours to write their dreams in their Dream Book. Tell your staff to dream without limitation—no dream is too big—and write their dreams in a sort of stream of consciousness. Ask them to write one hundred dreams, in any sphere of their life: spiritual, intellectual, physical, material, or emotional. As each dream is added to the Dream Book, tell your staff to write the date that they wrote the dream and when they plan to achieve it.

Once they have a list of one hundred dreams, ask your staff to add time frames for each dream. A short-term dream ("ST") is one that can be accomplished in less than twelve months; a moderate-term dream ("MT") can be achieved between one and five years; and a long-term dream ("LT") will take more than five years. Your staff should write "ST," "MT," or "LT" next to each of their one hundred dreams.

Step Two: Hire a Dream Manager

Ask your staff to pick one dream that is most important. Sure, you can't conquer the world, but you can help your employees achieve their most meaningful dream. Hire a dream manager (life coach) to meet once a month with your employees to create a plan for achieving their dream—these are "Dream Sessions."

> *"Just talking about our dreams moves us in the direction of them."*
> —Matthew Kelly, *The Dream Manager*

Let's say your receptionist's biggest dream is home ownership. Your employee meets with the dream manager to discuss a financial plan to save money from each paycheck for the down payment and continues having Dream Sessions with the dream manager for thirty minutes every month to review their progress.

> *"When we stop dreaming, we start dying."*
> —Matthew Kelly, *The Dream Manager*

The dream manager will hold your employee accountable and make sure they're complying with the plan. After six months, your employee is on their way to saving money for a down payment and hiring a realtor to find their first home.

Step Three: The Dream Fund

Tell your staff that you want to invest in their dreams. Create a Dream Fund and set aside some cash from every settlement into the fund. Maybe you're only adding $500 from each settlement to the Dream Fund, but you're showing your employees that there is money to help pay for their dreams.

When the Dream Fund is ready, you explain to your staff that they will vote to allocate the cash toward specific dreams. Let's say your secretary dreams of a three-week Italian vacation—the Dream Fund doesn't pay for the entire trip, and you don't give them a check. You pay for the airfare to Europe for them and their spouse, but if they don't go, they can't tap into the Dream Fund.

> *"Having dreams is what makes life tolerable."*
> —*Rudy's Friend, Pete, from the movie, Rudy*

Money doesn't motivate your employees, but if you help them achieve their dreams, they will do anything for you. There is nothing more powerful than helping your employees achieve their dreams.

A Crazy Idea that Might Actually Work

Your law firm is not the ideal fit for some of your employees' dreams and professional aspirations. Tell the ambitious twenty-two-year-old receptionist that you hope they move onto a bigger, better job, and you will help them. Perhaps you give your receptionist money from the Dream Fund for paralegal school or college.

> *"The pursuit of dreams creates passion, energy, enthusiasm and vitality."*
> —**Matthew Kelly,** *The Dream Manager*

Your receptionist might leave for bigger challenges, but you're showing your staff that you care about them, even if this means they leave for greener pastures. You will be rewarded with a staff that kicks butt and is devoutly loyal to your practice. And even when your receptionist leaves, you've built goodwill with your staff, which they will pay back in spades through their loyalty and commitment.

Make Dreams Your Unique Hiring Proposition

Don't keep the Dream Manager Program to yourself—make it one of the core benefits of employment with your firm. In your advertisements for a new secretary, show the candidates that you care about their dreams:

> We believe in your dreams and making your dreams come true. We want you to set new dreams and surpass them.

> You will have the opportunity to participate in the *Dream Manager Program* with a dream manager at your disposal (cost is 100 percent covered).

Once job candidates find out that you believe in dreams and the fulfillment of their dreams—both personal and professional—they will be knocking down your door for an interview. Here's the Dream Manual that describes our law firm's Dream Manager Program.

THE DREAM MANUAL

What's Your Dream?

Purpose of the Dream Manual

We believe in the power of dreams and helping you achieve your dreams. But you may not wish to participate and if so, we respect your wishes. The Dream Manager program is optional and may not be for everyone.

For those who want to take the leap, this Dream Manual outlines the process for the Dream Manager program.

Your Dream Book

Begin by writing a list of one hundred dreams in your Dream Book. Dream big and without limitation.

Next to each dream in your Dream Book, enter the date that you wrote the dream and when you plan to achieve it. The duration of a dream can be short-term ("ST"): less than one year, moderate-term ("MT"): one to five years, or long-term ("LT"): more than five years. When you achieve a dream, mark the date in your Dream Book and add bigger dreams.

Glance through your Dream Book for a few moments every day as a reminder of your dreams.

Your dreams may fall into any of twelve categories:

1. **Physical**: lifestyle habits, addictions, exercising

2. **Emotional**: relationships, security, helping others

3. **Intellectual**: reading, learning, continuous improvement tasks

4. **Spiritual**: peace with yourself

5. **Psychological**: overcoming fears and insecurities, developing willpower

6. **Material**: home ownership, purchasing a vehicle

7. **Professional**: a promotion, developing a new product/ service, sales/income goals, joining Toastmasters

8. **Financial**: becoming debt-free, investment goals, gaining financial freedom

9. **Creative**: exploring the arts, writing a book

10. **Adventure**: mountain climbing, exotic holiday, scuba diving

11. **Legacy**: instilling values in your children, volunteering, charitable giving, saving the world

12. **Character**: developing patience, walking the talk, earning respect, being worthy of trust

Your Dream Manager

The dream manager will help you articulate your dreams and formulate a plan for achieving your short-term, moderate-term, and long-term dreams. The dream manager will also help you design a savings plan and assess your financial situation.

The role of the dream manager:

1. Meet with every employee.

2. Discuss and give permission to pursue their dreams.

3. Avoid judgment of employee or dreams.

4. Provide employee with tools and accountability.

5. Develop a plan to help the employee achieve their dreams.

6. Meet to review the employee's progress.

Your Dream Sessions

You will meet with the dream manager for thirty minutes once a month to discuss your future and dreams. You may want to add more ambitious dreams to the list at the monthly dream sessions.

Your spouse and children can join in the Dream Sessions, and you may want your spouse and children to have their own Dream Book.

Our Dream Fund

For every case that gets resolved, our firm will deposit $1,000 into the Dream Fund. For each goal that a settlement meets, an additional $1,000 is deposited into the Dream Fund. The three goals consist of the settlement goal, legal fee to disbursement ratio, and duration of the lawsuit:

1. **Settlement Goal**: The amount of the settlement or judgment meets or exceeds the settlement goal for the case set forth in the Client/Retainer tab in Trialworks.

2. **Legal Fee to Disbursement Ratio**: The legal fee to our firm (after deducting referral fees) exceeds our disbursements by a ratio of at least 10/1.

3. **Duration of the Lawsuit**: The lawsuit is completed within one year and six months from the filing of the lawsuit until the first day of trial.

If all three goals are met, an additional bonus of $1,000 is deposited into the Dream Fund. When all three goals are met in a single case, $5,000 is deposited into the Dream Fund. In addition to funding dream grants, the expenses of the Dream Manager Program (e.g., fees of the dream manager and bank fees) are paid through the Dream Fund.

Dream Grants

Each employee can apply for a grant from the Dream Fund. The grant application should specify the amount being requested, the dream that the grant will be used to fund, and how the funds will be spent (e.g., airfare, hotel for trip). All participants in the Dream Manager program, including employees and management, vote to see who receives the grant.

The fund levels available for grants are:

- $250

- $500

- $1,000

- $2,500

- $5,000

A grant from the Dream Fund is not intended to pay all of the expenses of a dream, but to fund a portion of it, e.g., 25–35 percent of the total costs. We want to be your partner in achieving dreams, but the bulk of the saving and planning will be up to you.

When a grant is approved from the Dream Fund, payment will be made directly to the vendor providing the service; you will not receive a check from the Dream Fund.

A Few Final Suggestions

Read Matthew Kelly's book, *The Dream Manager*, and listen to the audio book—there is no better primer about the Dream Manager program.

Don't be shy about talking to others about your dreams. There is nothing more powerful than sharing your dreams with others and asking them to hold you accountable.

You might want to celebrate moments of progress by posting photos of dreams achieved in our conference room or sharing them with your friends on Facebook. We all need to celebrate small moments of progress and as you conquer small dreams, move on to bigger and bolder dreams.

There are just two final questions you have to answer:

What's your dream and why aren't you living it?

* * *

BECOMING A DREAM MAKER FOR YOUR CLIENTS

Have you ever spent time thinking about your client's goals and dreams? I know what you're thinking, "My clients want a boatload of cash." And you're partly right—your job is to maximize the financial recovery of your clients. But what do your clients really want? Have you ever bothered asking?

How to Discover Your Client's Dreams

The next time you accept a case, talk to your client about the R-Factor Question.* The "R" in the R-Factor Question stands for relationship.

"If you were meeting here (timeframe, e.g., two years) from today, looking back, what has to have happened during that period, both personally and professionally, for you to feel happy with your progress?"

The key to the R-Factor Question is that it always focuses on your client and not on you. Ask the R-Factor Question and write down the client's answer in their own words. Two years is a reasonable time for there to be significant growth and progress. Don't offer solutions or suggestions.

If necessary, prompt your client by asking about specific areas of their life, e.g., business goals, health, finances, family, etc. Ask, "What would you like to see happen in the areas of health, family, or finances?"

Most lawyers won't ask this type of question, so just by asking the question, you show that you care.

The Best Way to Show You Care

By asking them to visualize a bigger future, you're helping your clients contemplate what they need to be happy. Ninety percent of the conversation is spent on the client—almost nothing has to do with you.

By asking the R-Factor Question, you can learn what's most important in someone's future and how big their goals are. Try this out with one of your best clients at the beginning of the relationship. Ask the R-Factor Question and document the answer in a journal or in your case management system.

Documenting Your Clients' Dreams on Paper

Once you find out what's really important to your clients, you have to deliver it to them on paper. Summarize your clients' answers to the

R-Factor Question with a value creation letter. The Value Creation Letter* shows you actually listened.

Our Value Creation Letter

Dear Susan,

It was a pleasure learning about your visions, challenges, opportunities, and dreams. In our discussion, we identified three of the main challenges that need to be resolved toward these goals:

- You're afraid that you won't have money to pay for your daughters' college education.

- You're afraid you won't have money for retirement.

- You don't want to have any debts when your case is over.

You have identified these challenges during our meeting. By the end of your case, we will do our best to help fund your dreams and respond to your biggest challenges.

We hope we can help you grow a bigger future.

Sincerely,

John Fisher

At every meeting with your clients, you have a summary of their dreams on the value creation letter. You can remind your client of their dreams at every meeting, e.g., "I know it's really important to you that you have enough money to pay for your daughters' college education." At trial, you'll know why your client needs a specific monetary sum to pay for their biggest dreams and challenges.

*The R-Factor Question and the Value Creation Letter are reg-istered trademarks, protected by copyright and an integral concept of the Strategic Coach Inc. All Rights Reserved. Used with written permission. www.strategiccoach.com.

Part 2

Case Management

16

THE BEST WAYS TO LIMIT THE COSTS OF A LAWSUIT

Before you accept a case for litigation, make sure that you estimate the expenses and anticipated legal fee. Many times, the math just doesn't make sense (e.g., the case expenses are too high to justify a modest legal fee).

The case budget will help you determine whether the costs of the litigation are too high to justify the legal fee.

Case Budget

PURPOSE: To determine whether the legal fee justifies the expense of litigation.

There are three categories of case expenses: pre-lawsuit expenses, discovery expenses, and trial expenses. "Pre-lawsuit expenses" are incurred before the filing of the lawsuit. "Discovery expenses" are incurred between the filing of the lawsuit and the filing of the note of issue, and "trial expenses" are incurred between the filing of the note of issue and the completion of the trial.

The lawyer, paralegal, and secretary should prepare, review, and sign the case budget before the lawsuit is filed. The total expenses of the case budget, the settlement value, and the ratio of the legal fee to expenses should be entered in the Client/Retainer tab in Trialworks, and the Case Budget should be scanned into the Miscellaneous tab.

This is our checklist for a Case Budget.

Pre-Lawsuit Expenses

(Expenses Incurred Before Filing of Lawsuit)

Expert Witness Fee*: $_____

Medical Records Fees: $_____

Discovery Expenses

(Expenses between the Filing of Lawsuit and Note of Issue)

Filing Fees: $_____

Process Service Fees: $_____

Subpoena Fees: $_____

Medical Records Fees: $_____

Postage and UPS Fees: $_____

Fees of Consultant: $_____

Number of Depositions: _____

- Stenographer fees for depositions: $_____

- Videographer fees for depositions: $_____

Number of Expert Witnesses: _____

Treating Physician: _____

Medical Specialist: _____

Life Care Planner: _____

Neuropsychologist: _____

Economist: _____

- Review of File by Expert: $_____

- Lawyer's Meeting with Expert: $_____

TOTAL Expert Witness Fees*: $_____

Trial Expenses

(Expenses between the Filing of the Note of Issue and Trial)

Expert Witness Fees:

Number of Expert Witnesses: _____

- Transportation and Lodging: $_____

- Review of File by Expert: $_____

- Lawyer's Meeting with Expert: $_____

- Trial Testimony: $_____

TOTAL Expert Witness Fees*: $_____

Focus Group Expenses: $_____

Process Service Fees: $_____

Subpoena Fees: $_____

Fees of Medical Consultant: $_____

Fees of Trial Consultant: $_____

Editing Fees for Videotape Depositions: $_____

Playback of Videotape Depositions at Trial: $_____

Courtroom Exhibit Fees: $_____

Transportation, Meals, and Lodging Expenses for Attorney:

$_____

Transportation, Meals, and Lodging Expenses for Paralegal:

$_____

Court Reporter Fees for Trial Transcripts: $_____

Summary of Expenses

Pre-Lawsuit Expenses: $_____

Discovery Expenses: $_____

Trial Expenses: $_____

Total Expenses: $_____

Settlement Value: $_____

Total Legal Fee: $_____

Legal Fee to John H. Fisher, PC: $_____

Ratio of Legal Fee to Expenses: _____

(Goal: Ratio of ten to one for the legal fee of John H. Fisher, PC and the case expenses.)

Dated: _____

*An expert witness should not be retained until we receive a written estimate of their fee and the expert confirms that they will not exceed the amount of the estimate without prior authorization from us.

How to Limit the Costs of Expert Witnesses

You didn't see this coming. Your trusty expert witness sends you a bill for $7,000 for reviewing a new file. You trust that the expert spent the time, and you're happy with their work, but $7,000? You have no choice—you have to pay the bill. And you have no one to blame but yourself. You didn't get the expert to agree to a budget for their fees, and you essentially gave them carte blanche to spend as much time as they wanted.

The Only Solution for Limiting Outrageous Expert Fees

There is only one way to fix this problem: you have to put your expert witnesses on a budget. Before the expert spends a minute on the case, you have to explain your procedure for working with expert witnesses. Specifically, experts must estimate their fee for the case evaluation, and their invoice must not exceed the original estimate unless they receive advance approval from you.

The following is the agreement that sets forth our firm's expectations for expert's fees, invoicing, and their preparation and attendance at trial.

What We Expect from You

Thank you for agreeing to provide your objective and independent evaluation of the records. We appreciate the opportunity to work with you.

We hope you appreciate that we must budget carefully for the expenses of each case. In order to avoid unexpectedly large expert fees, we created this agreement for the purpose of setting forth our expectations for your invoices and, in those cases where you agree to testify at trial, what we expect from you in the preparation for depositions and trial.

This agreement covers

1. the budget for the initial case review,

2. what to expect after the initial case review, and

3. billing procedures.

If this agreement is acceptable, please keep a signed copy and review it from time to time as a reminder of our billing procedures and expectations. We look forward to working with you and appreciate your understanding.

#1: Budget for the Initial Case Review

We will send you the medical records in the format of your choice (email, Dropbox, or paper copy), and we ask that you send an email to our paralegal with an estimate of your time and anticipated fee for the initial review of the records, e.g., "Will need five hours to review the records at an hourly rate of $400. I expect to complete the review for $2,000." The estimate of your fee is the "budget" for the initial case review.

If your budget for the initial review of the records is acceptable, our paralegal will respond with an email that accepts your budget and authorizes the work. Please do not begin your review of the records until you receive approval from our paralegal.

Do Not Exceed the Budget Without Prior Approval

Please do **not** send an invoice exceeding the budget *without prior written approval* from John Fisher. For example, if the budget is $2,000, we do not expect to receive an invoice exceeding $2,000 unless you receive our prior approval.

We understand that there may be occasions in which you might underestimate the length of time needed to review the records. If you underestimate the length of time, please send an email to our paralegal with an estimate of the additional time and fees, e.g., "Seeking approval for an additional two hours at my hourly rate of $400 to complete the review of the records." With rare exceptions, we will authorize the additional time and expense.

If there are certain records that were not included in the records provided to you, please send an email to our paralegal and specify the records that were not provided.

#2: What to Expect After the Initial Case Review

If you express an opinion that the case has merit and you agree to be an expert witness, the three distinct phases of work after the initial case review are

1. the review of deposition transcripts,

2. the preparation for trial, and

3. the attendance at the trial.

We would like to create an estimate of your fees for every phase of the lawsuit. Similar to the budget for the initial case review, we ask that your time and fees stay within a budget for your review of the deposition transcripts, preparation for trial, and attendance at the trial.

Following your initial case review, please provide us with your "Fee Schedule." The Fee Schedule should provide your fees and hourly rates for the review of records, meeting(s) with the lawyer, travel and hotel fees, and your fee for your attendance at the trial. Your Fee Schedule should specify whether your fees are partially refundable in the event the case is resolved before the retainer fee is spent.

If you do not have a Fee Schedule, we ask that you send an email to our paralegal with an estimate of your time and anticipated fee as you continue to work on the case.

Review of Deposition Transcripts

Following the completion of depositions, we will send the deposition transcripts to you via Dropbox or regular mail, and we ask that you send an email to our paralegal with an estimate of your time and fee for reviewing them, e.g., "Will need five hours to review the deposition transcripts at my hourly rate of $400 for a total fee of $2,000." Our paralegal will respond by email in order to approve the additional time and work.

There are no depositions of expert witnesses in New York State.

Meeting with Lawyer Before Depositions

In almost every lawsuit, John Fisher will meet with you at a location of your choice one week before the deposition of the defendant. This meeting will help John Fisher prepare for the deposition in terms of the questions that should be asked as well as the defendant's anticipated excuses/testimony. We expect that you will be thoroughly prepared to discuss the deposition of the defendant at the meeting with John Fisher.

Scheduling Your Trial Testimony

We will notify you of the trial date, usually six to nine months in advance. We will notify you of the date on which the trial will begin, and in most cases, we will ask you to testify on the second or third day of the trial. For example, if the trial begins on January 16, you will be asked to testify on January 17 or January 18.

We have limited flexibility in terms of scheduling your trial testimony, and for that reason, you should call us (845-802-0047)

ASAP if you cannot testify on any of the dates that we propose for your trial testimony. We can arrange for your travel and hotel accommodations upon your request.

Preparation for Trial

At trial, we expect that you will be thoroughly familiar with the medical records and deposition transcripts. Being thoroughly familiar with the medical records and deposition transcripts is the most important thing you can do.

About two to three weeks before the trial date, John Fisher will meet with you at a location of your choice to prepare for trial. At this meeting, it is very important that you are ready to discuss your anticipated testimony, including:

- Specific deviations from the standard of care by each of the defendants.

- Whether the deviations from the standard of care were a substantial factor in causing the injury/death.

- Anticipated counter arguments/excuses from the defense.

Please do not come to the meeting with John Fisher if you are not prepared to address these issues.

Attendance at the Trial

After you have been notified of the trial date and you agree to set aside a day to testify, we cannot change the date of your trial testimony. If you cannot testify at the trial (for any reason), you must inform us in writing at least three months before the trial date.

Your attendance at the trial is not optional or discretionary. The lawsuit will almost certainly be dismissed if you do not attend the trial.

Retain the Case File

Please do not discard the case file until you receive our written permission.

#3: Billing Procedures

Please keep your billing current within thirty days of the date on which you spend time on the case.

Please itemize the time in your invoices, e.g., "forty-five minutes: review of deposition transcript of non-party witness, John Smith." We must be accountable to our clients for case expenditures, and consequently, we must be able to show that every expense provided some value to their case.

Please Sign Our Agreement

Thank you for your understanding and consideration of our need to carefully budget for the expenses.

If the terms of this agreement are unacceptable, we will respect your decision. If the terms are acceptable, please sign this agreement where indicated and return it to us via email.

Dated:

_____

[Name]

_____

John H. Fisher

How to Limit the Costs of a Videotaped Deposition

If a deposition isn't worth videotaping, it's not worth taking. Videotaping a deposition shows the witness's facial expressions, body language, changes in the inflection in the witness's tone of voice, and pauses before answering—the kind of stuff that will never show up on a transcript. Defense counsel are less likely to disregard the rules of depositions if they know you are videotaping them, and the jury will pay a lot more attention to the video of a deposition.

If videotaping a deposition is ten times more powerful than reading a transcript of a deposition at trial, why do so few plaintiffs' lawyers videotape depositions? Money. Plaintiffs' lawyers don't want to videotape depositions, and it's easy to understand why: videotaping can add $400–$800 to the cost of a deposition. There's a solution.

Videotape your depositions without a videographer. Some states, such as California, require that the video operator be a notary public, but there are no rules prohibiting a lawyer from operating the camcorder at the deposition. To videotape your depositions without a videographer, you only need a camcorder, basic skills in operating the camcorder, microphones, and an understanding of the rules in your state that apply to videotaping depositions.

This is a crash course for videotaping your first deposition.

Introduction at the Beginning of the Videotape Deposition

In New York, the rules for videotaping a deposition are set forth in Section 202.15 of the Uniform Rules of Trial Courts. You begin the video deposition by making the following statement on the record:

"We are on the record.

Today is [date], the time is approximately [time].

The location is [location where testimony is being taken].

This is index number [index #], captioned [caption], and the venue is [court and venue].

The deponent is [name and title], and this testimony has been noticed by [plaintiff or defendant].

Would counsel and all present please identify themselves for the record.

Would the court reporter please administer the oath or affirmation at this time?"

Going "On" and "Off" the Record

When you go on and off the record, you must make the following statements:

Going Off the Record at a Break: "We are going off the record at approximately [time]."

Going Back on the Record after a Break: "We are back on the record at approximately [time]."

At the End of the Deposition: At the end of the video deposition, you must give the witness the opportunity to watch the video of the deposition. Uniform Rules of Trial Courts section 202.15(d)(4). You should tell the witness/deponent: "You have the right to watch the video of the deposition. Do you wish to watch the video or waive your right?"

Ask all parties if you may conclude the deposition. Once all parties agree:

"Having heard the approval of all parties, this concludes the deposition of [name and title]. We are now going off the record at approximately [date and time]."

Setting Up for the Video Deposition

Arrive at the deposition location at least thirty minutes early to set up.

Position the Camcorder: The camcorder will be positioned on top of a tripod, and the camera should be positioned above the witness's eye level. As the operator, position the camcorder so that you are shooting across the table (as opposed to down the length of the table). You should be able to see the screen on the camcorder at all times to make sure it's recording.

Put the Camcorder in Automatic Function: The camcorder should be preconfigured so you don't have to worry about exposure, white balance, or focus (e.g., the camera should be on automatic function).

Microphones and Audio Mixer: There are three lavalier microphones that connect to the audio mixer (the audio mixer needs an external power source, just like the camcorder):

- Lavalier microphone #1 is for the plaintiffs' lawyer (you).

- Lavalier microphone #2 is for the witness/deponent.

- Table microphone (microphone #3) is for the defense lawyers.

When the defense lawyers speak, rotate the table microphone (microphone #3) in the direction of the lawyer who is speaking.

Sound Check: At all times, you must be able to see the video screen of the camcorder. The audiometer on the video screen of the camcorder will show that the audio is being received by the camcorder. Before you begin the deposition, listen to the audio through the audio jack on the camcorder to ensure the audio is being received and recorded by the camcorder (the "sound check").

Preserving the Video

Recording the Video on Memory Cards: The camcorder should have two slots for memory cards and should simultaneously record the video on both memory cards. If one memory card goes bad, you have the other one as a backup.

Preserving the Video on an External Hard Drive: Once the video deposition is over, transfer the video from the smart cards onto an external hard drive, and then place the external hard drive in a fireproof box in a vault. An external hard drive with two TB of memory will save about two years of video depositions.

Don't Forget the Deposition Notice

Defense counsel may object on the day of the deposition and claim that you did not provide sufficient notice of your intention to videotape the deposition. Your deposition notice must contain language alerting defense counsel that you will be videotaping the deposition.

The title of the deposition should read:

NOTICE TO TAKE DEPOSITION UPON ORAL EXAMINATION AND BY MEANS OF SIMULTANEOUS AUDIO AND VISUAL RECORDING

In addition, the deposition notice must have a sentence informing opposing counsel that the deposition will be videotaped.

> PLEASE TAKE FURTHER NOTICE that, pursuant to 22 NYCRR section 212.12 and 22 NYCRR section 202.15, the deposition will be videotaped by a professional videographer or a member of the law firm of John H. Fisher, PC.

When defense counsel objects, show them the deposition notice and remind them that you have the legal right to videotape depositions. If that does not solve the problem, get the judge on the phone for a ruling that you can't lose.

All the Equipment You Need

New York requires a video camera that contains a date and time stamp that is visible on the screen at all times. Other than this requirement, your video equipment will consist of (a) a camcorder, (b) mixer power cords, (c) sound/audio mixer, and (d) microphones and cables.

Here's the kit our video expert, Mark Whalen of Litigraphics, LLC, recommends:

- JVC GY-HM170 camcorder with extra battery

- Rolls MoreMics audio mixer

- Additional camcorder battery and wall charger

- Shure SM93 lavalier microphone (two)

- Audio Technica 891 boundary microphone for defense attorneys

- Thirty-two GB SDHC cards (two) (reusable, but good for about six hours of continuous recording)

- Pelican SDHC card case

- Lowepro Slingshot backpack

- 15' XLR audio cable

- Pelican Storm iM2500 case with Trekpak divider

- Magnus VT-4000 tripod

- f/64 tripod shoulder bag

- Impact 6' background stands

- Extension cord, power strip, and background clamps

- Botero gray photo background

The equipment costs about $1,500, or the cost of videotaping three depositions with a videographer. Just videotape three depositions, and the equipment will pay for itself.

Proof Positive that Video Depositions are Powerful

During a trial, Kingston, NY injury lawyer, John DeGasperis, Esq., masterfully used snippets of video deposition to show crucial admissions of hospital nurses to the jury. The video testimony contradicted the testimony of the attending physician and was very damaging for the defense. Not surprisingly, John's client got a fantastic settlement shortly after the playing of the video deposition.

This is proof positive that video depositions pay off. But don't take my word for this—just videotape a single deposition **without a videographer**, see how simple, cost-free, and powerful it is, and you'll regret that you didn't start videotaping all of your depositions years ago.

How to Limit the Costs of Medical Records

One of the biggest (and unnecessary) expenses of personal injury litigation is the cost of medical records. Most plaintiffs' lawyers request a complete set of medical records for all dates of treatment and get exorbitant invoices for the photocopy fees from third-party contractors. This should never happen again!

Tip One: Access the Records Through a Patient Portal

First, ask your client whether their doctor has a patient portal. Many medical facilities, including VA hospitals and primary care physicians, have a patient portal that allows their patients to obtain an electronic copy of their medical records.

Your client can give you access to the patient portal and you can print or download the medical records. This is the easiest and quickest way to get medical records.

Tip Two: Scan the Records During an Original Chart Review

Under federal and New York State law, you have the right to review and copy the original medical records (known as an "original chart review") at no cost. Call the medical records department of the doctor's office or hospital and schedule a date for an original chart review. Under federal law, you cannot be charged an "inspection fee."

Bring a portable laser color scanner to the original chart review and scan the medical records. You'll leave the hospital with a complete electronic copy of the medical records, in color, at no cost. Having "inspected" the original medical records, you'll know you have a complete copy of the medical records.

If the medical records custodian denies your request for an original chart review, ask to speak with a supervisor. If that fails, send the hospital/doctor a letter via certified mail citing the law and send a copy to the state's Department of Health. By showing the hospital that you know your rights, you'll get the original chart review.

Tip Three: Subpoena Medical Records

Serve a subpoena duces tecum for the medical records during discovery in a pending lawsuit. Under New York law, you can subpoena the medical records during the discovery phase of the lawsuit and the doctor/hospital cannot charge a photocopy fee, and is only entitled to the statutory and witness fees.

With a subpoena and the statutory witness and travel fees (usually costing less than fifty dollars), you will get a complete set of the medical records.

Tip Four: Request Medical Records in Electronic Format Only

Demand that the hospital/doctor provide the medical records in electronic format only. Under federal law, your clients have the right to insist upon the production of electronic medical records. The hospital/doctor can only charge for the actual labor fee of producing the medical records in electronic format.

NEVER request a paper copy of medical records unless your request is limited to less than thirty pages. In your cover letter, you should state in big, bold print that the hospital/doctor must receive prior written authorization from you for a photocopy fee exceeding twenty dollars.

Tip Five: Only Request the Medical Records that You Need

When requesting a paper copy of medical records, request only those parts of the records that you need. For a potential case involving a surgical error, you may only need the operative report, discharge summary, consultation reports, and certain dates of treatment, e.g.,

"We are only requesting the operative report, discharge summary, and consultation report(s) for the hospital admission on April 1, 2019."

By specifying the records that you need, you will save money for the initial case evaluation. You can always request a complete copy of the medical records (in electronic format) if you make the decision to accept the case for litigation.

17

HOW TO GET YOUR BEST CASES TO TRIAL

Go back in time to your first big case. You're a couple of years out of law school, and a thirty-something injury victim comes walking into your office. Within minutes of chatting with your new client, you quickly realize that you might have your first injury case with huge damages, clear liability, and oodles of insurance coverage. You can't contain your enthusiasm and have to rush home to tell everyone.

You have a vision for this lawsuit. Unlike your run-of-the-mill back injury cases, you will push this case through discovery and get it to trial in no time flat. You just know that a big payday is waiting for you, but you won't see a penny until the case gets to trial.

You have big dreams for this case, but once you file the lawsuit, you find that the defense is not quite playing ball with you. The defense lawyers aren't available for depositions for six months and they serve pro forma discovery responses that seem like they were copied and pasted from other cases. That's right, defense counsel isn't cooperating, and it seems that your vision for getting this lawsuit to trial quickly is nothing but a pipedream.

The Goal for Every Lawsuit

Let's begin with a simple, irrefutable truth: you will not get paid until the trial. Even in the most clear-cut, obvious cases, the defense will not pay your client until the day of the trial (or a day before trial).

This leads to one inescapable conclusion: your only goal is to get your case to trial as quickly as possible. The sooner you get your case to trial, the sooner you will get paid.

The First Step to Avoiding Delays and Adjournments

You can expect the same thing in every lawsuit—the defense will not schedule depositions of the parties until they have a complete set of your client's medical and employment records. And you can't blame them; the defense lawyers have a job to do, and without all of the medical and employment records, they won't even give you a proposed date for depositions.

> *"If you know what outcome you desire, the next step is to identify what type of behaviors will produce that outcome."*
> —**Matthew Kelly**, *Off-Balance*

The first step to avoiding delays is the *pre-litigation checklist*. The pre-litigation checklist is an itemized list of every medical record, employment record, and exhibit that you will need for trial.

Your secretary begins collecting these records on your pre-litigation checklist before you file the lawsuit. Yes, it usually takes a couple of months to get these documents, but it will be at least that long before the defense serves their answer and discovery demands. This way, you're not hustling to respond to the defendants' discovery demands; you have all of the other documents you need, and you provide discovery responses that are fully responsive to the defendant's discovery demands.

Being Proactive in Discovery

Don't wait to serve the medical and employment records with the plaintiff's discovery responses. As soon as you receive the defendants' answer, you should serve a complete set of your client's medical and employment records and release authorizations upon defense counsel. For paperless offices (and there is no excuse if you're not paperless), this is as simple as burning the medical and employment records onto a CD and dropping it in the mail.

Now there's no excuse for delaying or postponing the depositions—the defense lawyers have everything they need within days of their first appearance in the lawsuit. But make no mistake about it, the defense will almost always tell you that they don't have a part of the records they need for depositions—that's when you gently remind them that you gave them everything *months ago*.

So-Order Everything!

The preliminary scheduling conference is your chance to impose strict so-ordered deadlines for the completion of discovery, but most plaintiffs' lawyers agree upon outside dates for the completion of discovery that are eight to twelve months away. Big mistake!

At least one week before the preliminary scheduling conference, you should send a fax/email to defense counsel asking them for
alternative dates when the defendants are available for their depositions. Inform defense counsel that you will ask the judge to impose
specific so-ordered dates for the depositions of the defendants, and
you wish to schedule dates in advance of the preliminary scheduling
conference.

The preliminary conference order should specifically contain
dates for everything from depositions and original chart reviews to
site inspections and the defense medical examination (yes, always use
DME—not the bogus term, IME). With specific so-ordered dates
for discovery and depositions, discovery cannot be adjourned by
defense counsel without the court's approval.

Forcing the Defense to Comply with Discovery

Almost invariably, you will receive a set of pro forma discovery
responses from the defense lawyer that contain a list of meaningless, boilerplate responses. The defense lawyer will object to virtually
all of your discovery demands as seeking privileged or confidential
information, and even when they don't, the discovery response will
state that the "information will be provided later in a supplemental
response."

As soon as you receive the defendants' discovery responses, your
secretary should review the responses to determine what's missing. A
response of "will be provided later" is not really a response. Follow up
with a letter to defense regarding their worthless discovery response
and insist upon a meaningful response.

"Systems drive behaviors. Certain behaviors lead to certain outcomes."
—Matthew Kelly, *Off-Balance*

You want to document everything and follow up with another letter if the defense does not respond to the first. The defense won't comply with your discovery demands unless you hold their feet to the fire, and don't let them off easy—if the discovery response was due on July 8, remind them. If you are lax about discovery, you can't expect anything more from defense counsel.

No Adjournments Allowed!

It's easy to adjourn depositions with your busy schedule, and sometimes you want a break. When you're thinking about consenting to the defendants' request for an adjournment, kick yourself in the ass! If you consent to one adjournment, the preliminary conference order becomes meaningless.

Be tough! Tell the defense lawyer that the court has specific so-ordered deadlines and you cannot adjourn anything without a court order. The defense counsel will inevitably blame you for failing to comply with some aspect of discovery, and you have to be ready to respond (e.g., "We gave you a complete set of medical and employment records and release authorizations six months ago, and you have everything you need to proceed with depositions. Are you serious?").

Measure Everything!

We have a checklist of our key performance indicators that measure the number of days that it takes for the most important parts of discovery. By measuring your performance, you're not just hoping for the best—you're holding yourself and your team accountable.

"The thing that continually amazes me about the very best companies in the world is that they measure everything."
—**Matthew Kelly,** *Off-Balance*

In your key performance indicators, you should specifically measure the number of days

- between the receipt of the defendants' answer and the service of the plaintiff's discovery responses,

- between the service of the plaintiff's discovery responses and the completion of the depositions, and

- between the service of the defendants' answer and the filing of the note of issue.

The days that it takes to complete these three milestones are documented as each milestone is reached. Each milestone has a specific goal that we strive to reach. When we don't reach our goals, we analyze the problem to identify where the delays occurred and how they can be avoided.

The Twelve-Step Litigation Checklist

There are twelve simple steps to moving a new lawsuit from discovery to the desired goal: a trial date. The steps are not self-executing—you need to continually train your staff and reinforce and improve the processes. The best way to start is a "litigation checklist" that is signed, reviewed, and electronically filed in the case management system as each step of the process is completed.

#1: Pre-Litigation Checklist

Begin by creating a checklist for every new personal injury case. Your pre-litigation checklist should include the following:

- All medical records (pre- and post-incident)

- Employment records for the last ten years

- Tax returns and W-2 statements for the last five years

- Criminal background search

- Social medical search (e.g., Facebook, Instagram) for damaging content

- Photographs and video of injured person or decedent

- Names and addresses of lay witnesses re: liability and damages

Your secretary should check every box on the pre-litigation checklist, sign it, and submit it for your review and signature before every new lawsuit is filed.

When This Should Be Done: Your secretary should prepare the pre-litigation checklist as soon as you accept the case for litigation.

Why It's Done This Way: Once you receive the defendants' answers, you will already have all of the records you need to serve a complete set of medical and employment records upon defense counsel.

#2: Serve Medical Records and Release Authorizations (a.k.a. "Records to Defense")

You should serve a complete set of medical records and release authorizations as soon as you receive the defendants' answer.

Dear Mr. Defense Lawyer:

In order to expedite discovery, enclosed please find a complete set of the plaintiff's medical records and release authorizations in the above-referenced action.

If there are any additional medical, or nonmedical, records that you need, please notify us as soon as possible, and we will ensure that you have all of the records that are subject to disclosure.

Your cooperation will ensure that we are able to meet the deadlines that will be scheduled for discovery at the Court's preliminary scheduling conference.

Very truly yours,

When This Should Be Done: As soon as you receive the initial set of the defendants' discovery demands, you should serve a complete set of release authorizations and medical records upon defense counsel.

Why It's Done This Way: The service of medical records and release authorizations upon defense counsel will get the case moving while you prepare the plaintiff's discovery responses, Bill of Particulars, and discovery demands.

By serving the medical records and release authorizations as soon as you receive the defendants' discovery demands, you remove a common excuse used by defense counsel for adjourning depositions, namely, "We haven't had enough time to get the medical records."

#3: "Deposition" Letter

The "deposition" letter asks defendants' lawyers to provide alternative dates for the depositions of the parties and non-party witnesses.

Dear Ms. Defense Lawyer:

In an effort to establish a mutually agreeable timetable for the completion of all disclosure proceedings in this case, please provide the undersigned, within twenty (20) days of the date of this letter, with five (5) or more specific dates when your clients will be available to give their depositions in the above-referenced action.

In addition to your clients, please provide the same information regarding the following individuals, who I believe are current employees of your clients: [insert names of employees].

Upon receipt of your response to this request, we will proceed to schedule the depositions of such individuals.

If we do not receive a response to our request within twenty (20) days, we will select deposition dates that are convenient for the plaintiffs and will request that the Court enter an Order directing that the depositions be conducted on those dates.

We look forward to your anticipated cooperation in scheduling mutually agreeable deposition dates.

When This Should Be Done: You should fax, email, or mail this letter to defense counsel as soon as the preliminary scheduling conference has been scheduled.

Why It's Done This Way: The biggest obstacle posed by defense counsel will be scheduling the depositions. Often, defense counsel will have their secretary tell you that they refuse to even schedule the defendants' depositions until after the plaintiffs' depositions. For this reason, you should always get alternative dates for depositions from defense counsel before the preliminary scheduling conference.

#4: "Discovery" Letter

The "discovery" letter asks defendants' lawyers whether they claim there is any discovery owed by the plaintiff before the preliminary scheduling conference.

> Dear Ms. Defense Lawyer:
>
> This letter is sent to you in a good faith attempt to ensure that the plaintiff has complied with all of your discovery demands prior to the preliminary Court conference in the above-referenced action.
>
> We served upon you the plaintiff's medical records as well as the plaintiff's discovery responses and verified Bill of Particulars. Additionally, you were provided with release authorizations for the plaintiff's medical records upon our receipt of the defendants' answer.
>
> We believe that you possess all of the records and discovery responses that were sought in the defendants' discovery demands. However, if you believe that there are any out-standing discovery responses that are owed by the plaintiff or medical records that have not been provided, kindly respond in writing or via email by specifying the discovery responses and/or medical records that you believe are owed by the plaintiff.
>
> If you do not respond to this letter within ten (10) business days of your receipt of the letter, we will assume that there

are no outstanding discovery demands or medical records owed by the plaintiff and that you are ready to schedule depositions.

Unless you respond to this letter, we will assume that you will not raise any issues regarding outstanding discovery at the preliminary conference.

When This Should Be Done: The "discovery" letter should be mailed to defense counsel as soon as you are notified of the date for the preliminary court conference.

Why It's Done This Way: You need to know whether there are any outstanding discovery issues *before* the preliminary scheduling conference. This will allow you to be prepared to address any discovery issues at the preliminary conference, or you can hand-deliver the requested discovery responses at the preliminary scheduling conference.

#5: "Original Chart Review" Letter

The "original chart review" letter asks defendants' lawyers to provide alternative dates for the inspection and copying of the original medical records.

Dear Ms. Defense Lawyer:

Please contact us to schedule a mutually convenient date for the inspection of the plaintiff's original medical records at [insert name of hospital or physician's medical practice] in the above-referenced action.

Section 18(2)(a) of New York's Public Health Law states that upon the written request of any individual whose patient information is maintained or possessed by a health care provider, the health care provider must provide an opportunity, within ten (10) days, for that individual to inspect any patient information concerning or relating to examination or treatment of such individual in the possession of the health care provider.

If you have any objection to the inspection of the plaintiff's original medical records, please contact us within ten (10) days of your receipt of this letter

When This Should Be Done: In a preliminary scheduling order, you should insist upon a specific date for the hospital or physician to comply with your demand to produce the original medical records for inspection and that the original records must be produced at least two weeks before any depositions are conducted.

Why It's Done This Way: The worst thing is to be confronted with medical records at a deposition that you've never seen before. The only way to make sure this does not happen is to insist that the defense lawyer provide you with an opportunity to inspect the original medical records.

#6: "Discovery Owed" Letter

The "discovery owed" letter reminds defendants' counsel that there is outstanding discovery owed to the plaintiff.

Dear Ms. Defense Lawyer:

On [insert date], we served the plaintiff's combined discovery demands and demand for a verified Bill of Particulars upon you in the above-referenced action. To date, we have not received your response to the plaintiff's combined discovery demands and demand for a verified Bill of Particulars, and your time to object has expired, pursuant to CPLR section 3122(a).

In order to avoid a motion to compel discovery, we ask that you provide us with the defendants' response to the plaintiff's combined discovery demands and demand for a verified Bill of Particulars within ten (10) business days of your receipt of this letter. **We will not accept defendants' discovery responses stating that responsive documents will be provided at a later date.**

When This Should Be Done: This letter should be mailed to the defendants' lawyers on the thirty-first day after the plaintiff's combined discovery demands have been served upon defendants' lawyers.

Why It's Done This Way: If you do not possess the defendants' discovery responses before depositions, you will not be able to prepare for the depositions.

#7: Schedule Meeting with Client to Prepare for Deposition

You should call your client to schedule a face-to-face meeting at their home or your office (client's choice) in order to prepare for their deposition.

When This Should Be Done: You should call your client to schedule this meeting as soon as a date for their deposition has been confirmed with defendant's lawyers. The meeting with your client should be held about seven days before their deposition.

Once the meeting has been scheduled with your client, you should send an email to them to confirm the meeting and call them at least one day before the meeting as a reminder.

Why It's Done This Way: You need to meet with your client at least one week before their deposition in order to give you enough time to prepare for potential "danger points" (e.g., criminal convictions, substance abuse, etc.).

#8: Schedule Meeting with Expert Witness

A face-to-face meeting with your medical expert/physician is crucial for the preparation of the deposition of the "target" defendant.

When This Should Be Done: Once you have a confirmed date for the deposition of the "target" defendant (typically the first named defendant in the caption), you should contact your medical expert/physician to schedule a meeting at least seven (7) days before the deposition.

Why It's Done This Way: This meeting will help you prepare for the "target" defendant's deposition so the right questions are asked.

#9: Schedule Stenographer and Videographer for EBT

Always videotape the depositions of defendants and non-party witnesses.

When This Should Be Done: Once you have a confirmed date for the defendants' depositions, you should call a stenographer and videographer to confirm their availability for the deposition.

Why It's Done This Way: Videotaping the depositions of the defendants and non-party witnesses will show the witnesses' body language, facial mannerisms, pauses, and changes in voice inflection, which otherwise would not be captured.

#10: "Original Chart to Deposition" Letter

The "original chart to deposition" letter reminds the defendants' lawyers to bring the original medical records to the defendants' depositions.

> Dear Ms. Defense Lawyer:
>
> We ask that you bring the original medical records to the defendants' deposition on [insert date] in the above-referenced action.
>
> Please confirm that the original medical records will be present at the deposition on [insert date].

When This Should Be Done: At least one week before the defendants' deposition, you should call defendants' lawyer to confirm that they will bring the original medical records to the deposition. You should confirm by email and remind the defendants' lawyer one day before the deposition.

Why It's Done This Way: You cannot conduct an effective deposition of the defendants without the original medical records.

#11: "Additional Discovery" Letter

The "additional discovery" letter asks defendants' lawyers to advise whether there is any "additional discovery" that they need before you file the note of issue.

Dear Ms. Defense Lawyer:

In the plaintiff's discovery response, we identified several non-party witnesses, [insert names of witnesses], in the above-referenced action. Please advise us in writing whether you wish to conduct depositions of any of the non-party witnesses within ten (10) business days of your receipt of this letter.

If you do not respond to this letter, we will assume that you do not wish to conduct depositions of the non-party witnesses, and we will proceed based upon that assumption with the remainder of discovery.

When This Should Be Done: This letter should be served within five (5) days after the plaintiff's deposition. Following the plaintiff's deposition, the defense lawyers should have enough information to decide whether they want to depose the non-party witnesses.

Why It's Done This Way: It is very common that the defense lawyers will object to the filing of the note of issue, and scheduling of a trial date, by claiming that they need extra time to depose non-party witnesses. You need to anticipate this stall tactic by asking defendants' lawyers whether they want to depose non-party witnesses **after the plaintiff's deposition**.

#12: "Materials to Expert" Letter

While it makes sense to orally tell an expert what documents they might want to focus on, it is never appropriate to send them anything short of *all* the available documents that are relevant to their testimony.

The expert witness should receive the complete underlying file, including the following:

- All pleadings and discovery in the case

- Deposition transcripts of parties and non-party witnesses

- Medical records

- Expert responses

- DME reports

- Bills of particulars

You should keep an itemized list of what was sent to the expert so you can make certain that any expert who may be asked to testify on any of the same or related issues will receive identical materials.

When This Should Be Done: The complete underlying file records should be sent to the expert witness as soon as the expert has been retained.

Why It's Done This Way: If you do not send all of the documents relevant to the expert's testimony, the expert will be subject to a devastating cross-examination in which defense counsel will make it appear that the plaintiff's attorney is using the expert as a puppet to espouse the theories developed by the plaintiff's attorney, having only sent material to support that theory.

The Litigation Checklist

As each task is completed, check the appropriate box and bring the litigation checklist to our weekly goal meetings for review and signing by each team member.

#1: Pre-litigation checklist: _____

#2: "Records to defense" letter: _____

#3: "Deposition" letter: _____

#4: "Discovery" letter: _____

#5: "Original chart review" letter: _____

#6: "Discovery owed" letter: _____

#7: Schedule meeting with client to prepare for EBT: _____

#8: Schedule meeting with expert witness: _____

#9: Schedule stenographer and videographer for EBT: _____

#10: "Original chart to deposition" letter: _____

#11: "Additional discovery" letter: _____

#12: "Materials to expert" letter: _____

The Ultimate Goal: Eighteen Months to Trial

Getting the case to trial is your single most important goal for every case, because your client will not get the result they deserve until the trial. A victory for your client is getting the case to trial *within eighteen months* from the filing of the lawsuit.

How to Stop Defense Lawyers from Speaking with Your Client's Treating Physicians

New York law permits defense lawyers to have ex parte, private discussions with your client's treating physicians. Upon receipt of an "Arons" authorization from plaintiff's counsel, defense lawyers can schedule private meetings with your client's treating physicians.

Few defense lawyers inform the treating physicians that such meetings are voluntary and that they are not required to speak with the defense lawyers. Additionally, there is always a risk that the defense lawyer will attempt to engage in discussions with the treating physician regarding medical conditions (e.g., substance abuse, psychiatric conditions) that are not relevant to the injuries claimed in the lawsuit. The treating physicians may not know that such topics are off-limits under the law.

To avoid such private, ex parte meetings, we send the letter below to our client's treating physicians as soon as we mail "Arons" authorizations to defendants' lawyers.

Letter to the Treating Physicians re: Meetings with Defense Counsel

Re: Henry Jones

Date of Birth:

Dear Dr. Smith:

We represent your patient, Henry Jones, in a legal action which is currently pending. With respect to that case, you may have recently received, or you will shortly receive, requests from the law firms of [insert name of defendants] along with authorizations that we have signed on behalf of your patient.

Those attorneys wish to privately interview you, either in person or by telephone, concerning the medical condition, treatment, and prognosis of Henry Jones. Please be advised that, although we are required to sign the above-mentioned authorization, **Henry Jones prefers that you do not engage in such private discussions with anyone except us** concerning any aspect of his medical condition, treatment, or prognosis.

While such an authorization and request is permitted under New York State law, many federal courts have rendered decisions holding that such authorizations and ex parte discussions are prohibited by federal law (HIPAA) and that federal law preempts state law regarding these issues. In re Vioxx Prods. Lib. Litig. 230 F.R.D. 473 (E.D. La. 2005); Croskey v. BMW of N. Am. Inc., 2005 WL 1959452 (E.D. Mich. Feb. 16, 2005); Crenshaw v. Mony Life Ins. Co., 318 F.Supp.2d 1015 (S.D. Cal. 2004); EEOC v. Boston Mkt. Corp., No. CV-034227 (LDW)(WDW), 2004 U.S. Dist. LEXIS 27338 (E.D.N.Y. Dec. 16, 2004).

Hopefully, the defendants' lawyers will make it crystal clear in their request that you are in no way obligated to engage in private, ex parte discussions with anyone from their office. Rather, New York State case law and the authorization simply state that you are permitted (but not required) to speak with someone from their office, if you wish. It is your decision to make.

You may wish to consult with your own attorney before deciding whether or not to agree to any request by the defendants' attorneys.

Should you decide to discuss your treatment of Henry Jones with the defendants' lawyers, please notify us immediately, as our firm would like the opportunity to be present for any discussion.

Thank you for your attention to, and cooperation in, this matter.

18

THE SECRET TO BUILDING A MULTIMILLION-DOLLAR INJURY LAW FIRM

Injury lawyers face the same dilemma. You want the catastrophic injury cases with strong liability and tons of insurance coverage, but you feel compelled to accept slip and fall and soft-tissue motor vehicle wreck claims. You don't think you'll get the huge cases without taking the small ones that pay the bills.

There's one problem: this is a failed philosophy. You can't have a catastrophic injury practice and handle multi-million-dollar injury cases if you're accepting every broken pinky claim.

The Brutal Truth about the Monster Plaintiffs' Firms

First, let's face one fact: the massive plaintiff law firms have an established procedure for handling minor injury claims. The big plaintiffs' firms have multi-million-dollar advertising budgets and a small army of intake specialists working twenty-four hours a day. And for all of that money and hard work, the average value of a single case for the behemoth plaintiff firms? $4,500.

I'm guessing that you don't have that budget or system and you probably don't want that type of practice. You want your career to make an impact on the lives of the most seriously disabled. So, what can you do to build a catastrophic injury practice?

Do Less, Obsess More

Having a successful plaintiffs' practice is not about taking on more work and clients—it's about accepting fewer cases. Every minute you spend on a minor injury case is time you're taking away from your multi-million-dollar cases.

> *"To work smart means to maximize the value of your work by selecting a few activities and applying intense targeted effort."*
> —Morten T. Hansen, *Great at Work*

Focus on spending time every week on your biggest cases. Obsess about them. Get your biggest cases to trial in less than eighteen months—yes, this is realistic when you and your team have a laser-beam focus on taking steps every week to make progress.

Define Your Ideal Client

Be crystal clear who you want as a client. No, not just catastrophic injury and strong liability—go deeper in defining your ideal client. For our firm, the criteria for our ideal client is based upon five factors.

OUR "RULES FOR CLIENTS"

#1: Must have a Catastrophic Injury or Death

A "catastrophic" injury must meet one of five criteria to be considered by our firm:

- Death

- Brain injury

- Paralysis (partial or complete)

- Loss of limb

- Blindness (near complete in at least one eye)

If a new claim does not meet one of those five criteria, we refer the client to another law firm that handles minor injury cases (and get a referral fee for making the referral). Referral fees for minor cases alone can pay a good chunk of your firm's marketing budget.

#2: Must have a Minimum Settlement Value of $500,000

We categorize our cases based upon the settlement value, namely, the lowest settlement offer that we'd recommend that our clients accept. The cases are classified in our case management software (Trialworks) as follows:

- "A": Settlement Value in Excess of $1 Million

- "B": Settlement Value between $500,000 and $1 Million

- "C": Settlement Value between $300,000 and $500,000

- "D": Settlement Value Less Than $300,000

For cases having a value less than $500,000, they must have clear and undeniable liability, e.g., surgeon failed to remove a sponge or scalpel from the patient's body at the end of surgery. In the absence of clear liability, we steer clear of "C" cases and we avoid "D" cases at all costs.

#3: Decline Unreasonable or Rude Clients

Some clients are jerks. You've had clients that disagree with your advice, make unreasonable demands, and second-guess everything you do. If you're faced with an obnoxious, demanding client, do the right thing: fire them!

Whenever we've accepted a client who's a jerk, we've regretted it. Decline the jerks and you'll thank your lucky stars that you've got nice, humble clients.

#4: Do Not Accept Cases having Questionable Merit

One of our four core values for our law firm is that we do not accept cases having questionable merit.

If a catastrophic injury has questionable merit, we decline the case and wish the client well (also helps us sleep better). It makes no sense to invest a ton of money and time on a case that will likely fail at trial. Let some other lawyer make that mistake.

#5: Only Accept Clients Who Agree with Our Core Values

Our core values mean everything to us, and if they aren't important to our clients, we don't want to represent them. The conduct of our law firm is governed by four simple core values, including:

- We will NEVER agree to confidential settlements.

- We are brutally honest with our clients.

If our clients don't care about confidentiality, we don't want them as clients. If the client is money hungry, wants to sue to get rich or has a vendetta against a physician, we politely decline representation.

Sharing Your "Rules for Clients" with Your Team

If a new case does not meet the criteria for "Our Rules for Clients," we refer the client to another law firm. But you're not done yet— write down your Rules for Clients and share them with your team. Make sure your intake staff and paralegals are familiar with your Rules for Clients and use them to make decisions about new cases.

> *"You must obsess over your chosen area of focus to excel."*
> —Morten T. Hansen, *Great at Work*

Once your team embraces your Rules for Clients, you're one step closer to having a law firm that functions in your absence (a.k.a., the *autonomous law firm*). And isn't that the goal all of us should have?

The Question You're Dying to Ask

Don't you have to accept the minor injury cases while you're waiting for your biggest cases to get to trial? Au contraire, my friend. It's better to handle three cases than three hundred cases, and just one catastrophic injury case can pay your overhead and income for the entire year.

Just think, where do you want to be in five years? If you're happy where you are, keep doing things the same way. But if you're not, then start by writing down the Rules for Clients and share them with your team. Better yet, post your Rules for Clients in a framed picture in every room of your office and make them the centerpiece for discussion at your daily, weekly and quarterly meetings.

19

BURN YOUR ANNUAL GOALS INTO THE GROUND!

It's the day before your summer vacation. You have work that has to get done before you leave, and you are laser-beam focused on getting it done. You refuse to allow any outside interruptions or distractions; you refuse to take unscheduled phone calls, respond to email, or check your social media. You work like your pants are on fire and it's amazing how much you get done by 5:00 p.m.

Talk about a productive workday—you kicked ass and took no prisoners. Now, you can leave for your vacation knowing that you did those ultra-important tasks that had to be done, and you have peace of mind.

Why Isn't Every Day Like This?

Why do you wait until the day before your vacation to be ultra-productive? It's simple: on the last day before your vacation, you have a firm deadline—at 5:00 p.m., you have to leave with your family for your vacation, and there are no ifs, ands, or buts. You can't make any excuses or stay longer in the office.

> *"Top performers are great, not because their ideas are better,*
> *but because their execution disciplines are better."*
> —Brian P. Moran and Michael Lennington, *The 12 Week Year*

But why isn't every workday like your last day before vacation? You know goal-setting is important for your law practice, so you create annual goals in December, and every so often you remind yourself what you need to accomplish. But let's face it, even in August, you still have four months to accomplish your goals, so you can always focus on other things—your annual goals take a backseat.

Trash Your Annual Goals

It's no wonder you look at your annual goals in December and can't believe how few of them were accomplished. But you're not alone. Annual goals are often vague, abstract, and too far in the future to focus on.

What if you took your twelve-month goals and boiled them down to twelve weeks? Impossible, you say? Begin by setting twelve-week goals—that's right, list them right now—just three to five goals will do. These are the goals for your "A" cases—the ones that have the biggest injuries and best liability and that will make the most money for your firm.

Live in the Moment and Think Short Term

Let's say the Jones case has a settlement value of $1 million. It's a race to get this case to trial, because you know this is the case that will pay your overhead for the next six months.

What can you do in the next twelve weeks to get this case to trial? Break down the goals and tactics that you will need over the next twelve weeks to get a trial date. It's critical that you have a goal for each of the twelve weeks, with specific tactics.

> *"The weekly plan is a powerful tool that translates the 12-week plan into daily and weekly action."*
> —Brian P. Moran and Michael Lennington, *The 12 Week Year*

In week one, make sure all discovery demands and responses have been served on the defense. This is a start, but you need to identify exactly which member of your team will do each task—these are the tactics that are crucial to the success of your twelve-week plan.

By week twelve, you have executed on goals and tactics for each week, and the end result is a trial date. Amazingly, you got your best "A" case to trial in only twelve weeks. I know what you're thinking—fat chance of completing discovery in only twelve weeks. But just think: you've had cases that seem to breeze through discovery with few adjournments or delays. And isn't this at least *possible* for all of your "A" cases?

Your Scorecard for Success

But just setting weekly plans and tactics isn't enough—you have to keep score. You should have a twenty-minute weekly accountability meeting—a meeting every Monday that is strictly limited to ten minutes where each member of your team reports on their progress.

> *"It's nothing more than going around the table and asking every person at the meeting to report on the three primary activities on their plate for the week."*
> —Patrick Lencioni, *Death by Meeting*

With a twelve-week plan, you know what everyone is doing (or not doing) on a weekly basis and whether you're on track to reach your twelve-week goals. But don't stop there; give a grade for each of your team members. Have your assistant keep a log of every person's weekly scorecard and keep the grades for each week of the twelve-week plan. The weekly scorecard is a great way to keep track of the progress of each of your team members, and if there's a breakdown, you will know when and why it happens.

It's Time for a Big Kick in the Ass

Now, I know what you're thinking: the twelve-week plan is great in theory, but it won't work for you. You're ultra-busy with paperwork, depositions and trials and you don't have time to plan for the strategic success of your "A" cases.

> *"By working from a weekly plan and following your model week, you are setting yourself up for success."*
> —Brian P. Moran and Michael Lennington, *The 12 Week Year*

You can begin the twelve-week plan with only two or three of your "A" cases. Sit down with your staff and list the specific goals and tactics needed for each week over the next twelve weeks. No one ever said all cases are created equal—it's smart to focus on your highest-value "A" cases, even if you have to neglect the lower-value "B" and "C" cases. And if this doesn't improve your execution, speed, and progress, scrap the twelve-week plan and go back to your old way of doing things.

The Best Way to Prepare for Trial

Many (if not most) trial lawyers begin serious preparation for trial in the week, if not days, before trial. When you do this, your clients and witnesses won't be prepared to testify at trial, and you'll face legal and evidentiary issues that you're not prepared for. This is a recipe for disaster.

If the old school way doesn't work, what is the best way to prepare for trial?

The Magic of the Twelve-Week Plan

At least twelve weeks before trial, sit down with your team to document everything that needs to be done in the next twelve weeks to prepare for trial. Brainstorm and collaborate with your team— there are no bad ideas.

During the twelve-week-plan meeting, have a team member:

- Document every task that needs to get done.

- Assign a week for each task (weeks 1 through 12).

- Identify the person who will be responsible for every task.

With a twelve-week plan, there will be no uncertainty as to what must be done, when it has to get done, and who is going to do what.

Step 1: Drafting the Twelve-Week Plan

Every twelve-week plan will be different, but there are a few tasks that are necessary for almost every trial.

Week 1:

- Confirm dates and time for the trial testimony of the expert witnesses (secretary).

- Schedule focus group for at least two weeks before trial (secretary).

- Schedule meeting with expert witnesses (including treating physicians), clients, and lay witnesses to prepare for their trial testimony (secretary).

- Contact treating doctors to request updated medical records (secretary).

- Call our client to get an update about medical treatment (secretary/paralegal).

Week 2:

- Draft subpoenas duces tecum for medical and employment records (paralegal).

- Mail their deposition transcripts to our clients (secretary).

- Confirm with expert witnesses that they possess entire case file (paralegal).*

- Determine need for imaging films (e.g., MRI, CT, x-ray) at trial (paralegal/lawyer).

- Draft affirmation/affidavit for radiologist (CPLR section 4532-a) to authenticate imaging films for trial (paralegal).

- Contact trial judge's secretary to check for judge's trial rules (secretary).

Week 3:

- Serve subpoenas duces tecum for medical and employment records (paralegal).

- Schedule videographer for playback of videotape deposition at trial (secretary).

- Schedule meeting with trial/jury consultant (secretary).

- Contact expert witnesses to establish budget for fees (secretary/paralegal).

- Review defendants' expert response to identify name of their expert witness (paralegal).

Week 4:

- Call medical illustrator to discuss courtroom exhibits (lawyer).

- Review trial judge's trial rules (paralegal/lawyer) (*the trial rules differ for almost every trial judge).

- Schedule travel (e.g., hotel and airfare) of expert witnesses (secretary).

- Conduct background search of defendants' expert witnesses, including transcripts of past testimony and published articles/books (paralegal).

Week 5:

- Determine need to serve a supplemental verified bill of particulars (for updated medical treatment) (paralegal/ lawyer).

- Draft timeline of medical treatment for courtroom exhibit (lawyer).

Week 6:

- Edit the defendants' deposition transcript(s) for playback during trial (lawyer).

Week 7:

- Draft motion in limine for the danger points in your case (e.g., client's criminal record) (lawyer).

- Meet with trial/jury consultant (lawyer).

- Send the edited deposition transcripts to the video editor for video editing (secretary/paralegal).

- Draft supplemental verified bill of particulars (with updated medical treatment) (paralegal).

- Serve supplemental verified bill of particulars upon defendants' counsel (paralegal) (*must be done at least thirty days before trial).

- Serve updated medical records upon defendants' counsel (secretary).

- Draft list of trial exhibits (paralegal).

Week 8:

- Conduct focus group (lawyer).

- Highlight in yellow the portions of the defendants' deposition transcripts that will be played back via videotape during the trial (secretary/paralegal).

- Prepare content for trial notebook (paralegal).

- Prepare trial budget (paralegal).

Week 9:

- Meet with expert witnesses to prepare for their trial testimony (lawyer).

- Draft plaintiff's proposed jury charge, verdict sheet, and statement of contentions for submission to the trial judge (paralegal/lawyer).

- Review and approve courtroom exhibits with medical illustrator (lawyer).

- Follow up with defendants' counsel to request stipulation of exhibits (medical and employment records) (paralegal).

Week 10:

- Meet with clients and lay witnesses to prepare for their trial testimony (lawyer).

- Send letter to the trial judge requesting a *pre-trial* jury instruction regarding the burden of proof (paralegal).

- Call the court clerk to inquire whether the court provides audio-video equipment, such as an easel, video projector and screen, cables, and ELMO for the presentation of documents and photos (secretary).

- Confirm with the videographer the date and time of the videotape playback of the defendants' deposition testimony (secretary).

Week 11:

- Meet with clients at the courtroom to acquaint them with the courtroom (lawyer).

- Remind expert witnesses to bring entire case file (via email and phone call) (secretary).

- Prepare marked pleadings, plaintiff's verified bill of particulars, and list of witnesses (paralegal).

- Submit marked pleadings, plaintiff's verified bill of particulars, list of witnesses, plaintiff's proposed jury charge, verdict sheet and statement of contentions to the trial judge and defendants' counsel.

- Submit deposition read-ins and videotape of defendants' depositions to the trial judge and defendants' counsel.

Week 12:

- Review and pre-mark subpoenaed records with the court reporter at the courthouse (paralegal).

- Call medical and employment providers if the subpoenaed records are not present at the courthouse or are not properly certified (paralegal).

- Organize case file to bring to court (paralegal).

*The *entire case file* should consist of the medical and employment records, pleadings and discovery responses, deposition transcripts, and any other part of the case file that might be relevant to the expert's trial testimony.

The twelve-week plan should be printed and signed and dated by every team member and scanned into your case management software.

Step 2: Ensuring Compliance with the Twelve-Week Plan

At your weekly goal meeting every Monday, you should review the twelve-week plan for the previous and upcoming weeks. Did the team member do what they were supposed to? This is the time to hold them accountable. The twelve-week plan won't work if there is no accountability.

As the team members confirm that they did what they were supposed to do, check off the tasks on the twelve-week plan. Next, focus on the tasks that need to be done in the upcoming week. Make sure everyone knows what they are supposed to do.

Your weekly goal meetings are also the time to modify and update the twelve-week plan. There will always be unexpected tasks, such as the need for changes to the courtroom exhibits or a second focus group. Ask your team members whether anything else needs to be done.

And here's the beauty of the twelve-week plan: by the week before trial, you'll realize that everything is done. That's right—you're ready for trial, and you can't think of anything else to do. And that, my friend, is a nice feeling.

*The twelve-week plan is based upon Brian Moran's extraordinary book *The 12 Week Year*.

Part 2

Goal Setting and Financial Management

20

HOW TO MANAGE A LAW FIRM FOR PROFIT

You got into law for a noble purpose: you want to help people. And that's a beautiful thing, but you can't help people if you can't pay your bills. Yet, most lawyers refuse to acknowledge a simple fact: you are running a business and profit is your number one goal.

Knowing your numbers and getting into a rhythm of reporting them is the first step to running a profitable law firm. Begin with four numbers:

1. Gross Revenue

2. Operating Expenses

3. Salary Cap (aka cost of labor)

4. Pretax Profit

#1: Gross Revenue

The money generated by your law firm, including legal fees, referral income, book sales, etc. Gross revenue is every penny that is deposited into your operating account.

#2: Operating Expenses

Know exactly what it takes to run your law firm. The operating expenses will fall into one of six categories:

1. Salaries

2. Rent

3. Marketing

4. Payroll Taxes and Benefits

5. Insurance

6. Other Operating Expenses

Other operating expenses include office supplies, IT support, costs of software for case management, customer relationship management (CRM) and lead intake, telephone and internet, payments for debt (e.g., interest on your line of credit).

#3: Salary Cap (aka cost of labor)

You should know your law firm's salary cap or the cost of labor, including your market-based wage (salary and bonus). Set your market-based wage by asking this question:

> *"If you got run over by a bus today and your heirs decided they would keep the business going in your absence, what would they have to pay someone to do your job?"*

—**Greg Crabtree,** *Simple Numbers, Straight Talk, Big Profits!*

If it would cost $240,000 to replace you, then that is your market-based wage and that is what you should be paying yourself (e.g., salary and bonus). If you underestimate your market-based wage, you will overstate your firm's net income.

#4: Pretax Profit

The only thing that matters is profit, namely, how much money do you take home. Revenue is irrelevant. Many lawyers strive to get bigger and increase revenue, but when they do, overhead expenses grow and it becomes a continual battle to pay the bills. For my two cents, your philosophy should be: keep it small and keep it all.

Your pretax profit is the profit you make after you take your revenue minus costs and before you pay taxes. The pretax profit for a small firm will almost always exceed that of a large firm. A larger firm (twenty to twenty-five employees) might be thrilled with a pretax profit of 25 to 30 percent, while a small firm (five employees) can consistently have a pretax profit of 50 percent. When overhead expenses are low, profit is usually high.

> *"The goal, first and foremost, is to run a profitable company."*
> —Greg Crabtree, *Simple Numbers. Straight Talk. Big Profits!*

The amount of money that you pay the IRS is the only key performance indicator that matters. When you pay more taxes, your law firm is healthy. You should celebrate when you pay a big tax bill. Seriously. Paying a big tax bill means you're running a profitable law firm.

Three Numbers for Forecasting Your Income

To forecast your firm's net income over the next twelve months, you'll need three numbers:

1. **Trial Dates**: Number of confirmed trial dates over the next twelve months

2. **Settlement Values**: Settlement value for each case with a confirmed trial date

3. **Legal Fees**: Legal fee for each case (after the payment of referral fees) with a confirmed trial date

Let's say you have four confirmed trial dates over the next twelve months. Conservatively estimate the most realistic settlement value and your firm's legal fee (after paying referral fees) for each case that has a confirmed trial date. Once you tally the legal fees for the four cases, you know what your law firm's income will be over the next twelve months.

No trial dates over the next twelve months? That's a problem. Without a trial date, you cannot forecast income. Make it a priority to get confirmed trial dates for your biggest three to five cases over the next ninety days.

Keep a Scoreboard of Your Numbers

Buy a whiteboard and keep a scoreboard of your numbers. When it comes to your key financial numbers, less is more. Put the numbers on an actual Scoreboard—focus on the Scoreboard and make that the focus of your financial meetings. The Scoreboard will provide immediate, visual feedback.

Here's what your Scoreboard might look like:

1. Revenue: $1,100,000

2. Operating Expenses: $550,000

3. Salary Cap (aka cost of labor): $325,000

4. Pretax Profit: 50 percent

5. Income Forecast (for next twelve months): $750,000

Compare your profit and loss on a year to year comparison and month-by-month over the last twelve months (e.g., rolling twelve-month profit and loss). This will show whether you're doing better from year to year and whether your profit is trending up or down.

Know Your Budget and Target Allocation Percentages

How often do you review your profit and loss statement and balance sheet? Be honest. Meet with your financial team (bookkeeper and accountant) once every six to eight weeks to review your profit and loss and balance statement.

Go through the variable expenses, e.g., office supplies, and ask your financial team, "Do we really need this?" Cancel whatever is not absolutely indispensable to run your law firm, such as recurring monthly fees for things you don't use. Whenever possible, negotiate with your vendors to lower expenses.

Determine the percentage of every major expense relative to your gross revenue, e.g., if your revenue is $1,000,000 and salaries are $500,000, salaries are 50 percent of your gross revenue. Your bookkeeper should provide the current allocations, e.g. percentages for every category of your major expenses and pretax profit; this is a snapshot of where you stand right now. Your marketing budget might include sub-categories of your biggest expenses, e.g., TV advertising, seminars, etc.

Current Allocation Percentages (as a Percentage of Revenue)

Salaries: 50%

Marketing: 7%

Rent and Supplies: 23%

Net Income Before Taxes (Pretax Profit): 20%

Then, you should create Target Allocation Percentages ("TAP") for those categories—this is where you want to be in the future.

Target Allocation Percentages (as a Percentage of Revenue)

Salaries: 42% (down 8%)

Marketing: 15% (up 8%)

Rent and Supplies: 15% (down 8%)

Net Income Before Taxes (Pretax Profit): 28% (up 8%)

Your Target Allocation Percentages have reduced allocation percentages for your operating expenses, e.g., salaries, rent and supplies, and higher allocation percentages for the things that matter most, namely, marketing and pretax profit. Your goal as a business owner? Low overhead, high profit.

Thank you to Alex Nguyen, Esq., a numbers guru, former actuary and exceptional entrepreneur/injury lawyer in Atlanta, for sharing this tip!

Take Your Profit First

Create separate accounts for profit and taxes. The accounts are created at a bank (your "no temptation" bank) that is different from the bank where you have your operating and escrow accounts. You will call these accounts: profit hold and tax hold.

Every time you make a deposit, move 1 percent into the Profit Hold and Tax Hold accounts. By moving profit and tax into a separate bank account, you keep those funds out of sight and beyond your temptation to access them.

> *"Profitability isn't an event. It's a habit."*
> —Mike Michalowicz, *Profit First*

As you get used to setting aside money for profit and taxes, increase the amount that you deposit in those accounts and set targets (aka, target allocation percentages) for your profit and tax hold accounts. The goal is to pay yourself first from every dollar you earn and set aside money for taxes so you're not scrambling to pay taxes on April 15.

Three Simple Ways to Instantly Lower Your Taxes

Prepay Expenses: You can prepay expenses (e.g., rent, malpractice insurance, phone and internet fees, etc.) for up to six months at the end of the calendar year and deduct the expense in the year the expense was paid. This will lower your overhead expenses in the following year and increase your tax deductions (and lower your taxable income) in the year that you prepay the expenses. This is a no-brainer!

Do not increase your business expenses simply to increase your tax deductions. Spending money to save money makes no sense.

Max-Out Your Retirement Plans: Make the maximum contribution to your 401(k) and profit-sharing accounts or a defined pension benefit plan. For every dollar that you invest in your retirement account, you'll save about 40–50 percent on your taxes.

When you make a contribution to the retirement plans of your staff, you reduce your taxable income and get props for investing in their future. Your retirement contribution to your staff's 401(k) and profit-sharing accounts can be their end-of-the year bonus.

Defer Your Legal Fees in Personal Injury Cases: You can pay the future operating expenses of your law firm (or fund your retirement plan) by structuring the legal fees in personal injury settlements. For every dollar you put in a structured settlement annuity, you'll save about 40–50 percent on your tax bill.

One Caveat: You'll need the consent of counsel for the settling defendant to invest your legal fee in a structured settlement annuity.

Negotiate a Long-Term Lease

Don't just sign a three-year lease—think long term. Negotiate a lease that gives you multiple options (e.g., eight consecutive options to renew with a three-year term) to renew at the expiration of each term.

When you add options to renew to the lease, you have the right to remain in your office until the expiration of the last option to renew (e.g., long enough to stay in the office for your entire career). Just in case you have a change of plans, add a provision that gives you the right to terminate the lease at a fixed price (e.g., you can terminate the lease at any time for three months rent).

Eliminate Debt and Build Your Capital Reserves

Eliminate your personal and business debt and run your law firm from your capital reserves. This will take time and won't happen overnight, but just say "no" to debt. Build six months of capital reserves, so you have a cushion for the bad months and occasional defense verdict. If your operating expenses are $50,000/month, set a goal of having $300,000 in capital reserves.

> *"Businesses that have cash and no debt attract magical things."*
> —Greg Crabtree, *Simple Numbers, Straight Talk, Big Profits!*

If you pay yourself a market-based wage, you can live off that and won't have to take profit distributions (e.g., bonus compensation) from your law firm. You will be more frugal when you're paying expenses with your own money rather than a line of credit.

Create a Succession Plan for Your Law Firm

Create a succession plan that leaves nothing to chance. If you die today, your law firm will be worth money and your successor will be Shannon Jones, Esq. Agree upon a method for determining the value of your law firm. The economic value might be based on the last three years of pretax profit plus equity (assets minus liabilities) and the value of your case inventory.

If you do not have a succession plan, your law firm won't be worth a dime when you stop practicing law. Build a law firm based upon profit and no debt and other lawyers will be dying to buy you out.

21

MANAGING YOUR LAW FIRM BY THE NUMBERS

Whatever gets measured gets improved. If you don't measure your numbers for marketing, case management, and finance, you won't identify the flaws in your systems. And that, my friend, is a problem.

By identifying a few rocks for every department of your law firm, you have a scorecard that you can use to measure your progress. Is your website getting more traffic and converting more clients? Are you getting more lawyer referrals, and which lawyers are sending you the most work? You should know this.

The Most Important Rock for a Trial Firm

What is the most important number (a.k.a. "rocks") in your law firm? Our law firm's most important rock is the number of trial dates.

If we have nine to twelve confirmed trial dates over the next twelve months, we're going to have a good year. Of course, things don't always work out as you expect—your client might die or a defendant might file a bankruptcy petition, but confirmed trial dates gives us the best gauge of our outlook for the next twelve months.

> *"You will gain the power of being able to manage your company through a chosen handful of numbers."*
> —**Gino Wickman,** *Traction*

What rocks should you measure? Take your firm's growth chart (a.k.a. accountability chart) and identify the most important numbers for each department. You will have different rocks for marketing, case management, and finance. Keep things simple—less is better.

Finance

When measuring rocks for finance, you should compare the current year to the previous year in the following:

- Revenue

- Profit

- Salary cap (cost of salaries as a percentage of total expenses)

- Projected revenue (over next twelve months)

Marketing

To get an overview of your marketing results, you should begin by checking these rocks:

Number of active cases: An active case is either in litigation or has been accepted for litigation.

Number of potential cases: A potential case is under consideration but has not been accepted for litigation.

Number of new leads (last thirty days): A new lead is a lead from any source—digital, referral, et cetera, regardless of merit.

Next, you should take a deeper look at the sources of your leads by dividing your marketing into three categories, namely, nondigital/traditional, digital/internet and social media.

Nondigital/Traditional Marketing

- Number of referral partners
- Number of new referrals partners acquired in this calendar year
- Number of referred cases accepted for litigation/calendar year

Digital/Internet Marketing

- Number of website visitors (ProtectingPatientRights.com)
- Number of new website pages/last thirty days
- Number of links to website
- Number of new links acquired for website/last thirty days

Social Media Marketing

- Number of posts/last thirty days
- Number of followers

- Number of shares

- Number of engagement

Case Management

The rocks for our case management consist of three numbers:

- Number of active cases (An "active case" means a lawsuit has been filed.)

- Number of trial dates (A trial date means we have a confirmed trial date from the court.)

- Stage of every active case

The Four Stages of a Lawsuit

To make sure every lawsuit is making progress, you should establish rocks (deadlines for each stage of a lawsuit) for case management. For a trial law firm, there are four stages of a lawsuit:

- Filing of the lawsuit

- Paper discovery

- Depositions

- Trial

Stage I: Filing of the Lawsuit

What this is: Filing of the summons and complaint until receipt of the all of the defendants' answers

Goal: Sixty days

Stage II: Paper Discovery

What this is: Receipt of defendant's answer to service of plaintiff's discovery responses and discovery demands

    Goal: Sixty days

Stage III: Depositions

What this is: Service of plaintiff's discovery responses until the last deposition

    Goal: Five months

Stage IV: Trial

What this is: Filing of the note of issue to first day of trial

    Goal: Nine months

Tracking Every Stage of the Lawsuit

For every active lawsuit, we track three numbers, namely, the stage of the case (e.g., paper discovery, depositions, et cetera), the duration of the case in its current stage and the time remaining in the stage. If we've served the plaintiff's discovery responses and demands and are conducting depositions, the rocks would be reported as:

Client: Oddibe McDowell

1: Stage of lawsuit: Deposition

2: Duration in current stage: Two months, thirteen days

3: Time remaining for stage: Three months, seventeen days

The goal is to move a case to trial within eighteen months, and that won't happen if we aren't tracking our case management "rocks." Can we do better? Of course, but eighteen months is a realistic goal in almost all venues outside of New York City.

A Scorecard for Every Employee

With these rocks, you have a simple scorecard for measuring your law firm's progress, but don't stop there. Every employee should have rocks to measure their work. But where do you start? Just as with your law firm's rocks, go through your law firm's accountability chart (e.g., marketing, case management, and finance) to identify the most important rocks for your team.

Don't fret if you have trouble identifying your rocks. Take a day to sit down with your team to share with them your law firm's rocks. With feedback from your team, you can create their individual rocks to help accomplish your law firm's rocks.

You might measure your paralegals' rocks in the following:

- Number of completed discovery demands and responses

- Number of contacts with clients—potential and active

- Number of requests for online reviews

- Number of posts and shares on your firm's Facebook page

Case management—Number of completed discovery responses: For a litigation paralegal, you might measure the number of completed discovery responses and demands in the current month. What else can you measure?

Case management—Number of client contacts: Client communication (or the lack thereof) is a problem for all law firms. Ask your paralegal to document on a scorecard whenever they speak with a client. Every client—active and potential—should be contacted by your paralegal at least once every four weeks.

> *"These numbers must allow you to have an*
> *absolute pulse on your business."*
> —Gino Wickman, *Traction*

Marketing—Number of online reviews: Law firms should crave online reviews (focus on your firm's profile on *Google My Business*), but you can't do this alone. Ask your paralegal to document on a scorecard every time they request an online review from a client. This will keep online reviews top of mind for your paralegal.

Marketing—Number of social media posts and shares: Law firms should have a vibrant presence on social media, but this, too, is neglected. Have your paralegal document on a scorecard every time they post or share on your firm's business page on Facebook. Get your team involved in your firm's social media marketing.

Weekly Self-Reporting of Individual and Law Firm Rocks

Ask your team members to report their individual rocks at the end of the week on a Slack channel, and assign someone to report the rocks of each team member. With rocks that are reported on a weekly basis, you will have a pulse on your law firm unlike anything else.

> *"The unfortunate reality is that most*
> *organizations do not have a Scorecard."*
> —Gino Wickman, *Traction*

Some team members may balk at self-reporting their rocks—they're too busy and might tell you that they have better things to do. But these employees are not a good fit for a data-driven law firm, and it might be time to find someone who is.

Making Your Rocks Visible for Your Team

Every month, update the numbers and keep a physical scorecard in your conference room for your team to see. The tracking of the rocks on a visible scorecard will keep them top of mind, and your team will know how they're doing (and you will too). Has your secretary accomplished their rocks in the last thirty days?

> *"With vision clear, people in place, and data being managed through a Scorecard, you're creating a transparent organization where there is nowhere to hide."*
> —**Gino Wickman,** *Traction*

With a weekly scorecard, you know what has to be done over the next week/month. If your paralegal is not serving discovery responses and demands, your cases will languish (and you won't get paid). A scorecard also gives you data upon which you can base quarterly employee evaluations.

22

A LAWYER'S WORST NIGHTMARE

This is your worst nightmare.

You're out of town during a trial, and your trusty paralegal drives an expert witness to the courthouse. While driving to the courthouse, your paralegal blows through a red light and plows into an innocent pedestrian. The damages are huge, your paralegal is 100 percent at fault, and you are facing a monster lawsuit.

Days after the crash, the injury victim's lawyer discovers that your paralegal was driving to the courthouse as part of their employment with your law firm. The injury victim's lawyer begins hyperventilating, as they realize that your law firm is vicariously responsible for the crash. The injury victim sets their sights on suing your law firm, and without the right insurance coverage, you're screwed.

But there's a happy ending to this story. Your insurance agent shows you the policies insuring your law firm and assures you that you're covered for the motor vehicle crash. Your agent tells you that you have hired and non-owned auto coverage as part of your office business insurance, and this coverage insures your law firm against claims made against your employees while driving to the courthouse.

Six Coverages that All Lawyers Should Have

It's your job to make sure your law firm has the following coverage:

- Hired and non-owned auto coverage

- Data breach and cyber liability

- Commercial general liability insurance

- Employee theft/crime coverage

- Employment practices liability insurance

- Umbrella/excess liability coverage

Hired and Non-Owned Auto Coverage

Whether your paralegal was driving their personal vehicle or a rental car, hired and non-owned auto coverage insures your law firm for at least $1 million in damages and pays for defense costs. Even better, you can pay an extra fee for excess liability insurance providing an additional $5 million of coverage that applies to the hired and non-owned auto coverage. Not only is your law firm covered for the auto crash, you have $6 million in coverage and you won't have to pay a penny in defense costs.

Data Breach and Cyber Liability Insurance

Cyber liability and data breach insurance protects you when your clients' personal information becomes compromised, and includes third-party damages and defense costs. If you lose your smart phone, iPad, or laptop, your clients' private information might get into the wrong hands, subjecting you to damages for a data breach.

If your client sues for damages over the loss of private data or stolen identity, cyber liability insurance pays for legal fees, settlements, and court costs. If client information is stolen, there can be hefty fines of up to $250,000 for failing to notify clients of a data breach. With cyber liability insurance, your insurance company must notify your clients of the data breach.

Commercial General Liability Insurance

Commercial general liability (CGL) insurance covers property and personal injury claims that occur at your law firm. The costs of defending a lawsuit can cripple a law firm, and this coverage protects you from exorbitant legal fees. Your professional liability insurance (a.k.a. errors and omissions) will not provide coverage for property and personal injury claims that are unrelated to legal malpractice. CGL insurance is worth the expense.

Employee Theft/Crime Coverage

If your bookkeeper steals from your attorney escrow account or operating account, employee theft/crime coverage protects you. Employee theft/crime coverage pays for your losses as well as the legal fees for bringing your employee to justice. Employee theft/crime coverage can be bundled with office business insurance.

Employment Practices Liability Insurance

Employment practices liability insurance (EPLI) protects you against claims brought by employees alleging wrongful termination, sexual harassment, discrimination, and retaliation, including defamation, invasion of privacy, failure to promote, deprivation of a work opportunity, and negligent evaluation.

Excess Liability Coverage and Umbrella Coverage

Excess liability policies provide coverage above the limits of the underlying coverage. It offers no broader protection than that provided by the underlying policy. Your excess liability coverage should, at minimum, match the value of your firm's biggest case.

There is a difference between excess liability insurance and umbrella insurance. Umbrella policies are a type of excess liability that not only provide additional limits (as excess liability policies do), but also can provide broader coverage that is not available in the underlying coverage.

How to Avoid Three Fatal Mistakes with Your Errors and Omissions Policy

Your errors and omissions policy is a claims-made policy that protects you against claims that are reported when the policy is in force. Follow these three steps to maximize your coverage:

Step One: Maximize Your Prior Acts Coverage

Errors and omissions policies normally have a retroactive date for acts and omissions that result in a claim. If your errors and omissions policy has a retroactive date of May 1, 2019, your policy will not cover you against claims arising from acts or omissions that occurred before May 1, 2019.

Prior acts coverage that is defined as "full prior acts" covers acts occurring at any time prior to the current policy period and means that there is no retroactive date.

Step Two: Beware of Shrinking Coverage Limits

If your errors and omissions policy has claims expenses inside the limit (CEIL), all claim expenses are deducted from the liability limit first, and the balance is available for paying a judgment or settlement. If you have a liability limit of $1 million, and your claim expenses total $400,000, there will be $600,000 left to pay damages.

Claims expenses outside the limit (CEOL) means claims expenses are outside the limits of liability and won't lower the limits of liability. If you elect to have a CEOL endorsement on your policy for an additional fee, you are provided with a separate but equal limit of liability for claim expenses. On a $1 million liability limit, the full $1 million is available for payment of damages, and there is an additional $1 million available for claim expenses.

Step Three: Extend the Claim Reporting Period

The extended claim reporting period is an endorsement to your errors and omissions policy that addresses work performed during the policy period that gives rise to a claim after the policy has expired. This endorsement extends the period of time after the policy expiration in which a claim can be made and filed and still be covered. Typical options are one-year, three-year, and five-year reporting periods.

Become the Guru of Law Firm Insurance

Ask your insurance agent whether you have hired and non-owned auto coverage, cyber liability insurance, employee theft/crime coverage, employment practices liability coverage, and excess/umbrella coverage. By spending an hour reviewing your coverages, you can get back to doing what you do best—practicing law—and rest a little easier.

23

FINANCIAL PLANNING FOR THE SAVVY PLAINTIFFS' LAWYER

There's good and bad news with a huge settlement. It's always good when your bank account gets fatter, but the not-so-good news is that you have to share 50 percent of your legal fee with Uncle Sam (a.k.a., the IRS). For savvy plaintiffs' lawyers, there is a unique solution.

Since 1996, the IRS allows plaintiffs' lawyers to defer their legal fees prior to settlement. Childs v. Commissioner, 103 T.C. 634 (1994), affirmed without opinion, 89 F.3d 856 (11th Cir. 1996). Plaintiffs' lawyers can defer the receipt of a legal fee by using a structured settlement annuity that provides payments in future years. The legal fee structure is only available to contingent fee plaintiffs' lawyers. You can structure all, or a portion, of your legal fee.

The Benefits of Deferring Legal Fees

The benefits of deferring legal fees in personal injury cases include:

- Providing a source of income to match against future deductible business expenses, i.e., smoothing out future cash flow

- Avoiding massive tax liability on large cases

- Protecting assets for plaintiffs' lawyers

This translates into an investment return equal to your tax bracket. Instead of being taxed now on the entire amount, your income payments are reported to the IRS in the year you receive them. For those in a high tax bracket, you can save money in income taxes on the portion of your income that is deferred. Rather than paying taxes in the year of the settlement, you will pay taxes when you receive the funds from the structured annuity.

Stretching out payments over time yields a better tax result. Because of the tax-free compounding, the longer you stretch out the payments in a structured settlement annuity, the better the financial result.

You can spread out the payments in the future to pay for your firm's overhead expenses. In essence, you are prepaying expenses and smoothing out your firm's cash flow. With the right planning, you can ensure that your firm's overhead is prepaid with predictable income.

Deferring Legal Fees to Fund Your Retirement

Unlike traditional 401(k) retirement accounts, there are no limits on contribution amounts and no required minimum distributions. You can customize a retirement plan to fit your individual needs and construct a kind of unlimited individual retirement account. Struc-

tured legal fees can fund retirement in twenty years. This is an exceptional benefit that is available only for plaintiffs' lawyers.

You may want to structure a particular percentage of every settlement as a kind of retirement fund. If you structure 10 percent of
every fee, you get the benefits of tax deferral and retirement planning.

WARNING: Don't Sign the Settlement Agreement Just Yet

You must elect to defer the fees before they are "earned." You must
agree to a fee structure before your client signs the settlement
documents. Once the release agreement is signed, it's too late to
structure fees.

* * *

The Best Way to Finance Your Injury Law Firm

Starting a new injury law firm is a daunting task. You have overhead,
salaries, a boatload of case expenses, and you receive your fees in
drips and drabs. It's enough to make any young lawyer join a law firm
for the security of a weekly pay check.

But with all of the stress and anxiety of owning your own law
firm, there is one thing that outweighs all of the negatives: the satisfaction of knowing you're doing this for you and your family—
not for someone else. Rather than working your butt off to make
someone else rich, you're doing it for yourself, and that feels good.

When you work for someone else, even if you are an equity
partner with less than 50 percent ownership, you always run the
risk of being fired. Maybe the partnership dissolves, or the senior
partner has a bad day and wants to get rid of his junior partners, but

whatever the circumstance, there is always a chance that you will be shown the door.

Your Best Financing Options

Owning your own law business is the only option that makes sense for your long-term future. Okay, then, let's explore some financing options for opening your own law business:

- Credit cards

- Bank financing

- Legal fees

- Personal savings

It is always best to finance your law firm through fees so you're not tapping into your 401(k) or investment funds and are living off the income/fees you make. Estimate your law firm's budget for six months, and pay your expenses from the income and fees that you earn.

Get a Line of Credit with a Local Bank

The life of an injury lawyer can be a lonely one, and you won't always have enough income and fees to pay your expenses—you need a backup plan. A line of credit with a local bank will give you access to funds when your operating account is low on cash.

Use a local bank to get a line of credit. You will rarely get a line of credit on the first try, but a "no" is an invitation to try harder (e.g., the founders of Infusionsoft were rejected on their first twenty-five attempts to secure bank financing).

Avoid Credit Cards!

You should not use credit cards to finance your law firm. Credit cards usually have ridiculously high interest rates, and you'll be spending your hard-earned cash to pay down interest every month. A commercial line of credit will give you a much lower interest rate than any credit card. Avoid credit cards if you can.

You should avoid the temptation to tap into your personal savings (e.g., your 401(k), college fund for your kids, and long-term investment savings). You can be hit with penalties and taxes on withdrawals from retirement, pension, and 529 accounts.

Hire a Bookkeeper and Financial Manager

First, hire a bookkeeper to prepare a balance sheet and profit/loss statement. You will need a business plan and financial statements. Budget your expenses and estimate your annual income. Your bookkeeper will become invaluable.

Think Like Warren Buffett

Your financial worth is your net worth, which is what you own minus what you owe. The question is, do you know your net worth?

Keep a personal balance sheet for tracking your net worth. The wealthy are conscious players of the financial wealth-building game; they play it strategically and keep score by watching their net worth.

Invest your money in your practice—not expensive cars. Be very frugal. New stuff quickly becomes old stuff, creating the need for new stuff. The spending never ends, but the joy of it does.

24

HOW TO PREVENT YOUR CLIENTS' FINANCIAL RUIN

When that fat settlement check arrives in the mail, your clients can't wait to get their hands on it. Your clients have dreams of a Porsche 911, mini-mansions for their kids and mother, and might even toss in a yacht for their down-on-his-luck uncle. You're getting paid no matter what, so everyone's happy, right?

Not so fast, my friend. You cannot ignore your clients' stupidity, because if you do, their multimillion-dollar lawsuit recovery will be spent and wasted. At the final meeting, your clients will be in denial and tell you that excessive spending "*will never happen to me.*" That's when you tell them, "Oh, yes, it will."

Be Different from Every Other Lawyer

Share everything you know about the most common financial mistakes made by injury victims, what they can do to avoid these mistakes, and offer counseling from a trusted financial planner and trust attorney. Talk to your clients about the benefits of a structured settlement preservation trust.

Give your clients a free copy of Dave Ramsey's book, *The Total Money Makeover*. Ask your clients to read and sign your *Secrets to Financial Freedom for Injury Victims*, and continually reinforce the concepts of money management throughout the lawsuit.

Will this work? It's a lot better than giving a check to the clients, wishing them well at your final meeting, and knowing that (with near certainty) their money will be gone soon.

* * *

The Secrets to Financial Freedom for Injury Victims

We are grateful for the opportunity to represent you.

Unfortunately, we've witnessed many mistakes made by our clients, and we've seen multimillion-dollar recoveries squandered in less than a year. We know that you don't think this will happen to you, but unfortunately, that's what all of our clients say, and they are almost never right.

We want you to avoid these mistakes.

This is our best advice for avoiding financial ruin. If you follow these principles, your money will likely grow and could very well double or triple. We want you to become an expert in money management.

#1: Declare War on Debt: List your debts—from smallest to largest—pay them off and destroy your credit cards.

"You must draw a line in the sand and say, 'I will never borrow again.'"
—Dave Ramsey, *The Total Money Makeover*

#2: No Credit Cards: Cut up your cards and cancel your credit accounts.

"Broke people use credit cards. Rich people don't."
—Dave Ramsey, *The Total Money Makeover*

Avoid debt like your life depends on it. The goal is to get out of debt fast.

#3: Become an Expert in Money: Knowledge is power. Read all of Dave Ramsey's books and attend his Financial Peace University. Begin by reading these books:
- *The Total Money Makeover*
- *Dave Ramsey's Complete Guide to Money*
- *Financial Peace Revisited*

#4: No Loans to Family/Friends: Never loan money to family or friends. Guaranteed, you will not recover a dime, and your relationship will be ruined.

#5: Pay Cash: Pay cash for everything (if necessary, use a debit card). Never borrow again.

"We buy things we don't need with money we don't
have in order to impress people we don't like."
—**Dave Ramsey,** *The Total Money Makeover*

It's hard to make a big purchase when you're paying cash and you get better deals. *When you spend cash, you spend less.*

#6: Say "No" to Expensive Homes or Cars: Do not buy expensive homes or cars. New cars lose half of their value in only two to three years.

"Being willing to delay pleasure for a greater
result is a sign of maturity."
—**Dave Ramsey,** *The Total Money Makeover*

Delay big purchases—you'll be glad you did the next morning.

#7: Tell Your Money What to Do: Create a new budget every month and tell your money what to do.

"A budget is just telling your money where to go,
instead of wondering where it went."
—**Dave Ramsey,** *Dave Ramsey's Complete Guide to Money*

Your income minus your expenses is your disposable income. You can always spend more than you make; live below your means.

#8: Get Your Credit Reports: Check your credit score once a year.
- Experian: 888-397-3742 (www.experian.com)
- Equifax: 800-685-1111 (www.equifax.com)

- Transunion: 877-322-8228 (www.transunion.com)

Remember to build your wealth, not your credit score.

#9: No One Gets Rich Quick: Invest in companies that treat their employees like gold. *Fortune* has an annual "The Best Companies to Work For"—do not invest in a company that isn't on this list.

"Energy, thrift, and diligence are how wealth is built, not dumb luck."
—**Dave Ramsey,** *The Total Money Makeover*

Our favorite long-term investments are Adobe, Facebook, Apple, Novo Nordisk, Stryker, Costco, Amgen, Google, and Southwest Air.

#10: Hire a Financial Planner: Hire a trusted financial planner who will guide you through the process of money management, debt elimination, and budgeting. You need someone who will hold you accountable and stop you when you want to buy the seventy-five-inch TV.

"Wealth building is a marathon, not a sprint."
—**Dave Ramsey,** *Dave Ramsey's Complete Guide to Money*

I am a fan of Timothy Denehy, CFP (tdenehy@forgeconsulting.com), a certified financial planner. Tim is knowledgeable, trustworthy, compassionate, and has spent over twenty-five years working with injury victims and their families to develop comprehensive plans to manage and protect a lawsuit recovery.

Financial Options for Your Lawsuit Recovery

When you recover money from a settlement or judgment, your three options consist of

- cash settlement,

- structured settlement preservation trust, or

- structured settlement annuity.

Option One: Lump Sum Cash Payment

Your funds are delivered via an electronic deposit into your bank account or the hand delivery of a check. You are free to do with the money as you choose.

A lump sum cash settlement is almost always a recipe for financial disaster. Do not take a cash settlement unless you are willing to lose it all.

Option Two: Structured Settlement Preservation Trust

A structured settlement preservation trust is designed to prevent you from spending your money. You can access the money in the trust to pay for basic necessities, such as college tuition, health insurance premiums, or a down payment on a new home or car.

The structured settlement preservation trust provides you with periodic (e.g., weekly, monthly) income to pay your living expenses, e.g., gas, food, mortgage—this is the "job you can't be fired from."

The structured settlement preservation trust protects you from spending sprees and living beyond your means, and with some time and patience, you will be amazed at the growth of your money.

We love the structured settlement preservation trust as a tool for providing regular income, preserving and growing your money, and permitting access to the funds for the necessities of life.

Option Three: Structured Settlement Annuity

A structured settlement annuity provides a fixed benefit (e.g., $5,000 per month for life) in return for a large lump sum payment, i.e., $1 million. The rate of return on an annuity can be extremely low, e.g., 1–3 percent, and you will not get a better rate of return when interest rates increase. You are stuck with a very low rate of return for the life of the annuity.

A structured settlement annuity can make sense when the injury victim has a substandard life expectancy, known as a "rated age." If, for example, the injury victim is a five-year-old who, due to his injuries, has a life expectancy that is equivalent to that of a seventy-year-old, the annuity will have a far higher rate of return than a healthy child would get. In this example, the annuity makes sense due to the substandard life expectancy ("rated age") of the disabled infant.

Unless you get the benefit of a substandard life expectancy ("rated age"), we do not recommend structured settlement annuities.

The Decision Belongs to You

The decision concerning the management and investment of your lawsuit recovery belongs to you. This will be one of the most important decisions you ever make, and if you make mistakes, you probably won't have a chance to correct them. We are here to answer your questions and guide you through this process.

If you have a financial consultant, make sure he/she has at least five years of experience managing the money of injury victims. The needs of injury victims are much different from the needs of the independently rich.

Read, Sign, and Return this Agreement

Please acknowledge that you have read this document by signing where indicated and returning an original to us.

We are grateful for the opportunity to serve you.

Dated:

_____

Client

Part 3
THE ENTREPRENEUR

"Your job as a business owner is to leave a legacy. I don't care about the size of it—I care about the impact."

—Marcus Lemonis

Part 3

Non-Digital Marketing

25

HOW TO START A LAW FIRM FROM SCRATCH

A young lawyer asks for my number-one piece of advice for starting a law firm, but cautions that he has few clients, relationships with lawyers, or money. The lawyer believes that no one would refer a case to him since he's a novice, has no big settlements or verdicts, and no trial experience. In essence, the young lawyer is starting from scratch. We've all been there (and it's scary).

Step One: Hire a Marketing Director

Here's where I would begin: hire a part-time marketing director for ten to fifteen hours per week. Ideally, the marketing director has skills in graphic design and computer science. With a marketing director, the young lawyer is ahead of 98 percent of all lawyers who do not have a marketing plan, marketing skills, or a dedicated marketing specialist. Marketing is the highest and best use of the lawyers' time.

Block out two hours every week on a specific date and time to discuss marketing with the marketing director. At this weekly meeting, toss around ideas for the growth of your law firm. Eventually, you will come to the realization that the highest quality cases are referred to you by other lawyers, and you need a marketing plan to get referrals from lawyers.

Step Two: Create a Database of Your Contacts

Put together a list of existing and potential referral partners in a database. The database can be created using a Customer Relationship Management ("CRM") software, or a cost-free option such as an Excel spreadsheet.

The database will give the young lawyer instant access to his friends/followers and current and former clients. The young lawyer will use the database to launch new marketing tactics, such as email and print newsletters, speaking events, referral appreciation parties, and lunch dates.

Step Three: Lunch Twice a Week with Referral Partners

Have your assistant schedule one new lunch date with an existing and potential referral partner every week. Schedule specific dates and times for the lunch dates, and treat those appointments the same as a court appearance:

- Monday at noon: lunch with <u>existing</u> referral partner.

- Wednesday at noon: lunch with a <u>potential</u> referral partner.

Prominent lawyers love when young lawyers ask about their success. Just explain to the big-shot lawyer that you're starting from nothing and you've got no idea what to do. The hot-shot lawyer will relate to your struggles and vulnerabilities.

> *"The pinnacle of generosity isn't just helping*
> *others, but allowing them to help us."*
> —Keith Ferrazzi, *Who's Got Your Back*

At minimum, you will get tips from the best lawyers about building a law practice. And there's a decent chance that the big-name lawyer will begin referring cases to you.

Grassroots Marketing at Its Finest

Craig Goldenfarb, Esq., an ultra-successful injury lawyer in South Florida, spends 95 percent of his time on marketing. Craig's firm sponsors community events about public safety and he sets aside at least two hours every week to meet with his marketing director. Craig's investment of time and money on marketing has paid off big time.

Paul Harding, Esq., a prominent injury lawyer in Upstate New York, requires each of his 119 employees to join three charitable organizations. Paul sponsors the organization's charitable events, and his employees appear at their events on behalf of Paul's firm.

Joe O'Connor, Esq., an injury lawyer, supports biker rallies for Harley riders throughout Upstate New York. Joe goes to the rallies, chats up the bikers, and throws money behind their causes. Nice way to support the bikers, and it has paid off with referrals of seven-figure cases.

What Is Your Unique Value Proposition?

Lawyers are notoriously bad at telling the world about the unique value they offer. Every lawyer is unique in some way, but if you don't share this with the world, no one will know ... and you will look like every other "suit."

A long-time lawyer friend, Joe Lawyer, wants to get truck-wreck cases. Joe Lawyer's website looks like every other lawyer website with his pedigree, accomplishments, contact information, etc. But here's one thing that's buried in the fine print: Joe Lawyer worked as a tractor-trailer driver for ten years before going to law school.

Joe Lawyer should be shouting to the world: "There is no other lawyer in the marketplace who can match my real-world experience as a trucker. If you find another lawyer who can match my experience as a trucker, hire them!" But Joe Lawyer isn't sharing his unique value proposition with consumers, and predictably, he's not getting truck-wreck cases.

You Can't Say You're a "Specialist," But ...

You already know that you're unique, but this means nothing unless you tell the world. Begin by creating a ninety-second video for the home page of your website that features your unique qualities with infographics and video testimonials from former clients and referral partners.

For our plaintiffs' medical malpractice law firm in upstate New York, our unique value proposition is simple:

- We only handle medical malpractice for injury victims.

- We are extremely selective and accept very few cases.

- In most cases, your medical records will be reviewed by a board-certified surgeon.

While we're not allowed to say we're "specialists," the message is clear that we're not like any other law firm. Does this matter to most consumers? Probably not, but we don't want *everyone* to call us. We're looking for the more sophisticated malpractice victims who spend extra time researching the best lawyer for their case; we want consumers who are looking for a specialist.

26

THE LOST ART OF LAWYER-TO-LAWYER, REFERRAL-BASED MARKETING

You want to get big cases through glamorous, self-promoting ads that make you look like a superstar. You justify the huge outlay of cash with the occasional big case that strikes gold. And you think life is good: you're making some cash and paying the bills.

If you're happy, stop reading. But for some, this kind of self-promotion is too much. You want a more dignified approach to building your law practice, and you don't have the megabucks to compete with the big boys of lawyer marketing. And let's face it, if you do what every other lawyer is doing, you'll be like them: fighting for the marginal cases.

Lawyer Referrals Are Marketing Gold

Where do you get your best and most profitable cases? Are your best cases from your website or from TV and radio ads? No. You get your best cases from lawyer referrals. That's right, lawyers who have pre-screened the case for merit, obtained the medical records for you, and told the new client that you are the perfect lawyer for their case.

You know that you wouldn't exist without lawyer referrals. A single relationship with an influential, prominent lawyer can send referral after referral to you for the rest of your career, and you're not paying a penny for TV or billboard ads. You get good liability cases, spend no money on marketing, and get high-quality clients who think you're a rock star. There's almost no way you can screw this up.

We should all be focusing on getting more lawyer referrals, right? Okay, then why do you have no system for getting more lawyer referrals? You hope that lawyers will think of you, and you thank your lucky stars for any referrals. But you're merely relying on blind luck for lawyer referrals, and that is really no system at all.

Define Your Ideal Client with Laser-Beam Precision

Define the qualities of your ideal client: age, gender, geographic region, practice area, size of firm, etc. You already know who your ideal clients are—just take a moment to define them. Now, you have two assignments:

- Nurture and cultivate the relationships with your ideal referral partners.

- Create new relationships with your top twenty prospective referral partners (a.k.a. your "whales").

Your Online "Co-Counsel Program"

Begin by adding a unique landing page on your website for lawyer referrals (e.g., "Our Lawyer Referral Program"). Check out the Lawyer Referral Program on the website of the Mottley Law Firm, P.C. in Richmond, Virginia (MottleyLawFirm.com). The Mottley Law Firm, P.C. lays out their "Mottley Law Firm Referral Partner Communication System" and includes testimonials from their referral partners. Kevin W. Mottley, Esq.'s Lawyer Referral Program shows that he's serious about communicating with his referral partners and making sure they're aware of the status of the case.

But don't stop there. When new cases are referred, send an email to your referral partner explaining your process for reviewing the case and protecting their rights to a referral fee. Perhaps you send an email with a guide that shows them how to protect their rights to a referral fee and negotiate the best fee division.

Once you have the ball rolling, follow up with your referral partner with periodic updates. Every case has important milestones (e.g., filing of the lawsuit, etc.), and you should automate the process for sending case updates through a CRM software program. Your referral partners will never complain that you are giving them too much information.

Building Equity with Your Referral Partners

Once you've done a preliminary review of the case, send an email to your new referral partner with your evaluation. We send an update email (almost) every day to keep our referral partners informed. Perhaps you explain that you've reviewed the medical records and discussed the case with an expert.

I know what you're thinking: you're busy and don't have time for updates to your referral partners. But you don't have to conquer the world—simply focus on a single update, once a day. Your referral partners will love you for this, and even if you don't accept their referral, you're building equity with them that virtually guarantees you'll get their next referral. Your daily updates will instantly set you apart from the 99 percent of lawyers who ignore their referral partners.

Marketing Like No One Else

You have a crazy busy life and don't have the time to nurture the relationships with your ideal referral partners. No problem, my friend. You can automate the process of cultivating these relationships with a series of automated, multimedia touches that keep you top of mind.

A good start is a monthly print newsletter that is intended to educate and help your referral partners. Don't bother with a cheesy newsletter about your Aunt Betsy's apple pie recipes—instead, give away your best secrets for marketing and managing a law firm. Your referral clients will love that you're giving away all of your best secrets without asking for anything in return. *Never ask for anything—just give.*

Collect emails for an email newsletter on your website. Automate the process of sending a weekly email newsletter on the same day and time. Your tribe (a.k.a. raving fan base) will love that you are sending valuable information, and the database of your fans will grow daily.

A Warm, Personal Touch Is Everything

Do something special for your ideal clients when a case settles. Buy lunch for their firm, or drop off bagels for their staff. Small, personal touches will set you apart from the 98 percent of lawyers who ignore their referral partners.

Get crazy with a client appreciation party and invite all of your referral partners. Show your love with a free dinner or happy hour—take photos, hang out, and have fun.

Expanding Your Influence to Thousands of Ideal Clients

Once you've defined your ideal client, it's time to expand your base. Create a list of your top twenty prospective referral partners (i.e., those lawyers/referral sources with whom you'd like to have a referral relationship). Once you have a list of your top twenty "whales," begin reaching out to them with a healthy dose of your best advice and tips for running a law firm.

The law firm of Finkelstein & Partners (F&P) has mastered outreach to their referral partners. F&P is a certified CLE provider and sponsors free lectures about law firm management and marketing for lawyers. Judges and high-profile plaintiff lawyers speak at the CLE events. The base of referral partners for F&P expands with every new CLE event—this is how you become a rock star among your referral partners.

Outside-the-Box Stuff that No Lawyers Are Doing

Not quite ready to become a CLE provider? Hold a one-hour speaking event that provides value for your referral partners. You can invite your prospective referral sources to the demonstration of a focus group (e.g., the "Jury Project") and show them how a focus group can help them with their next trial.

You can hold a CLE about internet marketing for lawyers (e.g., "How to Get Your Law Firm's Website on the First Page of Google") or pick any topic about which you have special knowledge. Better yet, offer your speaking events to your county bar associations, and let them endorse and promote the event.

Write an article for the monthly newsletter of your county bar association. Your county and regional bar associations are always looking for good content for their newsletters, and once you become a guest author, you'll be spreading your influence among hundreds, if not thousands, of their members. There is no better way to stay top of mind with your ideal clients.

Run local or regional mastermind groups with your prospective referral partners. Trial Lawyers College graduate, Steve Shultz, Esq., offers monthly workshop meetings that build rapport and collaboration among the members. The ultimate beneficiary is Steve himself, with a nice flow of referrals and trial consultations.

Become a Rock Star with Your Ideal Clients

Build a legacy by writing a book with your best marketing and management tips. As a published author, you will have celebrity and credibility that will put you above every other lawyer in your market, and while the cost can be substantial, you'll have an asset that will last the rest of your career. Writing a book for your referral partners is the single most powerful marketing tool you will ever have.

"One of the things I love about writing a book is that once it is finished, it can never be taken away from me. It is there for anyone to read. It is ground that has been gained and won, and cannot be lost."

—**Matthew Kelly**, *Resisting Happiness*

John Powers, Esq., a prominent plantiff's lawyer in Albany, New York, expanded his influence by giving speeches at national CLE events for the American Association for Justice and received referrals of catastrophic injury cases from lawyers across the country. There was no immediate payback, but the long-term payback was worth the effort.

Speak at a regional, state, or national event to get in front of your prospective referral partners. Contact the organizer of the event/ summit, tell them about your content, and ask for a meeting. You might be surprised by the results—no other lawyers are doing this.

Don't Hold Back Any Secrets

Build a website just for your referral partners (e.g., www.UltimateInjuryLaw.com). Watch your influence expand as you blog weekly about the best marketing and management tips for your prospective referral partners. Create a mobile app that contains your best legal forms, books, and newsletters.

Create a shock and awe package for your referral partners, consisting of your books, newsletters, audio CDs, DVDs, office policies, legal forms, etc. Send the shock and awe in a gift-wrapped package when you receive a new referral or as a friendly introduction to a prospective referral partner. Giving quality content, rather than asking for referrals, is the most effective way to create new relationships with referral partners.

A Harsh Reality to Face

You're probably thinking, "How on earth can I get all this stuff done?" Don't try to do all of it—do one thing, and once you've done one, move onto the next. Even a slight improvement in your practice, once a day, will have the compounding effect of changing your law firm dramatically in twelve months.

But very few (if any) lawyers will take action, and that's a shame. Here's my challenge for you: if you do just one thing, send an email to jfisher@fishermalpracticelaw.com with the subject line, "I proved you wrong!" and I will send you a free, signed copy of my book, *The Power of a System*.

What You Can Do to Protect Your Rights

Michael McCready, Esq., an excellent personal injury lawyer in Chicago, has a great system for ensuring that his rights to a referral fee are protected. McCready's Rules of Engagement ensure that he gets notice from his referral partner whenever any of the following occur:

- Notice that the client has been contacted

- Filing of the lawsuit

- Updates about the status of a lawsuit

- Notice when the case is resolved via settlement or judgment

If you don't protect your rights to a referral fee, no one will. You can't simply trust your referral partner to do the right thing—you need ironclad Rules of Engagement for every case that you refer to another lawyer.

Our Rules of Engagement for Referrals to Other Law Firms

PURPOSE: To make expectations clear to lawyers to whom we refer cases.

1. All clients referred to attorney or firm (hereinafter referred to as our "referral partner") shall be contacted within 24 hours of the referral.

2. Our referral partner shall notify John H. Fisher, PC, that they

    • contacted client and declined,

    • contacted client and made appointment, or

    • were unable to contact. If unable to contact, John H. Fisher, PC, shall attempt to make sure such referral is not lost.

    Such notice to John H. Fisher, PC, shall be sent to our intake specialist via email at intake@fishermalpractice.com or via fax at 845-802-0052.

3. If the client is declined, our referral partner shall send written correspondence (e.g., print letter sent via regular mail) to our mutual client stating the attorney or firm as well as John H. Fisher, PC, decline to pursue the case, and a copy of such correspondence shall be sent to John H. Fisher, PC.

4. If the referral is accepted and the lawsuit will be filed in New York State, our referral partner shall enter into a retainer agreement with the client which complies with the New York Rules of Professional Conduct.

5. If the referral is accepted and the lawsuit will be filed in a venue that is outside of New York State, our referral partner shall enter into a retainer agreement with the client which complies with the Model Rules

of Professional Responsibility and/or the ethical rules applicable to fee sharing in the venue where the lawsuit will be filed.

6.   Upon request, our referral partner shall provide a copy of their malpractice insurance policy to John H. Fisher, PC.

7.   When referring a client, John H. Fisher, PC, expects our referral partner to keep in frequent communication with the client.

8.   If our referral partner accepts the referral for litigation, the summons and complaint shall be filed within forty-five (45) days of the acceptance of the case.

9.   A copy of the filed summons and complaint shall be sent to John H. Fisher, PC, via email and regular mail.

The date-stamped summons and complaint should be sent via email to our intake specialist at intake@fishermalpracticelaw.com or by fax at 845-802-0052.

10.   Our referral partner shall contact John H. Fisher, PC, at least once every six (6) months concerning the status of the referred case, e.g., "Depositions have been completed, a note of issue has been filed, and we will request a trial date at the next court conference."

We expect to receive an update from our referral partners when the following occur:

• Acceptance of the case for litigation

• Filing of the lawsuit

• Completion of discovery

- Scheduling of the trial date

- Settlement or jury verdict

John H. Fisher, PC, will appreciate more frequent updates from our referral partners about the status of the referred case.

11.   Our referral partner shall contact John H. Fisher, PC, before finalizing the settlement to confirm expenses and liens.

12.   Upon settlement, a copy of the Settlement Statement signed by the client approving the distribution of the settlement money shall accompany the settlement check. The Settlement Statement shall reflect attorneys' fees, disbursements, liens, and the client's net recovery.

AGREED:

_____

Dated: _____
Referral Partner
(Attorney and Name of Firm)

* * *

Your Rules of Engagement for Lawyer Referrals

Create Rules of Engagement for lawyers who refer cases to you. Your Rules of Engagement show your referral partners that you are serious about protecting their rights, and the rules explain your process for evaluating and updating them.

Our Rules of Engagement for Referrals are set forth below.

Our Rules of Engagement for Referrals to Our Firm

PURPOSE: To make expectations clear to lawyers who refer cases to us.

Introduction

We would not be in business without your referrals, and we are grateful that you entrusted your client's case to us.

We have three basic beliefs about lawyer referrals:

1. You will not hear, "We didn't know you referred it," from our firm.

2. Once a client has been identified in our case management system (Trialworks) as having been referred by you, any future case which that client, or the client's family members or friends, may refer also counts as a referral from you, even if they contacted us directly.

3. Since we only handle medical malpractice and catastrophic injury cases, we will refer all clients back to the referring attorney for all other legal matters.

Our Rules of Engagement are intended to lay out exactly what you can expect from us, as well as your rights as our referral partner.

#1: CONTACT WITH CLIENT

Clients referred to John H. Fisher, PC, shall be contacted within twenty-four hours of the referral.

John H. Fisher, PC, shall notify our referral partner that we
*   contacted the client and declined,

- contacted the client and the potential case is under consideration, or

- were unable to contact the client.

If the client is declined, John H. Fisher, PC, shall send written correspondence (e.g., print letter sent via regular mail) stating that John H. Fisher, PC, declined the case, and a copy of such correspondence shall be sent to our referral partner.

For cases that are under consideration, we will need more information to evaluate the case. Usually this means that we will need to review the medical records and/or consult with a physician. Cases are moved to under consideration in our case management system if we do not decline the case after the initial contact with the client.

If we are unable to contact the client, the client did not respond to our phone calls and/or emails.

#2: OUR CASE EVALUATION

In almost all cases, under consideration cases will be evaluated by John H. Fisher and a physician who is board certified in general surgery. The evaluation of under consideration cases involves a review of the medical records and a face-to-face meeting between John H. Fisher and the physician/surgeon.

For under consideration cases, you will receive an email specifying the work done on the case. In most cases, our email update will specify:

- That we obtained the medical records.

- We reviewed the records with a physician/surgeon.

- Our expert's opinion regarding the merit of the case.

With our case evaluation, you will be able to address the specifics of the case with your client as well as the status of our evaluation.

#3: RETAINER AGREEMENT

Upon acceptance of a case (e.g., a decision has been made to file a lawsuit), you will receive a Retainer Agreement and a Memorandum Concerning the Division of the Fee.

John H. Fisher, PC, shall enter into a retainer agreement with the client which complies with rule 1.5(g) of the New York Rules of Professional Conduct. An example of our retainer agreement is attached. The Retainer Agreement will specify that the case was referred by you and that you will share in the division of the legal fee.

The division of the legal fee will be specified in the Memorandum Concerning the Division of the Fee, and a signed copy will be attached to the client's Retainer Agreement. Our Memorandum Concerning the Division of the Fee is attached.

#4: STATUS OF THE LAWSUIT

For cases that we accept for litigation, you will be notified when the following occur:

- a summons and complaint are filed

- a trial date is scheduled

- a settlement or judgment occurs

Upon your request, we will provide you with a compact disc (CD) that contains the complete case file, including the pleadings, discovery responses and demands, deposition transcripts, and internal memoranda. Alternatively, we will send the entire case file to you via Dropbox.com.

#5: MALPRACTICE INSURANCE POLICY

Upon request, we will provide you with a copy of our malpractice insurance policy.

#6: *SETTLEMENT*

John H. Fisher, PC, will contact our referral partner before finalizing the settlement to confirm expenses.

Upon settlement, a copy of the Settlement Statement signed by the client approving the settlement shall accompany the settlement check. The Settlement Statement will reflect the attorneys' fees, disbursements, liens, and our client's net recovery.

AGREED:

JOHN H. FISHER, PC

_____

Dated: _____

John H. Fisher

* * *

The Anatomy of an Email Update to Your Referral Partner

The email to your referral partner always begins with appreciation for the referral:

"Joe, thank you for your kind referral of Henry Smith."

Your email briefly describes the facts of the new case and the critical issue that will be evaluated:

"By way of background, Henry Smith, forty-two years old, died of bacterial endocarditis three days after a visit to the emergency department of the hospital. Henry Smith was survived by his wife and two children. The critical issue is whether Henry Smith had any signs or symptoms of bacterial endocarditis at the ER visit."

The next paragraph of your email sets forth your evaluation of the medical records:

> "At the ER visit, Henry Smith complained of left ear pain and denied chest pain, had normal blood pressure, and had normal blood results. There were no signs or symptoms of bacterial endocarditis at the ER visit. I reviewed the medical records with our medical expert/surgeon, and he does not believe there was a deviation from the standard of care."

You decline the case and express appreciation for the referral:

> "For these reasons, I regret that we cannot accept your referral. We will confirm our decision with a letter to Henry Smith and you will receive a copy of our letter. Thank you, as always, for thinking of us with your referrals."

With three paragraphs, you gave a detailed update regarding your case evaluation to your referral partner.

27

AUTOMATING THE "WOW" EXPERIENCE

You work your butt off. Your day is full with meetings, depositions, trial preparation, and endless paperwork, and by the end of the day, you're exhausted. You've done everything imaginable to keep your clients happy, but no matter what you do, it's never enough. Your clients still complain that they don't hear from you.

And just maybe you get an occasional email like this one, entitled "Legal Malpractice":

> "My lawyer had not responded to my email that had been sent six weeks ago and a phone call that had been made two weeks ago, so I finally just showed up at his office at the end of the day. He very casually told me that he had not done anything on my case."

"I also see on the internet that most lawyers do not respond to phone calls for quite some time. I hear it is because they are busy and just don't want to be bothered."

This email is spot-on: the number-one complaint facing lawyers is lack of communication. You may be the greatest lawyer in your town, and you may get fantastic results for your clients, but if you're not in regular communication with them, they assume you're not doing anything.

The Magic of Automating Client Communication

You have to automate every aspect of client communication in your law firm. That's right, *everything*. CRM software makes it easy to communicate with clients. You just create a sequence of emails, direct mail, or text messages, and voila! You're following up with clients in your sleep.

Let's say a new personal injury client contacts you in the middle of the night through the live chat service on your website. It's 3:00 a.m., you're sound asleep, and you and your staff can't do anything about this new case for at least five or six hours. But your CRM is doing its thing while you're sleeping—your new client is getting an email that contains a welcome video, explains the procedures for evaluating the new case, and includes a copy of your e-book explaining their rights.

"Never before could you have your entire customer base literally at your fingertips, but now you can. Use it to your advantage."

—Peter Shankman, *Zombie Loyalists*

And even if you don't have a chance to call the new client that day, your CRM kicks into overdrive with a series of emails that are relevant to the inquiry over the next three weeks. Your new personal injury client is hearing from you every day. The CRM nurture campaign instantly separates your law firm from every other lawyer who relies on old-school tactics for client communication.

Taking the Next Step with Client Communication

Your CRM can be used to automate almost every aspect of client communication. Every lawsuit has important milestones, and with your CRM, you can update clients about the status of their case with the click of a button. You should update clients by sending them emails when you reach certain milestones in their lawsuit:

- Filing of the summons and complaint.

- Receipt of answers from the defendants.

- Scheduling of depositions.

- Scheduling of the defense medical examination.

- Scheduling of a trial date.

Each email explains the status of the case and what will happen next. With this automated follow-up, you are keeping your clients informed, educating them about the process involved in their lawsuit, and preventing needless phone calls for updates. You freed up a bunch of time, and your clients know that you're working on their case.

Staying in Touch Once the Case Is Over

But don't stop there—your CRM can keep you top of mind with your clients long after their case is over. Send monthly emails and birthday and anniversary cards to former clients. The emails are consumer-centric, with information that your clients might find helpful (e.g., "How to Prevent Lyme Disease" during tick season).

> *"Bring random amazement into normal situations."*
> —Peter Shankman, *Zombie Loyalists*

Your CRM can automate much more than client communication. We use Infusionsoft for these tasks:

- Follow up with purchasers of my books.

- Nurture inquiries during my wife's judicial campaign.

- Send follow-up email reminders to registrants for our events/seminars and subscribers of our email newsletter.

- Update referral partners on the status of a case.

You can use email, text messages, video, direct mail, and faxes as part of a nurture campaign with your CRM.

The Power of Your Herd

The biggest value of CRM software is that you are automatically collecting a database of every person who has ever contacted you (i.e., your "herd"). You can segment your list by similar interests— plaintiffs' personal injury lawyers in Albany County, New York—and send follow-up email campaigns that are specific to their geographic region and practice area.

"One of the biggest challenges to creating zombie loyalists [fans of your law firm] is managing customer relationships."
—Peter Shankman, *Zombie Loyalists*

With CRM, you can break down your groups of clients and referral partners into smaller groups, based on shared traits and interests ("segmentation"). Let's say a defense doctor has been indicted for crack possession in Albany County. With the click of a button, you can send an email that is limited to the plaintiffs' lawyers in Albany County to give them a heads-up. By segmenting your database, you can limit the follow-up email to only those people who might be interested.

What Can You Do to Stand Out?

In a perfect world, you could reach out to every client once a month and say "hi." But you're crazy busy, and you simply don't have time for this. A powerful CRM will do the work for you.

"Investing in a good CRM system is the equivalent of investing in good body armor: a necessity."
—Peter Shankman, *Zombie Loyalists*

You can access your CRM from anywhere, and you now have clear systems for communicating with your clients. The broken-down style of random communication with your clients is a thing of the past, and communication with your clients is no longer completely dependent on you and your staff.

28

SPEAKING YOUR WAY TO NEW CASES

With speaking events for your ideal clients, you steal the stage by delivering a unique message on a platform used by no other lawyer. But I know what you're thinking: no other lawyer in your town is doing this, so why should you? The fact that no other lawyers are using public speaking to market their law practice is precisely why you should.

The Secrets to a Knock-Out Speaking Event

Let's start with one irrefutable fact: unless you are F. Lee Bailey, Esq., you will probably not be asked to speak. Don't wait to be asked to speak—you will be waiting a long time if you wait for someone to anoint you as the expert. You have to create your own celebrity and expert status.

Begin by picking a date, location, and subject for your speaking event. Pick a subject that is relevant and provides valuable information for your referral partners (e.g., "How to Get Your Law Firm's Website on the First Page of Google") and then promote the event to your prospective referral partners. Mail and email invitations to your prospective referral partners, and follow up by calling the top ten targets on your list.

"Speaking—hands down—is one of the best ways to acquire clients."
—Adam Witty, CEO of Advantage Media Group

There is no better introduction to a prospective referral partner than face-to-face at a speaking event. As the speaker, you will be perceived as an expert, and you can meet new referral partners in an environment that is informal and social. Provide valuable information—perhaps a book—to your prospective referral partners at the speaking event, and in return, you will begin building new relationships to grow your law practice. This is the ideal setting to create new referral relationships.

Speaking on a Shoestring Budget

Okay, great, but speaking events must cost a fortune, right? Au contraire, my friend. You can promote and hold the speaking event on a shoestring budget with a little help from your county bar association and vendors.

Once you've picked a date, location, and subject for your speech, contact the county bar association to offer your free speech to their members. You will pay for the costs, and you'll even pay for the small cost of CLE credits for the attendees. The county bar association is always looking for special events for their members, and the executive director will usually respond with an emphatic "Yes!" Now the county bar association will promote your speaking event among its members with an email blast and in their newsletter—they'll do all the promotional work for you.

Next, call one of your vendors about sponsoring your speaking event. Let's say you want to videotape the speaking event (you should always do this): ask your videographer to videotape the event, and in return, you promise to provide a strong endorsement for them at the event. Your videographer will provide the audio and video services for your event, including video for your website, and once you endorse them at the event, they will be falling over backwards to sponsor your next one.

With the help of the county bar association and your vendors, you can reduce the cost of the speaking event. You have a great event that won't cost you an arm and a leg and will be promoted among your prospective referral partners at almost no cost.

Speaking Is Worthless Without Follow-Up

Let's say your speaking event is a big success. The attendees rave about your speech, you connect face-to-face with a few important prospects, and everyone leaves a happy camper. You're feeling good on the night of the event, but you've wasted your time unless you follow up with your prospective referral partners.

Follow-up begins by getting the names and addresses of the attendees at the initial registration. Follow up with the attendees by sending them a handwritten "thank-you" note and perhaps a free copy of your book. Perhaps you identify a high-value target and invite them to lunch. Most importantly, enter the attendees on the mailing list for your monthly print newsletter.

If you have twenty-three attendees at your first speaking event, you added twenty-three prospective referral partners. These are new referral partners who have seen you speak and had some face-to-face time with you. Now that your referral partner "in waiting" knows who you are and has seen you in action, you have the introduction that you need for a new referral relationship.

A Sequence of Processes that Will Get You Booked

To become a serious speaker, you need a system for growing your speaking events. The best place to start is a unique landing page on your website that is dedicated to one thing: promoting your speaking business. The web page should have videos showing you at speaking events and three to five bullet points about your background and speaking experience.

"Work so hard that someday your signature becomes your autograph."
—Steve Gilliland, *Enjoy the Ride*

You should not attend a conference unless you are a speaker. How, then, do you speak at the next major conference? Ask. That's right—few people bother to ask to speak, but if you pick a unique subject that will provide valuable information, you might attend your next conference free of charge (with hotel and meals included). And when you speak at a special event conference, make sure you do a book signing or have a gratis event for the members following your speech.

And once the conference is over, make sure you get a testimonial letter from the organizer on the organization's letterhead. You should put the testimonial letters on your web page and include them in the shock and awe package, which you can send to book your next speech. The package of testimonials from lawyer organizations will give you instant credibility.

How to Give the Speech of Your Life

There is nothing more fun than public speaking. You have a captive audience that hangs on your every word, and even before you say a word, you have a kind of celebrity status by virtue of being the speaker. You almost can't mess this up—or can you?

You've been through plenty of boring speeches where you couldn't wait for them to end. The speaker reads from notes, and you try to think of a discreet way to find the exit door. But public speaking is not taught in law school and many speakers just wing it.

The Essence of a Great Speech: Be Real and Deliver Value

The key to a great speaking event is to be real. Don't be someone that you're not, and deliver as much value as quickly as you can. Your referral partners in waiting will appreciate seeing the real you.

Scripting a Powerful Introduction

The introduction before you speak should be used to build up your credentials and celebrity status. With a powerful introduction, you're not just another speaker.

Don't let the organizer make up your introduction. Write your own introduction, and ask the organizer to use your script. Here's a snippet from the introduction for my speech at the Summit of The National Trial Lawyers:

> In 2015, I met this lawyer, John Fisher, at a mastermind meeting of elite plaintiffs' lawyers in Chicago. I found out a few things about John Fisher:
>
> - John runs a solo medical malpractice firm that is streamlined for maximum profit with a small staff and low overhead.
>
> - John was the National Marketer of the Year for Great Legal Marketing in 2013.
>
> - John speaks for national organizations like PILMMA and Great Legal Marketing about law firm marketing.
>
> Then I read John's book, *The Power of a System* [holds up the book for emphasis]. This book gives away all of John's secrets for the management and marketing of a multimillion-dollar injury law firm in precise detail. *Everyone in this room should read John's book!*
>
> Read *The Power of a System*, implement the policies and systems, and leverage John's failures, mistakes and successes, and one day, I might be introducing you as the National Marketer of the Year.

If you have a book, send your book to the organizer before the speech, ask them to read it, endorse it, and hold it up during the introduction. The book will give you celebrity, authority, and expertise that few speakers have.

THE SECRETS OF A STORYTELLER

Public speaking combines art, drama, theater, and a heavy dose of preparation. Just like practicing law, public speaking is an acquired skill that takes hard work, years of experience, and dedication to the craft. No one is a born speaker—it takes hard work and lots of trial and error. That said, there are common mistakes made by speakers that should be avoided.

Thirteen Tips for Delivering a Powerful Speech

Giving a powerful speech takes courage. You must have the willingness to share your innermost secrets and vulnerabilities.

#1: The Power of Storytelling

Stories are powerful. Stories are memorable, compelling, and build trust with your audience. Your audience will understand stories far better than a mountain of statistics and data or boring presentation slides.

> *"The truthful, inside story of almost any man's life—if told modestly and without offending egotism—is most entertaining. It is almost sure-fire speech material."*
> **—Dale Carnegie**

You just set the stage for a story and your audience wants to hear what comes next. Your goal should be to take your audience on an emotional journey with you. Stay vulnerable.

#2: Grab the Audience's Attention Immediately

You must grab your audience's attention in the first five seconds. With the first words out of your mouth, you should get immediately into your story. Don't waste a second.

> *"The holy grail of a presentation is to transport the audience to another place."*
> —**Carmine Gallo**, *Talk Like TED*

You can't ruin the most precious moments of a speech with, "I'm honored to be here," or "Wasn't that a great speech by Frank!" With this horrible start, you're sending the message that it's time for your audience to take a nap.

#3: Tell Personal Stories and Be Real

Zappos's founder, Tony Hsieh, created a simple formula for his speeches.

1. Be passionate.

2. Tell personal stories.

3. Be real.

From the very first words you speak, hook your audience's attention with a story. I began my speech at Max Law Con with a story:

> We're in a cramped conference room in a lawyer's office, where my mother, three sisters, and I are sitting across from each other and dreading what's about to happen.

Don't stop there. Use a story to illustrate every key point in your speech, i.e., if you've got five bullet points, illustrate each point with a story. Effective presenters use three to five stories as the outline for their presentation.

#4: Stay Off the Podium and Stage

The podium is a barrier between you and your audience. Speaking from the podium is almost as bad as covering your mouth or failing to make eye contact, as it suggests you are hiding information. Stay away from the podium.

The stage elevates you to the status of a king (i.e., above your audience). You want to be eye-level and close to your audience, as if you're sharing a campfire story with them (not looking down on them). Being on ground level with your audience, conveys that you're a real human being and you are no better than your audience. Stay off the stage.

#5: Share Your Vulnerability

By sharing your vulnerability and your biggest fears and failures, you're building rapport and credibility with the audience. Instead of talking about your biggest courtroom success, share your innermost secrets and fears. Can you share something about yourself that you've never told anyone?

When you reveal your biggest vulnerability and weakness, you're giving the audience permission to do the same. This is where trust is created. After your revelation, you might ask the audience, "Are any of you willing to share something about yourself that you've never told anyone?"

#6: The Beauty of Silence

Speak slowly. Most speakers speak way too fast and do not pause or modulate the inflection of their voice.

> *"Vocal delivery and body language make up*
> *the majority of a message's impact."*
> —Carmine Gallo, *Talk Like TED*

Pausing at a key part of your speech places emphasis on what you are about to say. Emphasize key points by slowing down, pausing, and speaking louder.

#7: Make Eye Contact

Connect with your audience members by making sustained eye contact. Don't move quickly from one member of the audience to another—let your eyes fix upon one person for twenty seconds before you move on.

> *"Don't deliver a presentation. Have a conversation instead."*
> —Carmine Gallo, *Talk Like TED*

Sustained eye contact sends the message that you're speaking one-on-one to every person in your audience. You want every person in the audience to feel like you're alone with them.

#8: Create Suspense with Tieback

Keep your audience anxious to learn the rest of the story using tieback. After your introductory personal story, tell the audience that, "At the end, I will share with you how this story changed my life."

This tieback will keep your audience in suspense for your surprise ending. At the end of your presentation, share the answer your audience has been waiting for.

#9: Purposeful Body Movement

Do not stand in one spot. Walk, move, and work the room. Connect with each member of the audience with eye contact and if you know them, call them by name.

> *"Transform verbal information to visual information as much as possible."*
> —Carmine Gallo, *Talk Like TED*

Don't wander or fidget aimlessly—every body movement should have a purpose. Use your body to emphasize a point.

#10: Use Pictures (Instead of Text)

Research shows that if you only hear information, you will recall about 10 percent of the content. If you hear the information and see a picture, you will retain 65 percent of the content. The combination of pictures and words conveys your message much better than words alone.

> *"It takes courage to show photographs instead of filling your slides with bullet points and text."*
> —Carmine Gallo, *Talk Like TED*

That said, limit your presentation slides to five pictures, no more than one or two thirty-second video clips and avoid presentation slides that contain a lot of text (no more than five words per slide). The TED presentation of Titanic explorer, Robert Ballard, contained fifty-seven slides and there were no words on any of the slides.

#11: Don't Use Notes

If you've rehearsed your speech and are well prepared, you won't need notes.

> *"The real magic of a memorable TED presentation relies on the speaker setting aside her notes and speaking from the heart, letting her audience get a peek of her soul."*
> —Carmine Gallo, *Talk Like TED*

Don't worry if you forget something—it probably wasn't important.

#12: Deliver a "WOW" Moment

At the end of a speech at Max Law Con, I visually constructed a scene of my father's final words on his deathbed. I visually created the scene by laying down on a table and re-enacting my father's body position and mannerisms, as he spoke his final words. Behind me was a photograph on a large screen of my father and I smiling in a happy moment.

> *"A showstopper might be something as simple as a short personal story."*
> —Carmine Gallo, *Talk Like TED*

Simply saying my father's final words would not have sufficed. Visually recreating the scene with props and my body language told the story in a way that words cannot. Every speech should have a "WOW" moment.

#13: Violate Expectations

Take your audience off-guard by violating their expectations. At the Max Law Con, I was supposed to speak about lawyer-based referral marketing. Instead, I began with a story about my family's intervention for my father's alcoholism. Not quite what the audience was expecting.

> *"Violating expectations is a superior communication strategy."*
> —**Carmine Gallo,** *The Storyteller's Secret*

I used the personal story to grab the audience's attention and build trust with them. Without their attention and trust, my words would have had little meaning.

Give a Speech that Will Never be Forgotten

Maya Angelou once said, "People will forget what you said, people will forget what you did, but people will never forget how you made them feel." Think about how you want the audience to feel.

> *"You must be prepared if you want to make life-changing, world-changing speeches."*
> —**Michael Port,** *Steal the Show*

There are few speakers following the tips that you have read and even fewer who have the courage to share their innermost secrets with total strangers. That, my friend, is the secret to a speech that your audience will never forget.

29

SEVEN STEPS TO BECOMING A MEDIA DARLING

When you brag about your huge verdicts and settlements, you are boring. No one cares about you (except your parents, kids, and spouse—and they might not even care). But when a newspaper, magazine, blog or TV station recognizes your authority, you have instant credibility.

The third-party validation lends credibility to you. If you're quoted in the *New York Law Journal* or *Trial*, that's a sign that you're an authority.

*"It's vaguely pretentious to call yourself an expert,
it's powerful when others do it for you."*

—Dorie Clark, *Stand Out*

Here's the problem: reporters get pitched, on average, dozens of times a day and will turn away blind pitches within four seconds of receiving your email. Fat chance that a random reporter will care about your big settlement or verdict. But there are tried and proven methods for getting press from the media that won't cost you a penny—they're not easy, but with time and patience, you might find your name on the front page of *USA Today*.

Step One: Create a Media List

Who are the key reporters in your practice area? Scour newspapers and media for reporters that cover your practice area or law reporters. Go online and identify the law reporters in the newspapers, industry journals, bloggers, TV, and radio stations that have influence in your practice area and create an Excel spreadsheet with their name, email address, and Twitter handle.

"Everything should be a potential media opportunity. Look at everything as a chance to get more media and more exposure."

—Peter Shankman

The key to finding the reporters is research. READ EVERY-THING. Search on Google for reporters in your practice area. If the reporter doesn't cover your practice area, they won't give you the time of day. Set up a free Google News Alert for the reporter's name, and when the reporter's name gets picked up by Google Alert, you will be notified.

Step Two: Build a Relationship with Reporters

Focus on building the relationship via social media. Reporters will love you if you retweet their posts and draw attention to their work. If you follow their tweets, you'll find out what events they'll be attending, and you can introduce yourself in person. Focus on building the relationship electronically at first and later advance to face-to-face.

Once you've created a media list of reporters in your practice area, follow reporters on Twitter and comment on and retweet their posts.

> *"1) Find a journalist that reports in your area of law/ business, connect with them on Twitter, and engage with them on Twitter. Regularly share their content and comment. Good way to become top of mind and build a relationship. 2) Promote and participate at major charitable events."*
>
> **—Nick Rishwain, JD, Experts.com**

Let the reporter know that you enjoyed their last story, and if they're planning to do a follow-up story, they're welcome to give you a call.

Hey, Chris, I saw your article about the dumping of sewage in the Hudson River. I really respect your strong position against dumping sewage in the majestic Hudson River. Well done!

You might share a link to a similar story that you wrote:

> Josepha, I enjoyed your article about the passage of a "date of discovery" law ("Laverne's Law") by the New York State Assembly and Senate. I thought you might be interested in this post I wrote that explains why the date of discovery law is so important to New York malpractice victims. Perhaps you might find it helpful.

And then proactively email links to your posts.

Step Three: Offer to Help Reporters

Offer to provide help and resources to reporters that will make their life easier.

> *"You should always try to give value before you receive it."*
> **—Dorie Clark, *Stand Out***

Send a friendly introductory email to a reporter in your practice area.

Dear [reporter]:

This is not a pitch. Quite the opposite—this is an offer of help.

The reason I'm emailing is just to offer myself as a source. I know many lawyers in medical malpractice, plus I have many examples of malpractice cases from my career as a medical malpractice lawyer.

So, if you ever find yourself on deadline, feel free to call—I can probably help or find someone who can.

Best always, John Fisher (jfisher@fishermalpracticelaw. com, 518-265-9131, cell)

You might pitch a follow up article, e.g., "How to Prevent the Dumping of Sewage in the Hudson River." The key is to make the reporter's life easier by providing resources.

> *"When connecting with reporters make sure they know you will make yourself available anytime and include your cell phone. I think it's helpful to also have a short video reel if you have been on the news before."*
> —**Thomas Wallin, Esq.**

You should send the reporter a few links to existing posts you've done, and you should create a mini-website that contains your past newspaper and magazine clips, audio files from radio interviews, and video clips from TV interviews.

Step Four: BE DIFFERENT!

Get to the point, be direct, and get your information out there. Don't be traditional—find an interesting way to make your point.

Email a reporter with the subject line "Jumping Out of a Plane for the Disabled."

Dear [reporter]:

Brace yourself for a crazy idea. On July 28th, I'm planning to jump out of a plane to benefit an incredible local orga- nization, Living Resources Foundation, based in Albany,

NY. I'll be jumping from 13,500 feet. Crazy, wild stuff (and I've never jumped out of a plane before).

Coolest part? This jump will raise money for an incredible organization, Living Resources, that provides career, educational, and vocational opportunities for more than 1,200 disabled individuals in fourteen counties throughout the Capital/Saratoga region of New York.

From services for brain injury victims and the deaf, to employment and residential programs for the disabled, Living Resources does a ton for the handicapped, and I figure it's time to say thanks for everything they do. We hope to raise awareness and money for this amazing organization.

Fun time, great organization, and just a little scary (at least for me). The sky jump will be videotaped on Facebook Live. You can watch this live on my Facebook page (www. Facebook.com/johnhfisherpc).

Up through the date of the sky jump, I will match every dollar that is donated to Living Resources. And to get things started, I'm donating $2,500 to this amazing organization.

Want photos, video, or have questions? Please feel free to reach out to me on my cell.

Thanks for reading!

John Fisher

jfisher@fishermalpracticelaw.com

Step Five: Think Small at First

Offer to write a column/article for your small, local newspaper. Nothing is too small or insignificant.

> *"PR is a process that takes time, and when done right, can yield spectacular results."*
>
> —Peter Shankman

Never turn down a request for an article—no matter how small the newspaper. It might be a small paper, but people read small papers, and the reporter at the small, local paper might be a *New York Times* reporter in a few years.

Step Six: News-Jacking Your Way into the Media

"News-jacking" (a phrase coined by David Meerman Scott) involves injecting your ideas or angles into breaking news in real-time in order to generate media coverage for yourself.

Tell a reporter about breaking news (e.g., a huge verdict) and connect the reporter with the victorious lawyer. Offer a few catchy suggestions about what you'd like to write for them. If there is a high-profile murder trial in your town, you might create a video or blog post that offers your viewpoint on an evidentiary issue. Above anything else, try to make the reporter's life easier.

> *"Taking the time to share yourself in a substantive fashion is an investment in your long-term reputation."*
>
> —Dorie Clark, *Stand Out*

Do you disagree with the way an issue is being presented? Here's your chance to right that wrong. Don't be bashful about expressing your views—for example, I strongly disagree with the legalization of marijuana (with the exception of medical marijuana) as this introduces another carcinogenic substance that will kill thousands. Who cares if most disagree—BE BOLD.

Step Seven: Don't Forget to Ask

Call the editor of a legal magazine or journal and ask them what type of articles they need. Editors of legal journals, magazines, and blogs are looking for fresh content, and if you inquire about their need for specific articles, there's a good chance they'll tell you.

I contacted the editor of American Association for Justice's *Trial* magazine to inquire about their need for specific topics for an article. The editor told me that the next edition would feature law firm management and she'd welcome an article about professional liability insurance. Great. I knew next to nothing about professional liability insurance, but I studied the subject, spoke with leading insurance experts, and two weeks later, presented an article that was accepted for publication.

Once your article is published, you can (with the publication's consent):

- Share the article on social media.

- Add the article to your shock and awe package for prospective referral partners.

- Post the article on the Press page of your website.

Follow the same strategy of contacting the editors of local and statewide magazines, journals, and bloggers about their need for articles. Once they see that you're a published author of an article in a national magazine, they will welcome your submission of an article or blog post.

The Perfect Pitch to get the Media Spotlight

If you do the prep for your pitch, that's 95 percent of your job. Shotgun pitches simply don't work. Your pitch should be tailored and personalized.

The Introduction

Dear [reporter's name]. Use "Jim" if that is how the reporter likes to be known, e.g., "James" vs. "Jim."

1st Paragraph: Lure the Reporter with a Great Story

What can you give a reporter that's interesting and exciting? A trend ties the reporter's past story to current news and grabs the reporter's curiosity.

"I have something interesting for you."

"I have a story for you that will fit with what you cover, interest your audience and offer some new information. I noticed you wrote a story about [wrote, produced, edited] on [exact date]. I loved that story! Because of that story, I think you'll find this [trend] interesting."

"You're the first journalist I've reached out to with this story." This line will give you more call backs than anything else.

2nd Paragraph: Blow Them Away with an Amazing Statistic

What can you give the reporter that's exciting and interesting? Use one line that blows them away or one amazing statistic—something the reporter has not seen before, e.g., stats about the number of deaths every year caused by preventable medical errors. Use quotes and anything that will let them know you have valuable information.

> "I've seen a trend for [what is the trend that will give the journalist a good story]. An interesting new trend [one line that blows them away] has been happening in medical malpractice trials. If you need more expert information, I can put you in touch with [name of expert]."

Give as much bait as possible to lure them in. Have four stories to tell. If one story fails, turn to the next.

3rd Paragraph: Promise Exclusive Access to the Story

Make the story exclusive for the reporter.

> "I'd be happy to offer you exclusive access to [source of information] or I'd be happy to speak with you personally as well as connect you with [competitor] to help you flesh out the bigger picture. I'm not pitching this around. If you want it, it's yours. I'm offering it only to you."

> "I'm available anytime at your convenience, either by cell, 518-265-9131, or via email, jfisher@fishermalpracticelaw. com. As I wrote, you're the first journalist to whom I'm reaching out with this story. As far as I'm aware, it's yet to be covered."

Do One Follow Up at Most

Wait three to four business days before following up. Send a follow up email: "Thought this might be up your alley. If not, I won't bother you. Feel free to reach out. Here's my cell." If you follow up too much, the reporter won't listen to future pitches.

How to Use a Press Kit

Do not send a press kit in your first email to the reporter. If you get a response from the reporter, you can send the press kit or a link to the press kit. Be funny in the subject line and follow up with, "I'm sending you the press kit we talked about."

Use the cloud for the press kit, e.g., post a link to Dropbox or Google Drive. Dropbox and Google Drive can sync; make sure you have at least two backups. With Airdrop, share the press kit on an iPhone. Swipe up from the bottom of the phone and share the press kit in a flash.

The Nuts and Bolts of a Press Kit

#1: Background: Less than one-page overview of you or your law firm. Shorter is better. Include things that give you extra credibility—not a resume, e.g., author of several books, awards, etc. Check out the bio of Ann Handley at www.AnnHandley.com/about for the short and long versions of a background.

Add a photograph and links to articles. Have a short and long version, and a booking page. Add your cell phone number at the top, a link to your website, and an icon for sharing. Every single page of the media kit should have your contact information at the bottom.

#2: Fast Fact Sheet: What's your one key call point? One sentence that is funny and intriguing. What is the one thing the media will call you for? Why do you matter? Is your story different?

- Who is John Fisher?

- What do we offer the world?

- What do we stand for?

If you have good video, give a link to it. Use an updated photograph that is 300 dots per inch (dpi) or better. Journalists need a high-resolution photograph and cannot improve the quality of the photo. The cloud is your friend. Journalists don't want attached files—use links only. Ninety-nine percent of attachments will be blocked.

30

HOW TO WRITE A BESTSELLING BOOK FOR LAWYERS

Alone in a cramped, musty motel room in Virginia, I get a phone call from a trusted referral partner. My referral partner gets right to the point by saying, "I've got a new case for you." The new case has everything: clear liability and massive damages; there is only one problem: I am in Virginia and the clients are in Albany, New York. I tell our referral partner that I will try to get back to New York ASAP.

This wasn't good enough. One hour later, I get the call that all lawyers dread. Our referral partner explains that our clients are lawyer shopping and they might retain other counsel. I manage to arrange a meeting with the new clients. A couple of days later, I spend an hour with the clients in the hospital and as I leave, I give them a copy of my book, *The Power of a System*. As I hand my book to them, the clients glance at me with a strange look and seem perplexed.

A couple of days later, I receive a phone call from our clients with the news, "We're hiring you." Out of curiosity, I ask why they chose our firm. The clients respond that they had no idea who to hire, but they spent the last two days reading the reviews/testimonials in my book and reached the conclusion that I must be the perfect lawyer for their case.

That is the power of a book. Even when you're not there, the book does the selling for you. The end result is a multimillion-dollar case … and there's no reason you can't do the same.

How to Get Started Writing Your Book

A common misconception is that a book should be written from scratch. If you write high quality blog posts, there's no reason you can't combine the blog posts into a book. Gary Vaynerchuk's best seller, *#AskGaryVee*, is simply a collection of his blog posts.

What are you more passionate about than anything? Once you identify your biggest passion, you know what your book should be about. If your passion is law firm management, write the definitive book about running a law firm. You won't have to do research because you already know the content.

> *"Don't ask yourself what the world needs. Ask yourself what makes you come alive, and go do that, because what the world needs is people who have come alive."*
>
> —Howard Thurman

Don't write a chapter or even a sub-chapter. Write two paragraphs at a time—that's all. Once you get in the rhythm of writing, it will be hard to stop and before long, you've written a new chapter for your book.

The Five Biggest Mistakes Made by Lawyer Authors

Ninety-eight percent of lawyers should not write a book. Most lawyers don't appreciate the time, effort, and money involved in a writing a high-quality book. But if you're ready to go all-in, writing a book could be the best thing you've ever done for your career.

Mistake #1: Failing to Give Actionable Advice

Most lawyer books are full of rah-rah motivational tips, e.g., work hard, persevere ... blah, blah, blah. Seriously, you don't need motivational tips—you need practical advice that you can implement. This is where 95 percent of lawyer books go wrong.

Albany, New York plaintiffs' lawyer, Patrick J. Higgins, Esq.'s, book, *The Plaintiffs' Personal Injury Action in New York State*, has forms for pleadings, discovery, subpoenas, jury charges, and a verdict sheet. Why does our paralegal keep Patrick's book on her desk? Our paralegal relies on Patrick's book almost every day for drafting discovery demands and responses.

Fill your book with forms and checklists, such as:

- Release authorizations for electronic medical records under the HITECH Act

- Stipulations of settlement with the conditions for liens, disclosure of the settlement, and deadlines for payment

- Stipulations regarding the client's decision to decline a structured settlement annuity

Lawyers want content that is quick and easy to use. If lawyers can copy and paste the content into their case management program, your book will never leave their desk.

Mistake #2: Using the Book as a Sales Pitch

Most lawyer books are nothing more than a glorified sales pitch for a product or service. If you sell anything in your book, your readers will be instantly turned off. Avoid selling and instead, give away your best tips and advice. If you give a lot of value and ask for nothing in return, your readers will love you.

Mistake #3: Creating a Mini-Guide

Self-publishers promise to make book publishing easy for you. With only a few hours of your time, the publisher will put together a mini-guide/book and turn you into a book author. Sounds good? Not so fast.

Mini-guides are a waste of time and money. Don't be seduced by the easy, low cost approach of many self-publishers. Writing a book is hard and can take years. Instead, write the definitive book for your ideal referral partners, namely, a hard cover book that will be a number one top seller on Amazon for years and turn you into a virtual celebrity.

Mistake #4: Charging Too Much for Your Book

Many authors think they will make money from book sales. At best, you'll make $4,000 per year from book sales and you won't even recoup the cost of making the book. Make your book affordable, e.g., $19.99 for soft cover and $26.99 for hard cover, or even better, give it away, e.g., ThePowerofaSystem.com.

Every business-to-business book should be hard cover. There is a perception of value and authority that comes with a hard cover book and for the minimal extra cost, this is an easy decision.

Mistake #5: Sending Book Purchasers to Amazon.com

Amazon will not share the name or contact information of book purchasers. When someone buys your book from Amazon, you'll have no information about them and hence, no ability to follow up. You want to avoid this.

Create a special website for book sales and sell them through e-commerce. Your local bank can create a merchant bank account for internet sales. With every purchase on your website, you will have the contact information for every purchaser and the ability to follow up with your fans.

Five Tips for Promoting Your Book

You won't have a lot of success at first, but the promotion of your book is a marathon, not a sprint. A book is a long-term asset of your law firm, but it can't be published and ignored. You have to continually promote your book.

Tip #1: Give Your Book Away ... to Everyone

Give your book away to as many of your ideal referral partners as possible. Create a display case and get permission from law schools and bar associations to display your books throughout your state. You don't want to make money from the book; you want to become a celebrity among your prospective referral partners.

Send a jumbo-style postcard with a free offer of your book to every lawyer in your state (ExactData.com can provide the contact information for the lawyers in your county, state or region). In return for their contact information, provide the lawyers with a free e-book or if they qualify as a potential referral partner, send a free signed copy of your book.

Tip #2: Turn the Book into Holiday Gift

Don't just send a generic holiday card. Send a holiday card in early December with an offer to send your book as a gift on behalf of your referral partners.

> Is there a better gift than the gift of knowledge? Let us make gift giving easy for you this holiday season.

> We will send five signed books to your referral partners as a special gift from you. Just tell us where you want to send the books and we'll take care of this for you.

Your referral partners will appreciate this special gesture to make gift giving easier.

Tip #3: Get Speaking Gigs with Your Book

Send your book to event organizers for national and regional lawyer organizations as part of your request to speak at their events. A book will give you instant credibility.

When you speak at a seminar, bring one hundred copies of your book and have a book signing after your speech. The audience will rush to the stage after you speak.

Tip #4: Build Your List of Email Subscribers with an Irresistible Offer

Offer your e-book as a free gift to those who subscribe to your email newsletter. Watch your list of email subscribers grow steadily with this irresistible offer.

Tip #5: Feature the Best Practices of Your Referral Partners

Featuring the best practices of other lawyers (and giving appropriate credit) is an advanced tactic for expanding your referral relationships.

In their book, *How Small Law Firms Can Obtain More Referrals*, Kara Prior and Jim Pawell (president and founder of James Publishing), spend eleven pages featuring our law firm's best practices for lawyer-to-lawyer referral based marketing. Truth is, I didn't know the authors were doing this, but they sent me a copy of their book with a jumbo-style postcard, "Done-for-you Legal Referral System." Flattered, I contacted the authors and we agreed to work together on a joint marketing project.

The Best Publisher (For My Two Cents)

Self-publishing gets a bad rap. With a self-publisher, you retain control over fees and marketing (no one can tell you what to do). But there's a downside—you must do all the work. Few lawyers know how to promote a book and most have no desire to learn.

My books, *The Power of a System* and *The Law Firm of Your Dreams*, are published by Advantage Media Group (AdvantageFamily.com), a hybrid between a self-publisher and traditional publisher, e.g., HarperCollins. Your manuscript must be accepted, but once approved, Advantage Media Group will do all of the work, including graphic design, copyediting, proofing, and distribution to both print and online channels. Advantage Media Group will help promote your book and create an audio book to compliment the physical copy.

Advantage Media Group is a strategic partner for book authors. Advantage Media Group costs much more than a self-publisher, but if you want to write a book that will last for the rest of your career, they are an excellent choice.

31

MARKETING YOUR LAW FIRM LIKE NO ONE ELSE

Perhaps you're looking for a unique marketing strategy that is dignified, enhances the image of lawyers and might bring a few cases to your firm. These powerful marketing campaigns will bring weekly media attention for your law firm, referrals of big cases and will boost morale in your community. With these campaigns, *you will be different from every other lawyer.*

How to be Different from Every Other Law Firm

Charles "Chuck" E. Boyk, Esq., a prominent injury lawyer in Toledo, Ohio, was looking for a way to promote his book about bicycle safety. Chuck came up with the idea of promoting bike safety through a weekly bike give-away. At first, the campaign received little media attention, but slowly it gained traction with the media.

Here's how it works: the firm has a thirteen-week program in the Summer when it gives away thirteen bikes. Every week, the firm reaches out for nominations for children who have done something positive for their community, e.g., *"Do you know a kid who deserves a new bike and has done something great for the community?"*

> *"The second you stop thinking how much money is this [community marketing] going to make, it becomes more authentic."*
> —Anneke Kurt Godlewski, Founder of Market Ink, LLC

Nominations can be made through a page on the firm's website. The firm's clients can nominate their own children and the firm gets prized "Google Juice" from the links to their website from the media and schools.

The nominations consist of short, feel-good stories that have a human interest angle that might intrigue reporters. The firm picks a winner with the most compelling story that reporters would like to share with their audience, e.g., "Joey brought a blanket to a homeless person in downtown Toledo."

A Public Service Announcement that the Media Craves

The firm has the bike give-away ceremony at the local bike shop at 3:00 p.m. (the best time for media to pick up the story) and invites the media to attend the ceremony. The firm sends a press release to the media (TV, radio and newspapers) the night before and the day of the award ceremony.

A local CBS affiliate sends a TV crew to video the award ceremony and share the winner's story, and the other three local TV stations often attend. Reporters sometimes take video of the ceremony on Facebook Live. The ceremony is a news story that is a gift to the local media, who crave feel-good stories.

The firm posts videos of the award ceremony of a kid winning the bike and shares the video with the media and on their Facebook page. On the morning after the ceremony, the winner appears live to share their story on the local CBS affiliate. The TV station mentions the law firm of Charles E. Boyk Law Offices, LLC at the beginning of the news clip.

A Return on Investment Unlike Any Other

How does this measure up cost-wise? Charles E. Boyk, Esq. spends $2,000 on display ads on the website of the local CBS affiliate and pays $150 per bike. The total cost is less than $5,000 per year.

And the time commitment? Once the system is in place, the law firm's marketing director shows up for the give-away ceremonies and creates a new press release every week. That's it—low cost, high return, and unique.

The Power of Community Marketing

The firm gets hundreds of media mentions, is in the news three times per week during the thirteen weeks of summer, and gets thousands of shares/likes/views on the firm's Facebook page. The winner's story is shared on the firm's Facebook page and in their print newsletters and e-newsletters.

Everyone nominated is added to the firm's newsletter list, and the firm gives away two thousand bike helmets obtained through a grant from the American Academy of Pediatrics. At the award ceremony, reporters are given a key tag with the phone number for Charles E. Boyk, Esq., *"Call us 24/7 if you need legal commentary"*.

> *"Earned media attention is worth more than paid ads."*
> —Anneke Kurt Godlewski, Founder of Market Ink, LLC

The media craves the public service announcements and as a bonus, an NBC reporter referred a six-figure injury case to the firm. The feel-good stories are fodder for the firm's newsletters and social media and creates goodwill with the media, reporters, and current and prospective clients.

Charles E. Boyk Law Offices, LLC, is not just another injury law firm—they are continually showing their love for their community through heart-warming stories. And the return on investment? You can be the judge.

Making a Difference in Their Community

Trying to keep the momentum going after the summer fun, Charles E. Boyk, Esq. thought of ways to help a local public high school (and his alma mater, Roy C. Start High School in Toledo) and came up with "TPS [Toledo Public Schools] Proud."

At the beginning of each month, the firm sends a videographer to the high school during lunch hour and the firm's marketing director asks students to provide twenty-second video clips about their favorite teacher. The law firm's marketing director asks three questions of the students:

- What is it about the teacher's class that you like so much?

- If you could tell your teacher one thing, what would it be?

- What is the one thing that your teacher taught you that is going to stick with you after graduation?

The students get a chance to show their appreciation for their teachers and add some humor, i.e., *"What do you think your teacher does after school?"* The videographer collects fifty to sixty video clips and uploads them to a YouTube channel ("TPS Proud"), where each student has a playlist. The students are given a paper handout with instructions for finding their playlist on YouTube and asked to share their video on social media.

Showing Teachers that Their Students Care

The videos are sent to the teachers via email. Perhaps for the first time, the teachers get to see that their students care about them and the impact that they've had.

In the email, the teachers are given a link to nominate their "Student of the Month" (e.g., "Go to this link to nominate your favorite student for the school"). The links for the nominations go to the law firm's website, which in turn delivers sought-after "Google Juice" for the firm's website.

From the nominations, the firm chooses winners based upon the most compelling stories. Many students come from broken families where no one attended college and the stories can be heartwarming. The impact of teachers on their students might otherwise remain an untold story, e.g., "Mrs. Richardson introduced me to the idea of college and now I'm going to Ohio State University ... Maumee campus."

A Feel-Good Story Like No Other

The firm schedules an award ceremony at the school and sends press releases to the local media and invites reporters and the local TV affiliates to attend; quotes from the winners are included in the press release. The firm videotapes the award ceremony, where the winning student and teacher are given a plaque and the teacher receives a $150 Visa gift card and the student receives a fifty-dollar Visa gift card. Some schools announce the winners at a school assembly.

This boosts enrollment, improves the morale of students, enhances the image of teachers and spreads a ton of goodwill to Charles E. Boyk Law Offices, LLC. The local community magazine, "Toledo Parent Magazine," features stories of the winners for free.

Priceless Branding of a Law Firm

The media craves the public announcements of the winners and the story is often the feel-good lead story on the nightly news. At first, the reporters were hesitant to mention the firm's name on the news, but as they came to realize the goodwill and positive impact, the reporters began embracing the firm's sponsorship and mention "Boyk Law Offices" when the story is introduced on the nightly news. As a side benefit, the campaign builds goodwill with reporters.

Once the firm finished the promotion for Start Public High School, it expanded the program among each of the nine public high schools in Toledo and then to the elementary schools. As the program expands, the firm shows video of prior winners and spreads the message through its print newsletter and e-newsletters, social media, and tells all of their clients. The firm has one thousand videos of students showing appreciation for their teachers.

What's Stopping You from Doing This?

How do you get started? Just go to the superintendent or the principal of your local high school, tell them that you will pay all costs and this will boost morale, improve attendance, and highlight the good work of their teachers and students.

Part 3

Internet Marketing

32

YOUR BLUEPRINT FOR A KICK-ASS LAWYER WEBSITE

You begin your quest for the ultimate lawyer website with a single question: Who is your target client? You want to be laser-beam focused on attracting only a very specific, target client to your website. And it's okay to repel everyone else.

You need to be very specific—"injury victims" is too general. Perhaps you want to get clients with malpractice cases involving a delay in cancer diagnosis (see Powers & Santola's website, Delayed-CancerDiagnosis.com), or you want traumatic brain and spinal cord injury cases (see Newsome Melton's website, BrainandSpinalInjury.org). Even the domain names of these websites have the magic keywords for the type of cases the lawyers want.

BrainandSpinalCord.org focuses on brain and spinal cord injury survivors. Yes, these are not your run-of-the-mill slip-and-fall cases—the law firm of Newsome Melton is going after the giant tuna of personal injury law. The content and design of BrainandSpinalCord.org conveys a clear message: if you have a soft tissue back injury or sprained ankle, we're not the law firm for you.

An Amazing Lawyer Website that Lawyers Should Emulate

BrainandSpinalCord.org is a model of a great lawyer website. The directory of BrainandSpinalCord.org is full of great resources:

- A list of the top ten rehabilitation hospitals in America.

- Directory of physicians specializing in spinal cord injuries (listed by state).

- Basic spinal cord anatomy, including statistics, treatment and rehabilitation options, and prognosis.

- A video library full of informative advice (e.g., "Special Needs Trusts: Things to Consider").

BrainandSpinalCord.org is the equivalent of Wikipedia for brain and spinal injury victims. There is a wealth of valuable information on BrainandSpinalCord.org that has absolutely nothing to do with the law firm of Newsome Melton—and that is the genius of this website.

Injury victims could care less about where you attended law school, your verdicts and settlements, and the number of years you've been selected to Super Lawyers. Injury victims don't care about you—they want answers, and if your website doesn't have them, they'll move on.

By focusing very specifically on providing information and resources for their ideal clients (e.g., brain and spinal cord injury victims), BrainandSpinalCord.org brings catastrophic brain and spinal cord injury clients to Newsome Melton from all over the country. And there's no reason your website can't do the same.

How a Fantastic Lawyer Website Can Get a Little Better

While nearly perfect, we might make a few subtle changes:

- Add video for every practice area (rather than putting all of the videos on a single website page).

- Add an "irresistible offer" on every page of the website (e.g., free e-book that requires the consumers to provide their name and email address).

- Add Ngage Live Chat to begin the dialogue with prospective injury victims as soon as they get to the website.

- Add a pop-up box that offers a free weekly email newsletter in exchange for the first names and email addresses of website visitors.

- Add video testimonials from clients (social proof is powerful).

Converting prospects into clients is the goal of a lawyer website. You want the prospective client to raise their hand and shout, "Yes, I want more." Once you have their permission, you can send a series of automated emails to the prospective client with even more valuable information (e.g., your weekly blog posts). Now you're not simply praying that consumers come back to your website—you're guaranteeing it.

One Basic Rule for Lawyer Websites: Quality Over Quantity

Many lawyer websites are crammed full of worthless content that no one cares about. There may be hundreds of pages on your website that no one has read. These web pages should be deleted from your website.

Even one web page that is chock-full of valuable, insightful information is ten times better than thirty web pages that no one will read. It's not the quantity of website pages that matters—*it is the quality of your web content that matters.*

> *"The more in-depth and informative your content is, the better your results will be."*
>
> —**Neil Patel**

Evergreen web content provides highly detailed, educational information. This could be a blog post, article, or a frequently asked question—it doesn't matter where you post the evergreen content, just that you post it. Your evergreen web content should be in-depth (1,000–2,000 words) and contain images, bullet points, an info-graphic, sub-headings, and (ideally) video.

How to Build Evergreen Content on Your Website

Begin by identifying the ten most popular web pages on your website—these are the web pages that are driving the most traffic to your website. Usually, the top ten pages on your website include

- the home page,

- the landing pages for your practice areas, and

- your professional biography page.

These are among the top ten pages of your website because they are full of information, contain photos, video, and images, and provide evergreen content that is educational. Once you know what's working, you want to update and refresh the content on these web pages.

Letting the World Know about Your Evergreen Web Content

Your next assignment is to add internal and external links to your top ten web pages. An internal link is a link to another page on your website, and an external link is a link to a different website. You want to keep visitors engaged on your website and view your site as resource that will answer their questions. (Check out the "Resources" at www.BrainandSpinalCord.org.)

You should boost your top ten web pages by adding links to those pages from new posts on your website. When you add a new blog post, add a call to action at the end of the post asking the visitor to click the link to one of your top ten web pages (e.g., "Want to learn more about bacterial endocarditis? Click this link."). Tell web visitors exactly what you want them to do ("Download my free e-book by clicking this link").

Make sharing your content on social media easy by adding sharing buttons at the top and bottom of the web page.

The Metrics for Your Website's Success

Create an account with Google Analytics and use it to track website traffic to your top ten web pages. On the first of every month, you should track three things:

- The number of unique visits to your top ten web pages.

- The average length of time that visitors are spending on your top ten web pages.

- The total number of unique website visitors to your website.

When you add fresh content to your top ten web pages, you'll see improvement in the number of website visits, bounce rate (percentage of website visitors who leave your website after visiting the entrance page), and length of time at your website.

A Simple Strategy for Internet Magic

Once you have the right webmaster, you only need to do one thing: *add a new web page once a day*. That's right, no secret SEO magic is required—if you only add a single new web page to your website every day, you will have new clients calling you within forty-five days. Within three months, you'll have close to one hundred new web pages.

> *"You cannot just slap together a website and call it a day."*
> —Dan Kennedy

Begin by writing answers to the top ten questions that your clients ask, and then write answers to the top ten questions that your clients *should be asking*. Voilà! You have content for twenty new website pages. Now, write answers for the FAQ for each of your practice areas.

Okay, sounds great, but you're busy and don't have time to write content for your website. You can always hire a team of law students from the local law school to write content for your website, and the law students will write better content than you.

33

THREE SIMPLE RULES FOR KILLER WEB CONTENT

Rule One: Have Attention-Grabbing Headlines

The first rule of compelling website content is to have a killer headline. An attention-grabbing headline should be short and sweet (ideally no more than six words) and hook the readers' attention, eg., "Attack of the Killer Ulcer."

The master of great headlines is the tabloid *National Enquirer*. Yes, it's junk journalism, but the visual images and the unbelievable headlines almost shout out to you, "READ ME!" Great website content counts for nothing if you can't get the visitor to read past the headline.

Rule Two: Write Conversationally

Don't use fancy legal words. Legalese makes your readers feel inferior, as if you are better than them.

Before you begin writing, imagine sitting across from your best friend with information that you want to share. Okay, now it's time to put pen to paper (or fingers to the keyboard). Your words will flow in a conversational tone, because there's no BS when chatting with your best friend, and when you're passionate about a topic, it's easy to write.

Rule Three: Keep Content Interesting

Website content should be short and right to the point. Each paragraph should be no more than two or three short sentences, and you should not have more than three sentences without a healthy dose of:

- sub-headings,

- bullet points,

- quotations, and

- infographics (a visual representation of a complex topic).

Market Your Website Like Your Life Depended on It

Just like anything else, you have to market a website for it to be successful. Start by using social media to drive traffic to your website and encourage your readers to comment, engage, and share your content.

Five Essentials for a Killer Blog Post

A blog should focus on current topics of interest that are relevant in your community. Share your opinions and add value. Two hundred to four hundred words per blog post are fine.

These are the five essentials for a killer blog post:

- Current

- Local

- Opinionated

- Informative

- Brief

#1: Current

A blog should focus on current events that everyone's talking about. Don't blog about general topics—blogs should focus on what's happening right now.

#2: Local

Blog about issues that are relevant to your geographic region. A blog post about federal malpractice reform law is okay, but it's better to focus on topics that are relevant in your local community e.g., sanctions against the local nursing home for sub-standard treatment of elderly residents.

"You can't afford for the best ideas to remain buried inside you."

—Dorie Clark, *Stand Out*

Blogging about a new law in New York State is informative and interesting (at least for lawyers). But it's better to focus your blog on a more regional topic, e.g., whether General Electric should be held responsible for dumping carcinogens in the Hudson River.

#3: Opinionated

Be brash and bold in expressing your opinions. Who cares if you're criticized—being politically correct is boring.

#4: Informative

Add as much value to your target audience as possible. Think—how can you be helpful to your followers?

> *"You should always try to give value before you receive it."*
> —**Dorie Clark,** *Stand Out*

#5: Brief

Blogs are not meant to be books. Get to the point in 200–400 words.

Your Voice Deserves to be Heard

You have to be constantly thinking of new ways to expand your list of followers. Share your blog on social media and build a mini-cult of followers with an email newsletter. If you want to build your tribe fast, use Facebook ads to entice followers to sign up for your blog. In return for a free book/guide, your Facebook ad can be used to entice a targeted audience of your ideal clients.

34

WINNING THE GAME OF PAY PER CLICK

For most lawyers, pay-per-click (PPC) is about making a quick buck. You give the marketing company your credit card and carte blanche to charge and anxiously wait for your PPC ads to bring new clients. But over the first six months of the new PPC campaign, your phone doesn't ring and you scratch your head wondering what happened.

This is a failed strategy for PPC. You should look at PPC as a long-term investment, not a short-term cost. A successful PPC campaign requires a long-term mind-set that tests and refines ad campaigns that are uniquely targeted to your ideal client.

Why Every Lawyer Should Have a Pay Per Click Campaign

There are six reasons why every lawyer should have a PCC campaign:

1. Instant results

2. Low cost of entry

3. Ideal client targeting

4. Referral targeting

5. Retargeting

6. Controlling the return on investment

Instant Results: The first listings are paid ads—called PPC. Forty-one percent of clicks go to the top three paid ads on the search results page. If you're not using PPC, you're missing out on 41 percent of potential internet leads.

Unlike organic SEO (which can take months or years), PPC offers nearly immediate results and puts your ad on the top of the first page.

Low Cost of Entry: For as little as $1/day, you can run a PPC campaign on Facebook or Google AdWords. The cost per click is much lower on Facebook than Google Adwords. You set the budget, duration, geographic location of the Facebook ads, and you determine whether the ads appear in the newsfeed, right column of Facebook, or mobile.

Check out these numbers from Lightswitch Advisors for a car wreck campaign:

Reach: 19,593
Clicks: 493

Total Spend: $146

Cost Per Click: $0.30

For only $.30 per click, you're reaching prospective clients about a potential car wreck case.

Ideal Client Targeting: Your ads can target people based upon geographic region, gender, age, etc. You are targeting the people most likely to click through to the ad.

Send your PPC ads only to those persons who have expressed an interest, e.g., persons on your email mailing list. Upload your email list to create a "Custom Audience" on Facebook. You can leverage the "likes" that you've already received on your firm's Facebook page. The top of your Facebook ad will show the "friends" who like your law firm, e.g., "thirteen friends like Ruane Attorneys."

Expand the reach with lookalike ads on Facebook. With a lookalike ad, you take the information on the custom audience and Facebook finds people who are very similar to your email list, e.g., the same criteria in their profile. Then you run Facebook ads to the lookalike audience.

Referral Targeting: Are lawyers your best clients for referrals? Now, target them. PPC ads can be a very cost-effective way to grow the list of your lawyer referral partners. Get an email list of the lawyers in your county, region, or state (ExactData.com can generate a list for you) and create a custom audience on Facebook for a lawyer-to-lawyer ad campaign.

Become the resource for other lawyers with free books, seminars and webinars and print and email newsletters. Here are the metrics of a Facebook ad campaign seeking lawyer referrals (courtesy of Lightswitch Advisors):

Reach: 1,192

Clicks: 89

Spend: $93

Cost Per Click: $1.05

For only $1.05 per click, there were eighty-nine clicks by targeted lawyers in a specific geographic region.

Retargeting: Retargeting gets the best bang for the buck. You can send your ads to those people who visited your website in the last 180 days. Put code (Facebook pixel) on your website that tracks people who have been on your website and your ads will be sent to those people.

Controlling the Return on Investment: The return on investment (ROI) from PPC ads is far easier to control than organic search (SEO). Every ad is set up with a conversion tracking and phone call tracking, such as CallRail.com and you can gauge the success, or failure, of every ad.

Let's say you're running twenty-five different PPC ads. With conversion tracking and phone call tracking, you'll know which ads are getting clicks and generating phone calls. With these metrics, you can track the click through rate and the cost per click.

The Secret to Lead Generation

The goal of the landing page is to convert visitors into leads. This means you want the visitor to call your special toll-free phone number right now. A phone call is much more valuable than a click.

Lead generation ads should focus on the benefits that you offer—not the history of your law firm or the services you provide.

Prospective clients will make decisions based upon one thing: how you can fix their problem.

The lead magnet for a PPC campaign for a car wreck should be customized to the specific ad, such as an e-book, e.g., *Everything You Need to Know to Win Your Car Wreck Case.*

The Biggest Mistake Made by Lawyers

Far too often, PPC ads send prospective clients to the home page of the lawyer's website. Big mistake. The home page is cluttered with information that is confusing. Make things simple for the consumer by creating a landing page that is specially designed for the PPC ad. A landing page is a page where the user lands after clicking the ad.

The PPC landing page should be separate from your main website and have a single goal: converting visitors into clients. The landing page should have:

- A strong headline that demonstrates the benefits you offer (not just a "Free Consultation")

- Three to five bullet points

- One video

- A Call to Action, e.g., "Download your FREE e-book now, *Everything You Should Know about Your Injury Lawsuit*"

- Your phone number should be easy to find

- Social proof, e.g., two to three testimonials from former clients

Getting Granular with the Keywords for Your Ad

Use highly specific keywords that are unique to your practice area. Rather than "best injury lawyers," use "best injury lawyers in Kingston, New York."

For a medical malpractice lawyer, you should use highly specific keywords, such as "spastic quadriplegia" or "athetoid cerebral palsy," rather than the more generic, "cerebral palsy." These specialized keywords will reduce the cost of the ad and increase the click through rate.

The Power of Negative Keywords

Negative keywords are words that you want to filter out of your PPC campaign. Your ads will filter out the results of searches that have those negative keywords. For a personal injury law firm, you should filter out searches that include "divorce" and "real estate."

You do not want your ad running to someone who is researching injury law in an academic setting—they are browsing and have no need for your services. Filter out those searching for research papers, classes, educational opportunities, etc., with these negative keywords (provided courtesy of Lightswitch Advisors):

> "about, definition, example, sample, free, inexpensive, compliance, discount, cheap, bargain, course, tutorials, guide, what are, what is"

This alone should increase the effectiveness of your PPC ad.

Testing and Refining Your Ads

Experiment with text and image ads (some placements only accept text ads). Create ads that are visual; text ads have a much lower click-through rate than image ads. Have your PPC campaigns target specific cities and towns, so your ads can be written for each one individually.

Constantly brainstorm ideas for improving your PPC campaigns. Figure out what consumers click on and test variations of your PPC ad. Once you know what ads are getting clicks, allocate more money to them and reduce your spend on ads with fewer clicks and less engagement. Test ads with images and video for Facebook ads.

Micro-Targeting to the Seriously Disabled

With managed placement ads, you select the specific website you want your ads to appear on. A placement can be on an entire website, a sub-set of a website or an individual ad within a specific page. Display ads are the visual banner ads you see on advertising supported websites.

"Hyper-targeting is so incredibly precise."
—Phillip Stutts, *Fire Them Now*

If you know of a website where your prospective clients spend time, you can place ads on the website. First, identify five to ten websites that are relevant to your practice area. Check out the websites and see it they run Google ads at the top and right column of the site; this is a quick way to determine whether the website participates in the Google Display Network (managed placements are supported for the Google Display Network only).

The Questions to Ask Your Digital Marketer

When the digital marketer asks for a budget of $4,000 per month, ask them to prove their worth with smaller budgets. Do not spend big money until you know which PPC ad campaigns will work. You don't need to out-spend your competitors—you only need to be smarter.

Do not sign a long-term contract (e.g., twelve to eighteen month contracts)—go month-to-month with the option to instantly terminate the contract if you do not get results, or at least a thirty-day out clause. Pay a flat fee per month, as opposed to an hourly rate, and force the digital marketer to prove their worth during a ninety-day probationary period.

Don't hire a digital marketer until you answer these three questions:

1. What is the exact return on investment (ROI) you're aiming for? (e.g., two to one)

2. How you are going to measure your ROI? (e.g., settlement values of new leads)

3. Are you on target to reach your goals at every stage?

Once you establish specific criteria to measure your success, you're ready to begin testing for your PPC campaigns.

Holding Your Digital Marketer Accountable

Make your digital marketer prove that they can get quality leads before you spend big money. Don't give the marketer their paycheck until they've proven themselves.

Give the digital marketer a concept to test in a limited amount of time, e.g., managed placement ads on the website of a construction union. Ask the digital marketer:

- Who will you target?

- What are your testing strategies?

- What metrics will determine the success of each ad?

Every month, have your digital marketer provide an itemized list showing the expenses. The expenses of a PCC campaign consist of the cost of placing the ad (a.k.a the "ad spend") and the management fee charged by your digital marketer. The management fee is typically 20 percent of the total ad spend; if you spend $1,000, the management fee will be $200.

The Only Way to Measure Your Success

The only standard you should use with a PPC campaign is whether it increases the number of your cases that you accept for litigation. A valuable lead is one that will make money.

It is not only the number of leads, but the quality of leads. Are you getting a flood of crappy leads? If you get ninety leads a month, but only one converts into a worthwhile client, your ROI might be lousy even though you're getting a lot of click-throughs.

> *"There is no quick fix, no magic pill. We're going to test and target, and spend lean until we know what works, and then carefully deploy a strategy of trust based specifically on what your customers have shown us what they want."*
>
> **—Phillip Stutts, Fire Them Now**

Tell the digital marketer from the outset: "If I don't have at least one new lead every month that I accept for litigation, we're done." You just set the standard to measure the success of your PPC campaign.

Plan for a Marathon

Success isn't going to happen overnight. There's no magic pill that will give you instant success. Most lawyers see little to no return on PPC campaigns and give up after six months. Hopefully, that's not you. You're building a marketing empire and Rome wasn't built in a day … and neither are great marketing campaigns.

35

MASTERING THE ART OF LINK BUILDING

You've heard the expression about internet marketing: *content is king*. But creating educational content on your website is not the only thing that Google wants—search engine optimization (SEO) consists of content plus links from authoritative websites.

> *"Who links to your site and how they link to it are more important to Google than virtually any other Google ranking formula."*
>
> **—Neil Patel**

If you master the art of link building, you won't need to add content to your website on a daily basis. Here's the proof.

The Anatomy of an Amazing Website

The website of the law firm of Newsome Mellon in Orlando, Florida, BrainandSpinalCord.org, contains resources and information for brain and spinal cord injury survivors. Government organizations and universities from across the country have links to this site.

Here's a sample of just a few of the websites linking to BrainandSpinalCord.org:

- Mn.gov/mnddc/resources/links.htm ("Minnesota's Governor's Council on Developmental Disabilities")

- Health.Utah.gov (Utah Department of Health)

- DrugLibrary.org

- MortgageCalculator.org

- Disability.Illinois.edu (College of Applied Health Sciences at the University of Illinois)

Where are these links found? Almost entirely in the "Resources" section of governmental agencies and disability providers. The "Resources" for the website of the College of Applied Health Science at the University of Illinois has one link, entitled "Resources for Brain Injury and Spinal Cord Injury Survivors" and guess where that link sends you? Newsome Mellon's website.

Twelve Simple Tips for Getting Links

Get some authoritative links for your website using these twelve simple steps:

#1: Give Testimonials

Write unsolicited testimonials for your vendors (e.g., Trialworks, Advocate Capital) and ask them to post the testimonial on their website with your name and a link to your website. Most vendors are grateful to receive the testimonial and happily post them on their high-ranking websites.

When you see a website with testimonial links, consider buying their product/service. If you have a good experience with the vendor, give a testimonial and get a link.

#2: Build Your Resources Page

Promote your vendors by sharing their expertise and stories and you'll earn links from them. List your best resources without asking for anything in return.

#3: Build Relationships with Bloggers

Scour the internet for the top bloggers in your practice area, e.g., American Bar Association's Top 100 Blawgs. Build relationships with the bloggers by sharing and liking their content on social media and let them post an article on your website.

> *"Don't build links, build relationships."*
> **—Neil Patel**

Send the blogger your book or guide and let them decide if it's worth a mention on their blog.

Your Outbound Email:

I enjoy reading your blog for updates on changes in New York law. Awesome stuff!

I just published a new book, *The Law Firm of Your Dreams*. I usually charge twenty-seven dollars, but I took the liberty of sending you a free copy. All I'd ask is that you consider mentioning it on your blog or writing a brief review.

Let me know how that sounds.

#4: Post Guest Articles

Write articles for county bar associations and ask them to share your article (with a link) on their website. Many lawyer organizations have online newsletters for the submission of articles. No one wants to link—they want to share valuable content. Linking is too technical. Stay away from "link"—*use "share," "mention," or "let your readers know."*

"Guest posting is one of the most effective approaches to building links."

—Neil Patel

Hire a graphic designer to create the infographic on 99Designs. com or Upwork. Reach out to bloggers and offer them the infographic as a guest post and submit the infographic to infographic sharing sites like visual.ly, DailyInfoGraphic.com, and AmazingInfoGraphics.com.

#5: Get Your Competitors' Links

Use Ahrefs or Majestic to get a backlink analysis of your competitors' websites. Each of the URLs has qualified itself by doing the one thing you want: linking out. Check out what links your competitors have and then go get them.

"Lost links" are links that have stopped pointing to your website in the last ninety days. Reach out to the website owner and get the links back.

#6: Fix Broken Links

A broken link (a.k.a. "dead link") is a link that is no longer working and that doesn't do the user or the website any good. Too many broken links can have a negative effect on your website.

Find broken links (e.g., "404 not found") on blogs in your practice area and suggest better content—your own—to replace it. Use DeadLinkChecker.com to find broken links. Send a personalized email, including the website owner's name in the subject line and use lower case for the subject line.

> *"Broken link building is perhaps the most effective white-hat link building strategy to come along in years."*
>
> **—Neil Patel**

Give the website owner help by letting them know about any broken links that you find.

Your Outbound Email:

I was just browsing your resources page today, and among the list of great resources were some broken links.

Here are a few of them: [URL #1]

Oh, and I have a website, ProtectingPatientRights.com, that regularly posts quality content related to healthcare and patient rights. If you think so too, feel free to share it on your resources page.

Either way I hope this helps and keep up the good work!

Broken link building is the easiest way to get links from educational portals.

#7: Link Out to Authoritative Websites

Linking out capitalizes on the principle of reciprocity. Promote the best content of others before they ask for it via links from your website and social media. When you write a post, link to external website pages that contain relevant content.

#8: Create a Scholarship

If you create something that colleges or high schools want to link to, you're golden. The holy grail of link building is .edu and .gov backlinks.

Step #1: Create a Scholarship Page that describes the scholarship.

Step #2: Find university pages that link to scholarships, e.g., .edu scholarships. Most universities have resource pages that link to websites that are helpful for students and faculty.

Step #3: When you find a scholarship page on an .edu website that seems like a good fit, send them an email.

Your Outbound Email:

We're excited to let you know about a scholarship opportunity for Saint Rose students. We value education and helping those in need. We also understand that school can be a significant expense for many students.

In an effort to make things a little easier for students and their families, we are pleased to be offering a bi-annual (February & July) $1,000 scholarship for individuals planning to attend college.

We would be honored if you'd be kind enough to add our award to your scholarship page [scholarship page URL].

Of course, we're here to answer any questions you may have. Thank you.

#9: Link Reclamation

Find mentions of your law firm that don't link back to you. When people mention you in an article, they (usually) like you. Use BuzzSumo to find mentions of you and your firm.

Then, email the person with a friendly reminder to add your link. Proactively reach out and ask them to share (link) your content. These are some of the easiest and most powerful links you'll ever get.

Your Outbound Email:

I just wanted to say thanks for mentioning me in your excellent article. I really appreciate it.

I'm reaching out today to ask if you could share an article that I wrote on this topic. That way, if people want more information, they can easily find us while reading your article.

Either way, thanks for the shout out and keep up the great work!

#10: Newsjacking for Links

Press releases can plant seeds for new backlinks to your website. Use *newsjacking* to create inbound links.

*"Newsjacking is the art and science of injecting your
ideas into a breaking news story to generate tons of media
coverage, get sales leads, and grow business."*

—David Meerman Scott

This gets you in front of a breaking news story, interviews by
the media and generates inbound links from the websites of highly
ranked media companies, e.g., TV, radio, newspaper. HARO (*Help A
Reporter Out*) is one the best ways to get backlinks from authoritative
news sites. You give a reporter a tailored response to a request for an
article and they'll give you a link.

Medium.com is a self-publishing website that has link opportunities. Publish an article or two on Medium.com and get links.

#11: Listings of Jobs & Events

Post a job listing with your local law school with a link to your
website. Law schools may be willing to link to pages that feature job
openings. Do this with events too.

#12: Content Is Still King

Long form content covers a topic extensively. In-depth guides attract
backlinks, particularly if they include graphs, charts, statistics, quotes
or video that others can use to validate their opinions. Go for the
"WOW" factor and spend time and money creating a powerful
infographic.

*"It's best to focus on creating and sharing excellent and engaging
content. Do this and everything else will fall into place."*

—Mitch Jackson, Esq.

Edgy, controversial content gets links, e.g., "*Why Structured Settlement Annuities SUCK.*" You will receive hate mail and links from structured settlement brokers.

36

THE MAGIC FORMULA THAT GUARANTEES FIVE-STAR ONLINE REVIEWS

At the end of a case, your clients are thrilled with the outcome, and they swear allegiance to your law firm. You're feeling good, and you don't want to ruin the moment by asking for a testimonial. A few months pass, and the case is forgotten by your clients.

Now, your chance of getting a testimonial for your law firm is almost zero. And this stinks—you know that testimonials are crucial for online marketing. Prospective clients *love* testimonials, but they won't believe a word *you* say.

If you're like most lawyers, you take the easy way out by sending an email request for a testimonial with a link to Google My Business,

Avvo.com, or Facebook. There is a far more effective approach that almost guarantees you will get a five-star review.

Step One: The Power of a Promise

First, get your clients to promise to give an online review. This begins by calling your client and asking four questions:

- Would you recommend our firm to a family or friend?

- Would you be prepared to post a five-star review?

- Would you be prepared to make time for my assistant to give you a call and help you write and post your review?

- Will you promise me that when my assistant calls you, you'll make the time to work with them and post your review?

Once your client promises to give an online review, the likelihood of getting the review is almost guaranteed if you follow the next two steps.

Step Two: Asking for Feedback

Your assistant should then call your client asking for their "feedback" about your law firm (feedback sounds much better than testimonial). Have your assistant ask, "What can we do better?" Chances are your clients will respond, "Nothing, you were amazing!"

Now, it's your chance to get some details: "What did we do that you liked about our law firm?" Make sure to get specifics from your clients—generalizations are useless for online reviews. The best online review consists of three parts in a sequence:

The Problem: The problem facing your client before they hired you.

The Action Taken: What you did to solve your client's problem.

The Benefits: The benefits received by your client (e.g., income, financial freedom, top-notch healthcare, etc.).

This sequence provides a story that is memorable and stands out from 99 percent of online reviews, which are generic and have little SEO value. You want your client to use the magic words from their case (e.g., "atrial fibrillation" or "perforated esophagus"). The use of keywords will help other injury victims find the online review.

Next, your assistant should rewrite the question and answer into a review for your client. This guarantees the content of the review. Now, move to Step Three—posting the review from your client's own computer.

Step Three: The Magic of Screen-Sharing

You want your clients to post the review from their own computer. Screen-sharing technology lets you connect to your client's computer and post the review from their IP address. Screen-sharing websites like LogMeIn Rescue or TeamViewer let you post reviews using your client's own PC, from their internet connection, with their own IP address.

Copy and paste the edited review into your client's web browser (because you have full access to their computer) and ask your client to click the "submit" button. This removes a big obstacle in getting a review and guarantees the content.

Where to Post the Online Reviews

Ninety-nine percent of law firms post testimonials on a single web page of their website. Big mistake. Ideally, you should create a unique web page for every testimonial—this will help the search engines find the review and, in turn, prospective clients will have an easier time finding it.

Every testimonial should be posted on review sites that will boost your website on the search engines. Begin by building reviews on the top three review sites:

1. Google My Business

2. Facebook

3. Avvo

Local rankings of websites are determined, at least in part, by the number of reviews. If you do nothing else, build reviews on Google My Business. If your clients do not have a Google account, you can help them create an account using screen-sharing technology.

37

THE ANATOMY OF A LAWYER VIDEO

It's impossible to deny: lawyer videos on the web are horrible. The internet is crammed with one lawyer talking head after another, talking about their big courtroom victories. But consumers don't care about you, and they sure aren't paying attention to the "talking head" lawyer videos.

How to Create Unique Lawyer Videos for Your Website

In a crowded marketplace full of lawyers screaming, "I'm the greatest," what can you do to differentiate the lawyer videos on your website from the pack?

Begin by writing content for the video; and no, we're not talking about a script. When you use a script for video and read from a teleprompter, your viewers can tell you're reading from a script—it's far better to go without a script, be yourself, and make mistakes. Mistakes are great for lawyer videos—in fact, your video bloopers will make you more credible.

The Best Place to Get Started

Before you start shooting video for your website, write down the ten questions that clients ask you the most. Now you have content for the first ten videos for your website. The questions might include, "How long do I have to sue?" or "How much is my case worth?"

Your videos shouldn't be documentaries—just sixty-second video clips will do. Remember, the attention span of consumers is ultra-limited, and you need to get to the point fast (no more than two minutes). And don't pitch or sell anything. If consumers want to call you, your contact information should be shown at the bottom of the screen.

Something Webmasters Will Never Tell You

Have fun with your video: be real, and don't be afraid of verbal hiccups and mistakes. Consumers will love seeing the real you, even if your video is not perfect.

Now you're connecting with prospective clients, and they're getting to know and like you, even though you've never met them. Once the video is uploaded to your website and YouTube channel, consumers from everywhere have instant access to you, and if your video provides helpful, valuable information, consumers will love you. This is the beauty of the internet—you can expand your reach far beyond your local community to the rest of your state, the whole country, and beyond.

Spreading the Word Everywhere

Great lawyer videos shouldn't be confined to your website. You should upload every video on your website to a dedicated YouTube channel. Remember, you want to spread your reach as far as possible, and if you're just putting video on your website, you're leaving a lot on the table.

Start by creating a YouTube channel, and then make one video, right now. You can create a customized URL for your YouTube channel that contains your name.

Engage and interact with others on YouTube, and you will drive new visitors and traffic to your videos. Just like social media, the key to success on YouTube is engaging in every relevant conversation you can and working to add value through commenting on other lawyer videos of "YouTubers."

Building Trust with Over 10,000 Consumers with Just Ninety-Three Seconds of Your Time

The nation's top lawyer video marketing expert, Gerry Oginski, Esq., shoots videos that are recorded in his office, his living room, and even in his beachfront condo. You might think, "That doesn't look very professional." But Gerry is recording video for consumers, not for you, and consumers don't care if the video was recorded in his garage. No one is doing lawyer video better.

Gerry makes informative videos (e.g., "What is Sepsis?") that attract malpractice victims to his law firm. "What is Sepsis?" is ninety-three seconds long and was uploaded to YouTube on October 7, 2009. This single video has had 10,618 views on YouTube—how's that for building trust with over 10,000 consumers? This single video is an asset that Gerry will have for getting new clients for the rest of his career.

> *"Video marketing is the best face-to-face conversation you
> can have with your audience, without even being there."*
> —Jim Folliard, Gearshift TV

Every new video gobbles up space on—and pushes your competitors' websites off—the first page of Google. Just adding ten or twenty videos to your website will give it an instant boost in the search engine rankings and the number of unique website visits. Even if you only add ten videos to your website, you will be far ahead of almost every other lawyer.

How to Create Website Video Without Doing a Lick of Work

There's an answer that's simple and won't require you to spend a second in a green screen studio: *videotape every speech you give.* When you give a speech, hire a videographer to record and edit your speech. Have the video editor break down your video into two or three minute clips and upload them to your website and YouTube channel. A forty-five-minute CLE speech can become ten to twelve video clips for your website and YouTube channel.

The Secret to Creating Video for Your Website

Schedule your own speech—that's right, tell the county bar association that you will speak about internet marketing for lawyers, and ask the county bar association to sponsor and promote your speech.

Even if no one shows up, give the speech and videotape it, and you will have new content for your website.

Speeches for lawyers kill two birds with one stone. You're building new relationships with lawyers (referral partners), and you're creating new video for your website.

Repurposing Video from the Defendants' Depositions

When you videotape the defendants' depositions (and you should be videotaping *all* of the defendants' depositions), you get compelling content. Post short clips from the defendants' depositions to show the good and bad practices of a deposition, e.g., volunteering information, bad body language, etc. Perhaps a defendant fails to make eye contact, covers his mouth with his hand, or folds his arms across his chest in a defensive posture.

You will have an educational video that you can use to prepare your clients for their depositions. You can add the video to your shock and awe package for new clients; it will impress them and help get them prepare for their deposition. Add the video to your website and YouTube channel, and give your critique about the verbal and nonverbal mistakes.

Part 3

Social Media Marketing

38

THE HARD, COLD TRUTH ABOUT SOCIAL MEDIA FOR LAWYERS

You haven't gotten a single new case call from social media, and you haven't made a dime from all of the time you've spent posting on Facebook and Twitter. So, you finally reach the conclusion that social media is not for lawyers and go back to the good old days of waiting for the phone to ring with your next case.

Why Lawyers Fail at Social Media

Almost all lawyers treat social media as a platform for sending press releases about their law firm, but consumers couldn't care less that you got a verdict or settlement or that you were selected to Super

Lawyers. You're wasting your time if you're only using social media for self-promotion.

Maybe you are posting informative articles about legal issues that might interest consumers on Facebook and Twitter. You're trying to help solve problems for consumers by answering the questions you get asked every day, and you post new articles every day on social media. Okay, not bad, but this alone won't get you any new cases.

The Secret to Success on Social Media

What is the magic secret to getting new cases from social media? *Engagement.* The concept is to listen to conversations, comment, and engage one-on-one with consumers and referral partners. Be real and creative—no lawyer talk allowed.

> *"You need to jump into every relevant conversation you can."*
> —Gary Vaynerchuk, *The Thank You Economy*

And don't just engage on your law firm's Facebook page—search Twitter and Facebook for conversations relevant to your practice area. Just enter a keyword in the search box of Twitter or Facebook, and you will find active conversations taking place in your area of practice. Get involved in this conversation, and keep the dialogue going.

Engaging on social media means retweeting, sharing, replying to conversations, and being active and participating in conversations—but no sales pitches allowed. You want to help others, and this does not mean, "Call me and I'll help." One little helpful tip can eventually lead to your next big case.

What Social Media Is Really About

Back in the good ole' days, word of mouth was everything. You gave great value to your clients, and they referred new clients to you. The key to your success was building strong, trusting relationships with your clients, who then became evangelists for your law practice. Care and commitment helped grow your law practice one client at a time.

The funny thing is, nothing's changed. Social media is all about relationship building, but now your relationships are not limited to your town or county, and talk of your good work is not limited to your small X on the map.

Yes, relationship building is what social media is about. But lawyers and their law firms don't get this—instead, they think social media is about the number of "likes" on Facebook and followers on Twitter. The number of "likes" and followers is meaningless.

> *"The quality of your fans and followers is vastly more important than the quantity."*
>
> —**Gary Vaynerchuk**, *The Thank You Economy*

How many of your friends and followers are actually paying attention to you? If you're not engaging with them one-on-one, your status updates will only be seen by a small percentage of your friends and followers in their news feed. That's right, Facebook and Twitters have filters that will not show your status updates to your friends and followers unless you have a dialogue with them (e.g., tweets, replies, sharing).

But when Facebook sees that more people are commenting on, sharing, or liking your posts, it will show your content to more friends in their news feed. So how do you get your friends and followers to engage with you? Before you post on social media, ask yourself: If you were to read this post, would you share, comment on, or like it? If so, great; if not, don't post it.

Never Let the Dialogue Die

You don't need to have a profile on ten social media platforms, and picking the right platform is not important. Because let's face it—if you're not engaging and participating in conversations on social media, you will get nowhere. Just pick one or two social media platforms, and engage in conversations there.

Give tremendous value and tips to your social media friends and followers. Don't hold back anything. Soon enough, you will have new relationships with strangers outside your local market, and you will begin getting new cases and making money from social media.

39

WHY EVERY LAWYER SHOULD BE ON FACEBOOK

Most lawyers don't understand Facebook. For most lawyers, Facebook and Instagram are mindless playthings for millennials and have nothing to do with the practice of law. If lawyers want to bury their head in the sand, it's their loss.

Facebook is everywhere. Just check out these numbers:

- There are 2.41 billion active users on Facebook—74 percent of which use the platform daily.

- 79 percent of Americans use Facebook (the platform with the second highest usage is Instagram—owned by Facebook—at 32 percent).

- 53 percent of Americans use Facebook "several times a day" and, on average, eight times per day.

- The average time spent per Facebook visit is twenty minutes.

(Source: Infodocket)

The average law firm posts nineteen times every six months and the "industry leaders" post forty-nine times every six months on their law firm's Facebook page (Source: Scorpion Marketing). That's not much. If you post just once per day, you will have 180-plus posts on Facebook in six months and blow away your peers.

But where do you get started? It's becoming harder to gain exposure on your friends' News Feed. The goal? ENGAGEMENT. Whenever your audience engages with your post in any way, e.g., comments, likes, shares and reactions, this sends one message to Facebook: I want more! And Facebook gives them what they want, with more exposure to your posts.

Five Rules for Posting Awesome Content on Facebook

Our law firm sees much less engagement on posts about legal issues. Generally, if you post about boring legal topics, your fans will ignore you.

Before you post, ask:

- Would I share this content with my friends?

- Will this get people talking?

- What type of content do my fans respond to?

We discovered that our firm's audience likes funny, entertaining, and informative content. Over a period of twenty days, a single post on our firm's Facebook page on National Hot and Spicy Day received 942 engagements, including fifty-one shares and sixty-five comments. This post had nothing to do with the law and had only a few surprising facts about the world's hottest pepper (the Carolina Reaper).

Turns out, our audience must have a thing for peppers and our business page continues to get likes, shares, and comments more than three weeks later. Now, we know what to post about, namely, nutty content that tweaks the curiosity.

Follow these five rules for posting content on Facebook:

Rule #1: Post on Your Business Page. Posting on your law firm's business page will add branding to your posts. Post on your law firm's business page, and then share on your personal page. This will expose your post to a larger audience on your personal page.

Posting on your business page will give you the ability to boost or promote the posts as well as access to statistics showing the level of engagement (e.g., comments, likes, shares) for every post. You will be able to tell which posts are getting engagement and spend more time and money on that type of content. You can't do these things with a post on your personal Facebook page.

Rule #2: Be Informative and Entertaining. Focus on sharing great content (as well as the best times to post). Your Facebook audience is not looking for a sales pitch, e.g., your settlements or verdicts, and they're not going to engage with one.

Rule #3: Ask Questions. Ask a question to kick off an active comments thread, e.g., "What's your favorite baseball movie? Let us know in the comments."

Rule #4: Keep it Short. Most posts will be viewed for only 2.5 seconds.

Rule #5: Follow the 70-20-10 Rule. Follow internet guru Neil Patel's, 70-20-10 rule.

- Post original content that is entertaining and informative 70 percent of the time;

- Post content relevant to your followers' interests 20 percent of the time; and

- Post self-promotional content 10 percent of the time.

Analyze your top ten Facebook posts. Go into Facebook Insights and rank your content by links, comments, and shares. Once you know which posts have the highest engagement, you know what you should be posting more about.

Fifteen Tips for Getting Engagement on Facebook

It's becoming harder for any post to gain exposure on the News Feed, but there are proven methods for getting engagement.

Tip #1: Post Regularly. This is easily the most important. *Posting at least once a day will increase your chances of being seen.* Ideally, try to post two or three times a day. Consistency is everything.

Tip #2: Use Images and Photos. An image takes up more space on the News Feed and an interesting image will get more likes, comments, and shares. A post accompanied by a high-quality photo is ten times more likely to get engagement than a post that only has plain text.

Tip #3: Comment on Other Pages. Always reply to the people who comment on your page. People will stop following your posts if you ignore them.

Tip #4: Tag Other Pages. When you tag another Page (by using the @symbol and typing the other Page name in a post), your visibility can increase with that Page's audience. Facebook sometimes shows tagged posts to that Page's fans in the News Feed. At the very least, you can increase your visibility with that Page so that your fans know you're talking about them.

Tip #5: Add Hashtags. By adding hashtags (keywords with the # symbol attached, such as #marketing), you have the potential to be seen by more people who are searching for that hashtag within Facebook.

Tip #6: Use Boosts or Promoted Pages. Boosting a post is a simple form of Facebook advertising that allows you to get your post in front of more people and thereby increase your chances of engagement. A Boosted Page is created from your Timeline and can either target your fans and their friends or an audience that you can choose with up to ten targeted keywords.

A Promoted Page is created from the Ads Manager and has more targeting options, such as targeting only your fans or an audience you choose with more targeted keywords.

Tip #7: Use Contests/Sweepstakes. A contest or sweepstakes is a fun way to get extra engagement on your Page because people like to win. When more people are engaging with your contest, more people have a chance to see your content.

Tip #8: Promote Facebook Pages with Your Blog. Embed Facebook Page updates in your blog posts.

Tip #9: Use Facebook Stories. Facebook stories appear at the very top of the News Feed. That's great placement for drawing eyeballs to your content. Sixty-two percent of people said they became more interested in a brand after seeing it in a story.

Tip #10: Add a Call to Action Button on Your Facebook Page. There's a little Call to Action (CTA) button on every Facebook business page. Adding a Call to Action button on your law firm's business page gives options beyond liking, sharing, or commenting. Your Call to Action button can give quick access to: "Download our Free App" or "Download our Free Book."

Your CTA button can link to a landing page on your website, a video, a contact form, or an opt-in page. Focus on what your Facebook visitors are most likely to click. You can even use the CTA image as the cover photo for your page (see @QuickSprout).

Tip #11: Promote Your Page Outside of Facebook. People who are already interacting with you are great sources of potential engagement. Make sure they know where to find you on Facebook, e.g., subscribers of your email and print newsletters or your email signature.

You might send an email to the subscribers of your email newsletter asking them to join you on Facebook with a link to your site. You can also share a post on your page when a user mentions you.

Tip #12: Use Video. Videos earn the highest engagement rate, despite making up only 3 percent of the content on Facebook.

Keep in mind that 85 percent of Facebook users watch video with the sound off. This means that captioning your video is essential for engagement.

Tip #13: Get Your Team Involved. Ask your staff to share and like your content with their audience. And go a step further, give your staff administrative rights that will allow them to post on your business page. This will be your secret weapon.

Tip #14: Complete Your Profile. Complete the "About" page on your business page. Connecticut plaintiff's lawyers, Ryan McKeen, Esq. and Andrew Garza, Esq. @ConnecticutTrialFirm, use their "About" page to tell their law firm's founding story and why they practice injury law.

You can add a video in place of a cover photo on your Facebook profile. Make sure your phone number and address are on your Facebook page.

Tip #15: Start a "Like" Campaign. Create a "Like" campaign on Facebook for $1/day. With a $1/day ad campaign over 365 days, you will get more likes every day and your audience will expand.

Avoid These Three Mistakes on Facebook

Mistake #1: Cross-Posting is a Bad Idea. Do not share posts across more than one social media platform. Each social media platform has its own unique audience and you want to post content that is relevant to them. Retweets and hashtags are a foreign language and shortened URLs get clicked less than long URLs.

Mistake #2: Avoid Engagement Bait. Do not ask for a share or like. This is considered "engagement bait" by Facebook and your posts will be downgraded.

Mistake #3: Making It All About You. It's called social for a reason—stop boasting about your settlements and verdicts. Social media is *not* about you.

The Best Time to Post on Facebook

The best data is always your own and Facebook has a ton of data available to all page owners and administrators. Use Facebook "Insights" to find your best time to post on Facebook. Click "Insights" at the top of your page. From the Insights dashboard, select "Posts" in the left-hand column menu. This will give you a detailed breakdown of the days and times your friends are most active.

- Is there a specific time your friends are online?

- When is your audience most active on Facebook?

Facebook Insights records the reach and engagement figures for every post you share to your business page. Head to your

"Page Insights" and click "Posts" and below the graph showing the times your fans are online, you'll see "All Posts Published." In the "Published" column, you can see the date and time when each post was published to your Facebook page. Do posts published around a specific time tend to receive more reach or engagement?

You have the potential to reach more consumers and drive higher traffic to your website during peak usage times, but people may be more likely to engage in the evening. Thursdays and Fridays between 1:00 P.M. and 3:00 P.M. are considered to be the best times to post on Facebook. On Thursdays and Fridays, engagement is 18 percent higher (Source: Bit.ly blog), and during weekends, most people spend more spare time checking out Facebook.

The Best Thing You Can Do Right Now

Want to take your firm's social media presence to the next level? It's hard to do this alone. Find an expert who knows what they're doing and let them show you the way.

There's no better place than *The Firm Flex Gym*. Jay Ruane, Esq. built the largest criminal defense firm in Connecticut through digital advertising and social media marketing and for the first time with *The Firm Flex Gym*, he's willing to share with you everything he knows. With daily advice, one-on-one coaching, and hands-on support in a private Facebook group, Jay and his team at *The Firm Flex Gym* can help take a dormant Facebook business page and transform it into an engaging social media powerhouse.

The Firm Flex Gym DIY program is a no-brainer for any lawyer looking to build a powerful social media presence. Go to GetFirmFlex.com to find out more.

40

THE POWER OF LIVESTREAMING FOR LAWYERS

Your friends on social media only care about one thing: *what can you do for them.* Give as much value as you can and ask for nothing in return—this is the key to becoming a star on social media. What actionable advice can you share that will make the lives of your friends and followers better?

St. Louis immigration lawyer, Jim Hacking, Esq., has a daily blog that offers his best tips for life (e.g., overcoming failure, hanging with high achievers, etc.). Jim's tips are simple but inspirational, and I read them almost every day because they deliver value (Jim Hacking, Esq.'s and Tyson Mutrux, Esq.'s podcast, *The Maximum Lawyer*, is loaded with fantastic interviews for lawyers).

The king of social media, Gary Vaynerchuk ("Gary Vee"), posts one or two videos a day with his best tips for social media. Gary Vee's videos are laden with obscenities, and most are not professionally edited, but who cares? Gary Vee delivers a ton of value for his fans, and the results are predictable: he has over a million rabid Facebook followers.

How You Can Become the King of Social Media

Facebook Live changed the game dramatically. Simply click and broadcast video to your audience—anywhere, anytime. Livestreaming is the closest you can get to talking to someone face-to-face. There are no fees for live broadcasting and no video editing or production is necessary.

All you need for a live broadcast is your phone and the right app. Facebook Live from the Facebook app is the easiest way to go live. The live button on your personal profile or fan page is all you need to go live.

It's Not About You

Hate being on camera? Too bad—you don't have a choice if you want to become a social media rock star. You have to allow yourself some leeway to be imperfect. Tell a story, talk like you would with your best friend, smile, and have fun.

Above anything else, *deliver value*. Think of ways that you can change the lives of your fans/followers, and get right to the point. The duration of your video is unimportant; what matters is that you give all of your best secrets away.

How to Build Your Fan Base

Set a Facebook Live event ahead of time so you can promote it. Have planned start and end times, and tell people when you are going to finish the live broadcast. You need to broadcast when your audience is most likely to be online.

Nothing beats an email list. Tell the fans on your email list when you're going to go live, and tell them when you are live. An email list is always the best way to get your content seen by others.

Share a livestream across multiple Facebook groups, and share the link on other Facebook pages, profiles, or groups. Ask your audience to share your broadcast if they think it would be of benefit, or ask them to register for your podcast or webinar. End the broadcast with a call to action (e.g., how to join your email list).

Leverage Live Video to Expand Your Audience

Facebook Live streams become replayable moments after you are done broadcasting live. Keep an archive of all your live content, and make it available after the stream. By making the content available, you will reach more people.

The majority of consumption of your live content will happen when you aren't live. When you're done with the broadcast, you have great material to reach another audience through redistribution. The people who watch the replay will be the fastest-growing segment of your audience. Add the replay of the livestream to your podcast and YouTube channel.

LIVESTREAMING YOUR ASS OFF

There's one lawyer who gets it: Mitch Jackson, Esq., a trial lawyer and livestreaming/social media guru in Southern California. Mitch is authentic, real, and livestreams his ass off. But what about the payoff? Through the power of his social media engagement, Mitch gets seven figure injury cases, but the payoff is far more than financial. Mitch has built relationships with some of the top celebrities, thought leaders, and marketers anywhere.

The Numbers Don't Lie

Livestreaming levels the playing field. And the statistics don't lie:

- People comment and engage on live video ten times more than regular video.

- The Facebook algorithm prioritizes live video.

Livestreaming costs nothing and helps build relationships and your status as a thought leader. The downside? Just a few minutes of your time.

The Ten Commandments of Livestreaming

Don't wait for anyone to appoint you as a thought leader—grab your smart phone and start the live broadcast. But before you do, here are a few ideas to get started.

#1: Smile, Damn It!

Begin every livestream with a HUGE smile. No one likes a sourpuss. No one has a bigger smile than Chicago trademark lawyer, Joey Vitale, Esq.

#2: Look at the Lens

Focus on the lens of your laptop/desktop and don't take your eye off it. Eye contact conveys honesty. Keep your hands away from your face.

Change your voice inflection and flow of your speech to emphasize key points. Pausing will have your audience anxiously anticipating your next word.

#3: Tell Personal Stories

Be real and personal. The story brings your audience into your living room and creates a powerful bond. You have great stories—you're just not sharing them.

I share the story of the day that I discovered that my mother was diagnosed with colon cancer ("A Story of Hope"). After spending hours questioning why God would let this happen, I decided to place my trust in God. My willingness to trust in God's plan helped me get through some anxious hours and become a source of strength and hope for my mother, sisters, and father.

"I truly believe that you can change the world one livestream at a time."
—**Jennifer Quinn**, *Leverage Livestreaming to Build Your Brand*

St. Louis immigration lawyer, Jim Hacking, Esq., shares the compelling stories of his clients when they receive their green cards or granted citizenship. There's nothing better than seeing Jim outside court with his client celebrating their win after years of struggle. Jim's audience is sharing his success with him.

#4: Share Your Fears, Faults, and Failures

Credibility is earned through the self-revelation of your biggest fears and failures. There is nothing more powerful or difficult.

"Give yourself permission to be real and be yourself."

—Mitch Jackson

#5: Welcome People by Name

What is your favorite word? Your name. That's because you (and everyone else) love to hear your name and if you are going to livestream, you better engage with your audience. Just two words will suffice, "Hey, Frank," when someone joins your livestream.

"Remember this basic truth about human beings and your livestreams will be magical: people want to be seen, recognized, and validated."

—Jennifer Quinn, *Leverage Livestreaming to Build Your Brand*

Can't focus on the topic of your speech and engage with your audience at the same time? Have a coworker or friend prompt you whenever someone joins your broadcast, e.g., have them hold up a note card, "Say, 'hi' to Charlie." With this little gesture, you did the most important thing of livestreaming: ENGAGEMENT.

#6: Let Your Hair Down

Going for a jog on the beach? Perfect time to livestream. Who cares that your hair is sticking up? Let the world see the real you.

*"When you take the focus off yourself and focus on
the viewers, that's where the magic happens."*

—Jennifer Quinn, *Leverage Livestreaming to Build Your Brand*

Perfection is the enemy of success. Even if your broadcast is full of mistakes, remember: no one else is doing this.

#7: Add Value

Always think, "What can I say that will ADD VALUE for my audience?" Don't hesitate to share your unique spin on a controversial topic. When you've got value to add to a news story, share your broadcast with members of the news media (or send them a tweet).

Confidential settlements cover up the crimes in sexual harassment claims, but are the victims partly at fault for taking hush money? Don't shy away from sharing your unique view on a controversial subject.

#8: Become the Host of Your Own Show

Alabama injury lawyer, Morris "Mo" Lilienthal, Esq., has his own Facebook Live show ("The Mo Show"), where he interviews prominent members of his community. The interviews have little to do with the law and focus more on newsworthy topics. A show featured the problem of football-related concussions and as a former college football player, Mo offered his own unique insights.

Missouri lawyers, Tyson Mutrux, Esq. and Jim Hacking, Esq., livestream their shows for their podcast, *Maximum Lawyer*. The livestream makes the podcast far more personal and engaging, even with the occasional technical hiccup. The results? *Maximum Lawyer* is one of the American Bar Association's Top 100 Blawgs.

#9: Show Love for Your Community

The Wheel of Giving is a weekly Facebook Live show by New Jersey injury lawyers, Rich Grungo, Jr., Esq. and Bill Colarulo, Esq. The favorite charities of the firm's clients are listed on clicker spots on a spinning prize wheel and a team member spins the wheel to randomly pick a winner. The winning charity gets $250 and Rich and Bill get a heavy dose of Facebook goodwill.

Mo Lilienthal, Esq. used a Facebook Live show to announce the winner of a drawing for Alabama football tickets. The scheduled announcement on Facebook Live resulted in over seven hundred likes for his law firm's Facebook page.

#10: Consistency Is King

The key to any form of marketing/relationship-building is consistency. Livestreaming on a consistent basis will build your audience. Legendary marketer/business guru, Gary Vaynerchuk, has a video crew following him seemingly all day and he posts video twice a day. As long as you have something valuable to share, there's no reason you can't follow Gary Vee's lead.

Livestream whenever you have anything of value to share with your audience. When you don't want to go live, feel the fear and do it anyway.

Once You've Mastered the Basics

Want to become known with bloggers and members of the media? When you like their articles, send them a tweet, i.e., "Loved your article about Laverne's Law," and retweet and share their posts on your social media channels. Nick Rishwain, JD, of Experts.com, generously shares and retweets valuable articles.

Georgia injury lawyer, Rebecca Kay Sapp, Esq., uses Facebook Live to show her law firm's holiday parties and announcements of new hires. Rebecca's live videos are funny, off-the-wall, and give you real-time access to the inner workings of her firm. How many lawyers are doing this?

The Best Way to Grow Your Digital Footprint

Let's face a brutal reality: you can't do this alone. Sure, you might be okay for a few weeks, but eventually other commitments will get in the way and before long, livestreaming will be long forgotten. You need accountability—a group of peers who will make sure you do what you say you'll do.

There is no better place than Mitch Jackson, Esq.'s online mastermind, LegalMinds (LegalMinds.lawyer). I've been a member since Mitch created LegalMinds and I can't think of any reason to leave. LegalMinds has online meetings twice a week and has interviews with special guests in the world of social media. The members share best practices and each other's posts, and continually challenge each other to "go live."

Part 3

The Entrepreneurial Lawyer's Secret Weapons

41

HOW TO BUILD TRUST AND CREDIBILITY IN A CYNICAL WORLD

To strangers, you are another suit. For the most part, consumers (including jurors) have a negative perception of lawyers, and even your warm smile, charming personality and good looks won't change a thing. But there's one thing that can build credibility and trust with total strangers: sharing a personal story that explains why you do what you do. Sharing your innermost feelings with strangers (and even jurors) shows you're a real human being and, just like them, you have fears, failures, and mistakes. There is nothing more effective at building trust and credibility.

One Lawyer's Powerful "WHY" Story

Louisiana personal injury lawyer, Keith Magness, Esq., shares the heart-wrenching story of a phone call informing him of a car wreck involving his parents. Keith rushed to the hospital and when he got there, he was told that his mother did not survive.

As a young, inexperienced lawyer, Keith had little idea what to expect in the wrongful death lawsuit. Through his experience handling the wrongful death claim, Keith saw the dirty underbelly of insurance companies and their go-for-broke strategy designed to minimize (and avoid) payment of legitimate claims. This deny-at-all-costs experience with insurance companies fueled Keith's ambition to do one thing: protect the rights of those negligently injured in car wrecks.

> *"People don't buy what you do, they buy why you do it."*
> —**Simon Sinek,** *Start with Why*

Keith created a video of his "WHY" story and shared it on the home page of his website and social media. Because he shared his WHY story, clients often tell Keith that they feel a personal connection with him. The WHY video creates credibility and rapport with clients and continues to bring new clients to Keith's firm. Keith will tell you that sharing his WHY story was the best thing he's done.

A Story of WHY that Needs to Be Told

Awhile ago, someone happened to pose the following question at a partners' meeting at my old law firm in Albany, NY: "*Why do you practice law?*" One by one, each of the lawyers took a turn giving the same stock answer: "I love the thrill of the courtroom" or "I get a rush out of cross examination." When my turn came, I reflected on the question and then shared my WHY story.

> In the late 1990s, a senior partner gave me the assignment of handling a wreck that caused horrendous physical injuries and severe brain damage to our client, Dale. Every time I visited Dale at his home, he did not appear to recognize me due to the severity of his brain damage and sadly, the bulk of his day was confined to staring blankly at the TV. Handling such a case was an enormous responsibility for a young, inexperienced lawyer and, truth be told, I made more than my share of mistakes.

> *"When you tell people why you're doing what*
> *you're doing, remarkable things happen."*
> **—Simon Sinek, *Start with Why***

About a week before trial, the case settled for a modest sum and I dwelled on the thought that the outcome would have been better had I done a better job. Days later, Dale came to our law firm to sign the settlement papers. As I walked into the conference room to greet him, Dale got out of his chair, walked over and gave me a bear hug. As I stood there awkwardly not knowing what to say or do, Dale softly whispered three words that I will never forget, "*I love you.*"

That is WHY I practice law. I don't practice for the love of money or the thrill of the courtroom. I practice to make a profound impact on the lives of severely disabled people—this is what gives me the courage to go to trial.

What is Your WHY?

Each of us has our own WHY and your WHY will almost certainly be different from everyone else's. Once you define why you practice law, take a chance by sharing your story. Hire a videographer to videotape your WHY story and share it on the home page of your website and social media.

> *"All great leaders have clarity of why, an undying belief in a purpose or cause bigger than themselves."*
> —**Simon Sinek,** *Start with Why*

Your clients will appreciate that you're like them—a human being with fears, weaknesses and vulnerabilities—and in the process, you might create something that is especially elusive for lawyers: trust and credibility. There is nothing more valuable.

42

HOW TO MOVE BEYOND MEDIOCRITY

You return from a seminar full of energy and excitement. You can't wait to get started with your grandiose plans for world domination. But when you get back to the office, emergencies start popping up, and before you know it, you're back to the same ole' grind. And after a few weeks, your big plans are a distant memory.

There is a reason why seminars fail and it's the same reason why you don't follow through on your New Year's resolution: there is no system for ongoing accountability. Of course, you have the best of intentions and a strong commitment to make changes, but your self-discipline (just like mine) is far from perfect, and you quickly lose sight of the big dreams and goals that you had when you left the seminar.

It's time to change this.

Success Can Only Be Achieved with Accountability

There is only one path to long-lasting success: ACCOUNTABILITY. Alcoholics Anonymous and Weight Watchers provide peer accountability that have proven to make life-long changes in seemingly hopeless situations.

> *"Wanting to improve ourselves is one thing;*
> *actually following through is another."*
> —**Keith Ferrazzi**, *Who's Got Your Back*

My best friend, Vince DeCicco ("Vin-Man USA"), lost seventy-two pounds (in only six months) at Weight Watchers through the power of weekly weigh-ins and an accountability system that virtually forces compliance with goals. Vince knew that he couldn't take off the weight alone and had the courage to ask for the help ... and the rest is history. Today, Vince is no longer a diabetic, and he eats healthy, nutritious meals that will add ten to twenty years to his life. The power of peer-to-peer accountability changed Vince's life.

Everyone should have a small group of trusted peers (a.k.a. your "Board of Advisors") who you meet with regularly, share your biggest goals and dreams, and give them permission to kick your butt.

Strive to be the Dumbest Person in the Room

Rule out family and friends. They are too soft and will never hold you accountable. You need a peer group who won't hesitate to kick your butt when you're slacking off.

"Work with people who've been where you've never been, to help you learn from the mistakes they've made and see opportunities differently than you do."
—Keith Ferrazzi, *Who's Got Your Back*

Look for peers who are doing things much bigger and better than you—if you aren't the dumbest person in the room, you're in the wrong room. If you are earning $100,000, you'll never get to $1 million by hanging around people making $100,000–$300,000. Join forces with peers who are living big lives, making a boatload of cash, and living a life that seems unattainable.

Masterminds that Are Kicking Ass

William Eadie, Esq., a nursing home abuse lawyer in Cleveland, created his own monthly mastermind group consisting of seven to ten lawyers. Will's mastermind members meet face-to-face once every three months and bring guest speakers to their meetings via videoconference. There is no cost, and there is ongoing accountability among the members.

Mitch Jackson, Esq., an injury lawyer and social media guru in Southern California, created an online mastermind, *LegalMinds*, for lawyers who want to grow their practice through social media. The mastermind has two weekly calls via videoconference, where the members share marketing and social media concepts.

The Ingredients for a Powerful Mastermind

For a mastermind, accountability is everything. Begin by creating a private Facebook group, where members can share best practices and challenge each other. The private Facebook group will be a daily resource for collaboration. Create an online directory consisting of the address, email, and phone number of the members. The members can create a video narrative that tells their backstory for the online directory.

Schedule monthly video conference accountability meetings, where the members can share their progress and biggest challenges. Zoom.us is great for video conferencing. The monthly accountability meetings should be recorded for those members unable to attend. Document the progress and goals of the members at each accountability meeting and share your notes with the members.

> *"Having someone hold you accountable for your
> goals is a powerful reinforcing mechanism."*
> —**Keith Ferrazzi,** *Who's Got Your Back?*

Meet in person at least once every four months. At each meeting, every member must give a "Hot Seat" presentation about their biggest marketing or management challenge. The group will share their best advice and offer solutions. Each member must set specific goals that they want to accomplish by the next mastermind and the goals are shared collectively.

The Top Four Tools for Promoting Your First Mastermind

The promotion for your first mastermind will take three to four months, so be patient. Few lawyers will be receptive at first. Most are unfamiliar with the concept of a mastermind and many will balk at spending even one day away from their busy practice. You need to find lawyers who think like you, i.e., entrepreneurial-minded lawyers who are life-long learners and ideally, highly successful lawyers willing to share everything they know.

#1: Referrals: The best source of members will always be referrals and warm leads, e.g., lawyers who already know, like and trust you. Create a list of your referral partners, newsletter subscribers, and social media friends (e.g., contacts on LinkedIn). Write a list of your ideal people for the mastermind that are a good fit; then call them and offer a spot—it's as simple as that.

> *"Sharing your best ideas with the world is a powerful way to help others and give meaning to what you do."*
> —Dorie Clark, *Entrepreneurial You*

#2: Direct Mail, Email, and Webinars: Reach out to your friends and warm leads through a series of personal touches—the more personal the better. You should create a sales letter explaining the benefits of the mastermind and follow up with a webinar with a special guest, e.g., "How to Become an Authority with the Media." Promote the webinar and mastermind in your monthly print newsletter.

Invite those on your email list with a series of emails that provide valuable content and a special offer to your mastermind, e.g., "What is your biggest professional challenge right now?" Ask for their phone numbers and get their permission to call them to follow up (this is a proxy—if they say yes, they are more interested and likely to become buyers). Use the subject line, "quick question," in lower case so it looks as personal as possible.

#3: Sponsors and Joint Ventures: Get sponsors for the mastermind, e.g., Advocate Capital. Ask your vendors to promote the mastermind on their social media channels and offer to co-host a webinar on a subject relevant to the mastermind, e.g., internet marketing or hiring and firing.

You might do a joint venture with another trial lawyer organization or firm with a complimentary event, e.g., The 7-Figure Attorney, and co-promote each other's events.

#4: Speaking Engagements: Use speaking engagements to promote your mastermind. Once attendees see the value you offer, they will be lining up to attend your mastermind.

Offer to sponsor conferences in return for the endorsement of your mastermind. The Mastermind Experience was a sponsor of the Max Law conference and just from that event, our mastermind received ten new applications.

The Top Six Mistakes of a Mastermind Organizer

Don't wait to launch a mastermind—start now and make improvements at each mastermind. But here are a few tips (which I've learned through first-hand experience) for avoiding common mistakes.

#1: Failing to Attend a Mastermind: One rookie mistake is lawyers who want to launch a mastermind group, yet have never participated in one. It's hard to run a mastermind when you've never attended one.

Spend a few bucks to attend a high-live mastermind and learn what they do—good and bad. I attended a mastermind known as Elite Forum at Infusionsoft and received invaluable ideas for creating a mastermind for lawyers.

#2: Unsolicited Mail: Mailing a sales letter to cold leads (e.g., lawyers who don't know you) will have a very low return on investment. I once sent one thousand sales letters to a cold list and got no response. Cost $5,200. Big mistake.

Like unsolicited mail, digital advertising has a low response rate when you send the ads to cold leads. If you have a budget for digital advertising, target a list of lawyers who already know, like and trust you, e.g., your email subscribers or referral partners.

#3: Spending without a Budget: Set a budget and stick to it. When you add special events, have the members pay extra, e.g., baseball game. Your goal is to break even financially in the beginning. If you're losing money at every mastermind, the longevity of your mastermind will be in jeopardy. This is a mistake I've made more than a few times.

When possible, ask one of the members to host the mastermind at their law firm. This alone will save a lot of cash.

#4: Letting Anyone in the Mastermind: Don't simply admit anyone who is interested—you have to be selective. The collective wisdom of the mastermind will suffer if unscrupulous, low-achieving lawyers are admitted to your tribe.

If one of the members has a problem with an applicant, you have to give them veto power to reject their application. Some want to attend the mastermind only to get the secrets of the other members.

#5: Failing to be Unique: What would make your mastermind distinctive in the marketplace? Unlike other lawyer masterminds, the Mastermind Experience is a one-day event that has no recurring fees and is limited to less than thirty lawyers. There is no commitment or fees beyond the one-time registration fee. No other mastermind does this.

*"In-person experiences are an incomparable
form of community building."*
—Dorie Clark, *Entrepreneurial One*

The Mastermind Experience separates the members into three groups by practice area and firm size and brings special guests to the mastermind to present cutting-edge concepts in law firm marketing and management.

#6: Failing to Charge a Fee: Failing to charge a fee has been the death of many masterminds. If you don't charge a fee, your members will not be invested and your attendance rates will suffer, e.g., lower than 50 percent. When you charge a fee, your members will be invested and your attendance rates will exceed 90 percent.

"The world needs your ideas and you need to be paid for them."
—Dorie Clark, *Entrepreneurial You*

#8 Tips for An Amazing Mastermind

Over-promise and over-deliver. You want the attendees to be blown away by the content you deliver; when you over-deliver, the mastermind will sell itself.

#1: Be Ruthless with the Schedule/Time: Start on time and keep close watch of the time limits for the hot seat presentations. Being strict with time shows respect for the time of your members.

#2: Desirable Venue and Meals: Find desirable venues and don't skimp on meals or entertainment. Your members want to be in South Florida or Hawaii in the winter.

#3: Bring Guest Speakers: Bring the best speakers in person to speak at your mastermind and expose your members to marketing and management concepts they won't find anywhere else.

#4: Vary the Format: Vary the format of your mastermind so that every mastermind is different, e.g., themed masterminds about hiring and firing or internet marketing.

#5: Expand the Offerings: Create a members-only website with your best video presentations and a membership registry, so new members have an archive of your best presentations and legal forms. Add special offerings, such as a private Facebook group and a health and fitness Facebook group.

#6: Keep it Small: Keep the mastermind to less than thirty attendees. When you exceed thirty members, there is not enough personal attention for your members.

#7: Separate Groups: Separate into small groups by size of law firm and practice area. Your members want to work with others in the same practice area, who face the same challenges.

#8: Video Testimonials: Capture the video testimonials at the mastermind and you'll never have to sell the event again.

The Best Thing You Will Ever Do for Your Career

You might be thinking, "sounds nice, but this is not for me." And you're right, the mastermind is not for most lawyers—in fact, most do not see the benefits. But for those who are active and engage in the mastermind, it is nothing less than transformative, both professionally and personally.

43

THE HIDDEN TRUTH ABOUT THE PRACTICE OF LAW

At the annual meeting of my former law firm's partners, the question posed by the senior partner was simple: "How many trials do you have scheduled in the next twelve months?" The news wasn't what anyone wanted to hear. Each of the partners took turns staring down at the table as they softly mumbled that they only had a couple of trials over the next year, and it quickly became apparent that our firm's future was far from promising ... until the youngest partner spoke.

The junior partner unabashedly announced to his partners, "I've got eleven trials and some are double booked. *Can you help?*" The junior, non-equity partner was booking trial dates, hustling, and bringing in new clients. Business looked good for at least one of the lawyers, but therein lies the problem: every lawyer in your firm has to bring in new clients because your magnificent trial skills mean nothing without clients.

Getting clients is your business—yes, your law firm is a *"marketing business."* This is the one thing that most lawyers struggle to accept more than anything.

The Ultimate Wish-list for Lawyers

Think of new and inexpensive ways to market your firm, e.g., community marketing programs ("Bikes for Kids") or an email newsletter. List all of your marketing tactics and then list them by order of priority.

> *"You know what they say about the definition of insanity: doing the same thing over and over and expecting a different outcome.*
>
> *So, stop the insanity by looking at your marketing tactics with a whole new perspective. You must ask yourself, where you want to be this year, next year and in five years."*
>
> —Harlan Schillinger

Marketing all is about building relationships. You are not marketing, you're building relationships one at a time. When you build relationships with prominent, influential referral sources, you may not have to spend another dollar on advertising.

The Marketing Plan for John H. Fisher, PC

Our Target Market:

Plaintiffs' personal injury lawyers in New York State between the ages of thirty and fifty-five, who have high volume caseloads, but do <u>not</u> handle medical malpractice.

These are the *ideal clients* for our law firm.

Historical Data:

Our best financial results have been based upon recoveries in non-medical malpractice catastrophic personal injury cases. Even with the same gross recovery, the legal fee in a catastrophic personal injury case is almost double the legal fee for a medical malpractice case.

We need to expand our practice into catastrophic personal injury in order to achieve our goal of annual income of $2.5 million.

Current Marketing Position:

We have 388 referral partners; our main website (ProtectingPatientRights.com) gets 12,000-13,000 visitors per month and we have 1,651 subscribers for our email newsletter on UltimateInjuryLaw.com.

While we have 388 referral partners, almost all of our revenue is generated by four plaintiffs' law firms. We need to expand our referral relationships to plaintiffs' personal injury law firms in the Hudson Valley, Capital District, and Central New York.

We derived about 80 percent of our revenue from internet marketing. We need a better system for following up with prospects who do not have a case and nurture and cultivate leads through a 365-day follow up campaign.

Future Predictions:

Unless the statutory legal fee in medical malpractice increases to one-third, it will be difficult to achieve our goal of annual income of $2.5 million. I do not believe the statutory legal fees will be increased in the next three to five years, and hence, we need to expand our practice to three catastrophic injury cases per year.

In order to achieve this goal, we should launch a new website that provides resources and information for the victims of traumatic brain injury and spinal cord injuries in New York State. While we will not see immediate results, I expect to expand our practice area into catastrophic personal injury within three to five years.

Marketing Tactics & Strategies for John H. Fisher, PC

Our firm's marketing goals and tactics are broken into six categories:

- Law office operations
- Referral marketing
- Internet marketing
- Social media and email newsletter
- Mastermind Experience
- Community marketing and press relations

Each marketing strategy/tactic is listed top to bottom in the order of their priority, so our marketing director knows where to focus her time and money.

Law Office Operations:

- Send holiday cards for clients and members of the Mastermind Experience.

- Create a mini-book consisting of photos and testimonials from the Mastermind Experience.

- Provide birthday cards and phone calls for current and former clients and referral partners.

- Update and finalize the Office Manual into a mini-book as a gift for referral partners.

- Create a client portal on a mobile app to provide access to the plaintiff's Bill of Particulars, client's shock and awe package and deposition transcripts.

- Create an infographic for the lobby with our mission (basecamps for 2020, 2021, 2022, and 2023 and 1,000 referral partners by October 19, 2023).

- Create a brochure describing the Dream Manager Program and the Dream Manual.

Referral Marketing:

- Schedule lunch dates once a week with an existing referral partner and a prospective referral partner.

- Schedule a two-hour meeting every Friday to meet with our marketing director to review our progress and new marketing initiatives.

- Promote book sales through Facebook ads.

- Make books, *The Power of a System* and *The Law Firm of Your Dreams*, part of the curriculum in the legal practice management classes of all fifteen law schools in New York State.

- Give a one-hour speech for law students about managing and marketing their own law practice in every law school in New York.

- Expand speaking engagements to trial lawyer organizations outside of New York with a focus on the American Association for Justice.

- Create a brochure/press kit for speaking engagements consisting of testimonial letters, photos from past speeches, etc.

- Gift-wrap the books for online purchasers and promote our email newsletter with book purchasers.

- Acquire 250 reviews of *The Power of a System* on Amazon. com.

- Create an audiobook for *The Power of a System* and add to the shock and awe package.

- Meet with the professors of law practice management at every law school in New York State to introduce *The Power of a System* as part of the curriculum.

- Ensure that every lawyer in the State of New York possesses *The Power of a System* and *The Law Firm of Your Dreams.*

- Add video testimonials of *The Power of a System* on John's Amazon author profile.

- Finish shock and awe package for referral partners.

- Create CD of interviews of Ben Glass, Esq., Adam Witty, and Richard James Strauch for inclusion in the shock and awe package.

- Create a mini-book of *Our Best Legal Forms for Personal Injury Lawyers.*

- Contact the New York State Bar Association about an article submission.

- Send a print newsletter containing quarterly updates for referral partners about the changes in the law of New York evidence and procedure.

- Identify the top one hundred legal bloggers and send them a signed copy of *The Power of a System* and *The Law Firm of Your Dreams.*

Internet Marketing:

- Launch new website for victims of traumatic brain injury and spinal cord injuries in New York State.

- Create a website featuring my speaking profile with video testimonials.

- Create a "Lawyer Referrals" page on ProtectingPatientRights.com.

- Create a "Community" page on ProtectingPatientRights. com with a list of the charities that we support, e.g., HWNN.com/community-program.

- Create nurture campaigns that are relevant to initial new client inquiry, e.g., nurture campaigns for each practice area on ProtectingPatientRights.com.

Social Media & Email Newsletter:

- Update the firm's Facebook page with photos, trivia contests, and inspirational quotes on a daily basis.

- Produce monthly Facebook Live shows based upon the marketing and management of law firms.

- Revamp firm's Facebook page into an educational resource for Facebook Live shows and webinars.

- Upload more videos to our YouTube channel.

- Track YouTube performance with analytics.

- Add introductory ten emails for new email subscribers for email newsletter.

Mastermind Experience:

- Create sales funnel (a.k.a., campaign) for promotion of the Mastermind Experience.

- Create CD of podcast interview on the Maximum Lawyer for inclusion in the shock and awe package for referral partners.

- Expand the Mastermind Experience to Hawaii.

- Create webinars (e.g., "Lawyer to Lawyer Referral Based Marketing") and Facebook ad campaign for the promotion of the Mastermind Experience.

- Implement a three-tiered coaching program.

Community Marketing & Press Relations:

- Create a press kit for media relations and put the press kit on the website.

- Create a media list for members of the legal community in the Hudson Valley and Capital District.

- Give legal commentary in local and national TV stations.

- Implement community marketing programs, e.g., suicide prevention scholarship and "Kingston Proud."

- Build relationships with the local media through community marketing programs.

44

HOW TO CREATE ENTREPRENEURIAL-MINDED ASSOCIATES

It is the classic mistake made by law firms: the partners are the rainmakers and the associates do the grunt work (e.g., depositions, trials, etc.) There's only one problem: this doesn't work.

If only a few lawyers are bringing in the business, the law firm is dependent on a few lawyers to survive. Every lawyer, paralegal, and team member must be devoted to bringing new clients to the firm. And it's your job as the principal to create systems that incentivize associates to bring new clients to the firm.

Tell a new associate that they can make $50,000 or $400,000—it's up to them. Bonuses are based upon revenue generated by the cases brought to the firm by the associate. If the associate brings big cases to the firm, there's no limit to what they can make.

Here's our policy:

FEES ON CASES

1. All attorneys agree to devote themselves to the practice of law exclusively for the firm of John H. Fisher, PC (hereinafter referred to as "the firm"), and shall devote their full time, attention, efforts, and skill to the affairs of the firm and will use their best efforts to promote the interests of the firm.

2. No attorney shall directly or indirectly engage in any other business or occupation without the written consent of the principals of the firm.

3. All attorneys shall be required to submit any new legal representation offered to them to a principal of the firm for acceptance or rejection by the firm.

4. No attorney is authorized to accept any new legal representation offered to that attorney without first obtaining the written consent of a principal of the firm.

5. An attorney will be considered to be the original source of a file only if the attorney establishes to the satisfaction of a principal of the firm that it was the attorney's contact with the potential client that was the exclusive cause of the file coming to the firm.

6. In the event John H. Fisher, PC, accepts a file, and it is agreed that the attorney was the original source of the file, the attorney will receive a bonus. The amount of the

bonus shall be computed by multiplying the total amount of the attorneys' fee received by John H. Fisher, PC, on that file by an amount that is equal to the percentage of the **net sum recovered** by the client that is received by John H. Fisher, PC, as their total attorneys' fee in the matter.

7. For example, if the total amount of John H. Fisher, PC's attorneys' fee is $90,000 and that fee represents one third of the net sum recovered by the client ($270,000), then the amount of the bonus shall be one-third of the $90,000 attorneys' fees recovered by John H. Fisher, PC, or $30,000. If, however, the total amount of John H. Fisher, PC's fee is $137,500 and that fee represents 27.5 percent of the net sum recovered by the client ($500,000), then the bonus shall be 27.5 percent of the $137,500 attorneys' fee recovered by John H. Fisher, PC, or $37,812.50.

8.   If the attorney was not the original source of the file, the attorney will receive no bonus on that file.

9. In the event John H. Fisher, PC, declines to accept a file, but elects to refer the file to another law firm, and it is agreed that the attorney was the original source of the file, to the extent permitted by the New York Rules of Professional Conduct, or any successor code of ethics in effect from time to time in the state of New York, by applicable rules and regulations governing lawyers' professional conduct and by applicable law, the attorney will receive a bonus equal to two-thirds of the net attorneys' fees received by John H. Fisher, PC, on that

file. If the attorney was not the original source of the file, the attorney will receive no bonus on that file.

10.   John H. Fisher, PC, as additional salary, shall pay any bonuses due to an attorney, pursuant to this policy, within sixty days of John H. Fisher, PC's receiving final payment of its fee on the applicable file.

11.   If the employment of an attorney with John H. Fisher, PC, terminates, any payments due to the attorney shall be paid to the attorney, or to the estate of the attorney, within sixty days of John H. Fisher, PC, receiving final payment of its fee on the applicable file.

12.   For the purpose of enforcing an attorney's right to any payment due pursuant to the provisions of this memorandum, the only admissible evidence shall be an "Acknowledgement of Original Source Letter," in the form annexed hereto, signed by both a principal of the firm and the attorney within ten days of the case first being offered to the firm. It shall be the responsibility of the attorney to immediately, upon the same being signed, deliver an original copy of such Acknowledgement of Original Source Letter to the firm's bookkeeper for filing and to have a copy placed in the specific file to which it pertains.

13.   Nothing contained in this memorandum is intended or shall be construed to create any partnership or joint venture between or among the firm of John H. Fisher, PC, and any attorney or attorneys.

14. This memorandum and the rights of the parties hereunder shall be governed and construed in accordance with the laws of the state of New York.

15. For purposes of this agreement, the "principal" of the firm is John H. Fisher.

16. For the purposes of this agreement, an "attorney" shall mean any attorney employed by the firm and who is not a principal of the firm.

17. In the event that any one or more of the provisions of this memorandum shall be determined by a court or other judicial or administrative body to be illegal or unenforceable, such illegality or unenforceable provisions shall not affect the validity or enforceability of the remaining and enforceable provisions hereof, and any such illegal or unenforceable provisions shall be deemed amended so as to make such provisions legal and enforceable in the determination of such court or other body and shall, as so amended, be enforceable among the parties.

_____

John H. Fisher

_____

Attorney

* * *

Acknowledgement of Original Source Letter

Date:

Re:

The undersigned hereby agree that the attorney whose name appears below was the original source of the file referred to above and is entitled to receive a bonus or other payment, subject to all of the terms and conditions of the firm's memorandum, entitled "**FEES ON CASES**," which are hereby incorporated by reference, and that the principal signing below hereby accepts that case on behalf of the firm.

_____

John H. Fisher

_____

Attorney

45

THE TWENTY-FOUR-HOUR-A-DAY LAW FIRM

Imagine a day where your law firm operates twenty-four hours a day, even while you sleep. Work gets done while you sleep, and you arrive the next morning with work already done.

When you outsource work, it gets done overnight, and you can go to bed knowing that completed assignments will be in your inbox at 9:00 a.m. You've entered a world where your work gets done by a team of superstars who work long after business hours are over.

Find your own "A" team that will make your law firm tick like clockwork. But to get started, I am listing our team of "A" players—feel free to give them a call.

A Team of Superstars at Your Disposal

Accountability Coach: Joey Bridges, JAB Consulting, joey@marketingfanpages.com, 562-396-5633, Long Beach, California

Big plans mean nothing without accountability. Joey Bridges is an internet marketing expert who kicks my butt every week during our weekly fifteen-minute accountability phone call. My weekly accountability calls with Joey are a great way to toss around new ideas, fix marketing obstacles, and redirect my focus.

Joey helps me set goals, implement, and watch big things happen. And best of all, Joey is ten times smarter than me, and if he doesn't know how to fix a problem, he's connected with experts who can. Our special events (e.g., Mastermind Experience, Jury Project, etc.) would not happen without Joey.

Websites for Lawyers: BluShark Digital, LLC, 1826 Jefferson Pl. NW, Washington, DC 20036 (202-871-1509; blusharkdigital.com)

Since bringing BluShark on-board as our webmaster, our firm's internet presence has changed dramatically. We receive a level of service that is unmatched in the industry. Our account manager contacts us at least weekly with new ideas and content for the website, scholarship projects, links to government and educational websites and ideas for improving our profile on Google My Business.

Every couple of months, I visit BluShark to discuss the status of their link building, content creation and ideas for improving the website. It seems that the team at BluShark is obsessive about our firm's internet presence and truth be told, I couldn't be happier.

Case Expense Funding: Mike Swanson, CEO, Advocate Capital, mswanson@advocatecapital.com, 615-577-5461, Nashville, Tennessee

Ever wonder where all of your money goes? Most of your money doesn't cover overhead or payroll—it's spent on case expenses. What if you had a partner to pay the case expenses for you and pass on the interest expense to your clients?

Advocate Capital has been the perfect partner for our law firm. Our law firm doesn't spend a penny on case expenses, and this frees up cash flow for marketing, special events, and the occasional vacation. Mike Swanson and his team at Advocate Capital are a pleasure to work with and can adjust your line of credit as your cash flow needs change.

Graphic Designer: Julee Hutchison, Hutchison-Frey, juleehutchison@yahoo.com, 970-327-4565, Placerville, Colorado

Where would I be without Julee Hutchison? LOST. Julee creates original and creative designs for our newsletters, direct mail, and special invitations. I don't have to tell Julee what to do—she takes over each project with gusto and turns out amazing work. Consider yourself very lucky if you get a chance to work with Julee.

Julee Hutchison and Michelle Foster are a *phenomenal* team for a monthly print newsletter.

Printing and Fulfillment Provider: Michelle Foster, Help Without Hassle, michelle@helpwithouthassle.com, 620-628-4902, McPherson, Kansas

Through trial and error, I found the best fulfillment provider in the market: Michelle Foster of Help Without Hassle. Michelle Foster handles the printing and fulfillment for our newsletters, direct mail campaigns, and shock and awe packages.

Michelle never misses a deadline, is extremely responsive (e.g., twenty-four-hour turn-around time), and has never said no when we are in a jam.

Infusionsoft Expert/Marketing Implementer: Brett Farr, Blick Digital, brett@blickdigital.com, 480-278-6216, Queen Creek, Arizona

Brett Farr is a master at the implementation of Infusionsoft (now known as Keap) and he is one of a handful of technology and marketing experts whom I trust implicitly. When I was frustrated and ready to terminate Infusionsoft, I was referred to Brett, and he created new campaigns that manage our marketing, intakes, client communication, book sales, and special events.

Structured Settlement Consultant/Financial Advisor: Tim Denehy, tdenehy@advocacywealth.com, 860-239-0094, Forge Consulting, Connecticut

I've worked on structured settlements for injury victims for more than twenty years, and I've yet to find anyone who comes close to Tim Denehy, CFP. Tim will meet with you and your clients to find the best long-term solution that is tailor-made for their needs, and most importantly, he will stay in touch with your clients.

Trial Consultant: Steven P. Shultz, Esq., 2 Ridge View Road, Gansevoort, New York 12831 (518-791-7221)

Steve Shultz, Esq., a plaintiffs' trial lawyer and graduate of Gerry Spence's Trial Lawyers College, generously shares his time and knowledge with plaintiffs' lawyers and will work one-on-one with you. Steve offers unique, outside-the-box solutions for addressing the most challenging part of your case (a.k.a. the "danger point"). By the time you get to trial, you will be prepared for anything.

Business Coaching for Entrepreneurs: Strategic Coach, 10255 W. Higgins Road, #420, Rosemont, Illinois 60018 (800-387-3206; strategiccoach.com)

Strategic Coach is the training ground for entrepreneurs and high achieving business owners. At Strategic Coach, you will learn to focus on your priorities—both personally and professionally—on your Unique Ability, namely, those things that you are passionate about and do better than anyone else. Living the life you want, rather than the one imposed on you by the outside world, is what Strategic Coach is about.

Book Publisher: Advantage Media Group, 18 Broad St. Suite 300, Charleston, South Carolina 29401 (843-414-5600, AdvantageFamily.com)

If you are serious about publishing a book, you won't find a better partner than Advantage Media Group. Not only will Advantage help you publish a book, they will show you everything you need to know about marketing and promoting your book. I wouldn't publish a book with any other book publisher.

Lien Resolution: Precision Resolution, LLC, 4134 Seneca Street, Buffalo, New York 14224 (716-712-0417, PrecisionLienResolution.com)

Negotiating a lien resolution—whether it's Medicare, Medicaid, or an ERISA lien—can be frustrating, time-consuming, and is not the best use of your time. Let the experts do this for you.

I couldn't be happier with the personal attention and results from the lawyers at Precision Resolution.

Lead Intake Management System: Lead Docket, LLC, 341 Chaplin Rd., 2nd Floor, Morgantown, West Virginia 26501 (304-381-1849; LeadDocket.com)

What is the most neglected aspect of running a law firm? Following up and tracking new leads. You have to tackle this problem head-on. Lead Docket provides an intake management system for tracking and following up with new leads. This robust software is a must for any plaintiff's law firm.

Lead Docket provides for tracking of the new leads and their marketing source, automated text messages and emails sent to keep in touch with leads, and real-time customizable data and reports.

You can export the lead details in your case management program and customer relationship software. Lead Docket provides a user-friendly dashboard with the data about new leads, so you know which marketing sources are generating the leads.

Dream Leadership Consulting: Dan Ralphs, CEO/founder, Dream Leadership Consulting, 2019 E. Mia Lane, Gilbert, Arizona 85297 (480-272-2244; DreamLeadershipConsulting.com; dan@thedream-blog.com)

Do you want to start the Dream Manager program for your law firm? You should speak with Dan Ralphs, the founder of Dream Leadership Consulting and one of the world's foremost experts on dreaming. Dan Ralphs was the facilitator of the Dream Manager program at Infusionsoft, where he helped its employees identify, articulate, and accomplish their dreams. Dan Ralphs has an amazing ability to help people discover their own dreams and learn to go after them.

Community Marketing: Anneke Kurt Godlewski, Market Ink, (419-283-5573, anneke@themarketink.com)

Have you considered launching a community marketing program that is inspirational, raises your profile in your community, and gets a lot of free press? There is no one better at community marketing than Anneke Kurt Godlewski, owner of Market Ink.

Anneke sets the standard for innovative community marketing programs, such as Bikes for Kids and Teacher of the Month, and can walk you through the steps for your own program or do it for you. Anneke is generous with her time, creative and wonderful to work with. I love working with Anneke.

Strategic Planning for Lawyers: Michael Smith, SBC & Associates, Inc., 7419 Ascot Court, Bradenton, Florida 34201 (303-472-0101, michael@sbcassociates.com)

Have you ever considered forming or dissolving a partnership? Want to incentivize an associate to bring more cases to your firm? Have you considered creating a strategic plan for the growth of your law firm? If you've answered "yes" to any of these questions, you should speak with Michael Smith.

Michael Smith is the foremost authority on law firm management strategic planning. Michael specializes in helping lawyers and law firms enhance the business side of their practice. Michael will do a comprehensive review of your firm's organizational structure, staffing, staff morale, financial performance, and business focus, including business development, strategic planning, and recruiting, motivating, and retaining staff.

When it comes to strategic planning for lawyers, you won't do better than Michael Smith.

Superstars You Should be Following

Internet Marketing: Neil Patel, an internet marketing guru, gives away his best advice in a weekly email that is subscribed to by tens of thousands. Go to www.NeilPatel.com and sign up for the free weekly email newsletter.

Law Office Management: Lee Rosen, Esq. has ingenious tips for law office management that I haven't seen anywhere else. Go to the website for "Divorce Discourse" and get the free "Rosen's Rules."

Lawyer Podcast: Want to build the law firm of your dreams? There is no better place to start than the "Maximum Lawyer" podcast (MaximumLawyer.com).

The weekly podcast of St. Louis attorneys, Jim Hacking, Esq. and Tyson Mutrux, Esq., features guests and experts in legal marketing and management. The candor and generosity of Jim and Tyson make this podcast one-of-a-kind. I won't miss a single episode.

Part 4
THE TRIAL LAWYER

"Going to court to gain justice for your clients is heroic."

—Susan Saladoff, *Hot Coffee* documentary

Part 4

Trial Preparation

46

HOW TO (ALMOST) GO INSIDE THE JURY DELIBERATION ROOM

You see your case through rose-colored lenses and overlook the warts. But jurors won't be nearly as kind. You're shocked that the jurors' view of the evidence is completely different from your own and you're tempted to write off the defense verdict as the result of a crazy jury.

Here's the problem: you perceive the evidence as a plaintiff's lawyer advocating for an injury victim, but jurors perceive the case from a different perspective. The average juror has no medical or legal background, little education, and while they've answered the subpoena for jury duty, they're anxious to go home. You have two choices: deal with this harsh reality or lose your case.

*"The longer most attorneys practice, the less they
tend to see things the way jurors do."*

—David Ball, PhD, *How to Do Your Own Focus Groups*

It doesn't have to be this way. A focus group provides invaluable insights into the weaknesses of your case, questions that must be answered and even problems with trial exhibits. Based upon the feedback from the focus group, you form a new trial strategy, tackle the weaknesses head-on, and answer the questions that jurors will be asking in the jury deliberation room. For $500, *there is no better investment for a trial lawyer.*

How Focus Groups Change the Way You Prepare for Trial

Just weeks before a trial, I was supremely confident in a medical malpractice case alleging a delay in the diagnosis of cancer. Our medical experts could not have been stronger in their opinions and I was feeling great about our client's chances … until the focus groups began.

At the first focus group, the "jurors" pointed out holes that I never expected. The jurors in the focus group almost unanimously agreed that the plaintiff was at fault for failing to follow medical instructions, despite the overwhelming evidence that the defendant/doctor did not order the appropriate test. We could see for the first time that our client's failure to follow medical advice would almost certainly result in a defense verdict.

"Focus groups are an awesome but underused tool in the trial lawyer's toolbox."

—Phillip H. Miller, Esq. & Paul J. Scoptur, Esq., *Focus Groups: Hitting the Bulls-Eye*

At the second focus group, we presented evidence of the doctor's responsibilities when faced with a patient who is not following their instructions. We showed that the doctor did not follow their protocols for non-compliant patients and made the case that the violation of the protocols places at least some responsibility on the doctor. Again, the jurors in the focus group disagreed.

Owning the Weaknesses of Your Case

We knew we had a serious problem. Rather than denying or ignoring the weakness, we formed a plan to make no excuses during jury selection.

> *Jason is not perfect.* You will hear from the defense that they have excuses for not getting the test done and we want to be fair, some of the defendant's excuses are legitimate.

> *Jason has no excuses.* Jason should have followed the doctor's advice and I'm sure he wishes he had done things differently.

> But is there any other information that you'd like to know?

> If you've made up your mind, that's okay, just tell us.

Safe to say that the defense lawyer has never heard a plaintiff's lawyer admit that the plaintiff made mistakes and has no excuses.

The plaintiff's mea culpa defuses the weakness and puts the focus back on the doctor's responsibility for not following their protocols.

Problem solved? We'll never know because the case settled. But we never would have realized the serious weaknesses facing our client unless we held focus groups. The feedback from the focus groups changed our strategy for jury selection, opening statement, and our preparation of the lay and expert witnesses.

How to Do Your Own Focus Group

Scheduling a focus group is easy. Have your secretary call the local high school or civic organization (e.g., volunteer fire department) and tell them that you need at least twenty people to attend a "jury research project" for two hours. Explain that you will provide a free pizza dinner and a $500 donation, and ask the organization to provide the jurors and physical space. Ideally, the participants will not know each other.

> *"Some attorneys still believe they do not need focus groups. These attorneys are dangerously and mistakenly reliant on their ability to project themselves into the minds of various kinds of laypeople."*
> —David Ball, PhD, *How to Do Your Own Focus Groups*

You will need three forms for the focus group: (a) a confidentiality agreement, (b) a verdict sheet, e.g., "Was the defendant negligent?," and (c) a questionnaire inquiring about the strengths and weaknesses of the case. The confidentiality agreement states that the jurors agree to be videotaped and will not talk to anyone about the case when they leave.

Your questionnaire should be simple and ask no more than three to five questions:

- "If you were writing a headline for a newspaper article about this case, what would the headline say?"

- "After hearing the facts in this case, was there anything missing that you would have liked to hear?"

- "If the judge would allow you to ask questions of the witnesses: What would you want to ask the plaintiff? What would you want to ask the defendant? What would you want to ask the experts?"

For the questionnaires and confidentiality forms, I recommend these excellent books, *How to Do Your Own Focus Groups*, by jury consultant, David Ball, PhD, and *Focus Groups: Hitting the Bull's-Eye*, by Phillip H. Miller, Esq. and Paul J. Scoptur, Esq.

Insights from a Jury You Won't Find Anywhere Else

Bring another lawyer to present the opposing side of the case and act as formally as you would in a courtroom. After each side presents its best arguments to the "jury," have a neutral moderator (a.k.a. the judge) divide the jurors into two or three juries, instruct them on the law and insist that they must reach a unanimous verdict.

> *"If done right, focus group research offers tremendous insights into your case's strengths and weaknesses."*
>
> —**Phillip H. Miller, Esq. & Paul J. Scoptur, Esq.,** *Focus Groups: Hitting the Bulls-Eye*

Watch the jury deliberations (or better yet, video them); explain that the video camera is there because you have to make a record and what they have to say is important. There's a good chance you will be shocked by the arbitrary manner that juries decide cases, but more importantly, you'll get fresh insights into the issues and questions that are critical.

Test Your Exhibits and Witnesses

If you want to test the credibility of your client, do a mock direct and cross examination at the focus group. Test your opening statement and see if the jurors get it. Test your trial exhibits at the focus group. Show your trial exhibits to the jurors and ask:

- Is the timeline misleading or incomplete?

- Does the medical illustration clarify the injuries or is it confusing?

- Is the video reconstruction of the wreck realistic?

Based upon the feedback, you will realize the weaknesses of the trial exhibits and make changes.

Getting Jury Feedback During Trial

You can use "mock jurors" (a.k.a. shadow jurors) during trial to get feedback on the evidence. The shadow jurors are not told who hired them and they act like jurors. When the jury leaves the courtroom, so do the shadow jurors. The shadow jurors do not speak to the lawyers and you should not let them know who you represent. You may limit the shadow juror to key parts of the trial, such as the opening statement or the plaintiff's direct examination.

At the end of the day, the shadow juror is taken to a neutral site for a debriefing about their views of the evidence. If the shadow juror is confused about the evidence, you have the opportunity to go back to court the next day to clarify the issue.

A Challenge for You

Trials are expensive. From the exorbitant fees of expert witnesses, to the costs of trial exhibits and transcripts, and the fees of stenographers and videographers, your costs will be substantial. And then there's the less quantifiable cost of your time, anxiety, and time away from the office in preparing the case for trial.

There's only one question: *Is it worth $500 of your hard-earned money to do a focus group?* Do one focus group and you won't do another trial without one.

47

HOW TO EDUCATE YOUR CLIENTS ABOUT THEIR DEPOSITION AND SOCIAL MEDIA

What are the things you do repeatedly at your law firm? For trial lawyers, we prepare our clients for their depositions, and each time, we do this almost exactly the same way. There's a good chance you've met with clients to prepare them for their deposition hundreds (if not thousands) of times.

What if you educated your clients about the deposition in writing and video before the deposition? Your clients will know what to expect at their deposition, and your pre-deposition meeting will simply reinforce concepts. Your clients will be better prepared and you'll have less work.

We give our clients the form "What to Expect at Your Deposition" at the initial client meeting and again before their deposition.

What to Expect at Your Deposition

We've created this document to help you prepare for your deposition. If you follow these instructions, you will do great at your deposition. If you do not read this document or ignore our instructions, your deposition will not go well. It's up to you.

I will meet with you about one week before your deposition in order to help you prepare so you will know what to expect. We strongly recommend that you read this document repeatedly before I meet with you.

What Is a Deposition?

At your deposition, a defense lawyer will ask questions, under oath, about the claims made in the lawsuit, and the questions and answers will be typed by a court reporter (a.k.a. stenographer). Your deposition will be held in a lawyer's conference room (not in a courthouse). You do not win your case at a deposition—you win your case at trial.

I will be present with you throughout the deposition, along with a court reporter and the defendants' lawyer(s). I will be present with you during the deposition in order to protect your rights, and make sure the defense lawyer does not ask inappropriate questions.

The defense lawyer hopes you speak endlessly and volunteer as much information as possible. When you volunteer information and answer simple questions with lengthy answers, you are helping the defense lawyer.

Our goal is to get you in and out of the deposition as quickly as possible. If you follow these instructions, your deposition will likely be brief (less than three hours). If you ignore these instructions, your deposition could take an entire day (seven hours) or even two to three days.

Questions that Will Be Asked at Your Deposition

Your deposition will cover three main topics: (a) your background, (b) events in dispute, and (c) your injuries/damages.

Your Background: The defense lawyer will begin by asking about your background, namely, where you live and work, your family, your income, etc. The background questions typically last one hour.

Events in Dispute/Medical Treatment: The defense lawyer will ask you about the medical treatment/event in dispute that is the basis for the lawsuit. By way of example, the questions about the medical treatment might include:

Question: When did you arrive at the emergency room?

Question: What were your symptoms when you arrived at the hospital?

Question: What did you tell Dr. Jones about your symptoms?

Question: What did Dr. Jones tell you about your diagnosis?

The questions about the medical treatment/events in dispute typically take two hours.

Injuries & Damages: The defense lawyer will ask about your injuries and loss of income, and these questions typically take one hour.

What to Wear at Your Deposition

You want to dress your best. You should wear conservative clothing that would be appropriate for a job interview or a funeral. Do *not* wear jeans or T-shirts, and if you have earrings (or nose rings), remove them, and cover any tattoos (if possible).

Dress Attire for Men: Men should be clean shaven and wear a dress shirt and pants. There is no need to wear a suit and tie (unless that is how you normally dress for work).

Dress Attire for Women: Women do not have to wear a dress (unless that is what you prefer). At a minimum, women should wear formal dress pants.

If you have any questions or do not have formal attire, call us, and we will help.

Objections by the Attorneys During Your Deposition

Objection to the Form: During the deposition, there will be times that I will object to a question, but instruct you to answer the question, e.g., "Objection to the form of the question, but you may answer." When I "object to the form" of the question, I am objecting to a technical error in the question, but you must still answer.

Instruction Not to Answer: There might be an occasion that I object to a question and give an instruction not to answer the question, e.g., "Objection. Do not answer the question." When I object and instruct you not to answer the question, the defense lawyer asked a highly improper question that is either irrelevant to the issues in the lawsuit or violates a court order or privilege, such as the attorney-client privilege.

Your Rights at the Deposition

Take a Break: You have the right to take a break during the deposition (as long as a question is not pending when you ask for a break). I prefer that you take a break at least once every hour in order to ensure that you are mentally sharp. To take a break, you only need to ask, "May I have a break?"

Speak Privately with Your Lawyer: You have the right to speak privately with me. If you have something that you'd like to discuss with me, or believe that your testimony is inaccurate, you only need to ask, "May I have a break?" You and I can speak privately in a separate room, and the privacy of our conversation will be protected by the attorney-client privilege.

If I ask you, "Would you like to take a break?" you should always answer, "Yes." When I ask whether you want to take a break, I want to speak with you in private.

How to Act at Your Deposition

Make Eye Contact: Sit up in the chair and make eye contact with the defense lawyer.

Do not look up at the ceiling or down at the conference table. The lack of eye contact is a non-verbal sign that you are not telling the truth.

Hands Away from Your Face: Keep your hands away from your face. Ideally, your hands should be on your lap and never go near your mouth, head or face. When you hand is covering your mouth or face, that is a non-verbal sign that you are hiding the truth.

No Small Talk or Jokes: Do not laugh or make small talk with the defense lawyer. The deposition might be the most important thing you do in your lawsuit, so it is important to take it seriously.

How to Answer Questions at Your Deposition

Pause Before Answering: Let the defense lawyer finish the question before you answer, and pause before you answer the question. The court reporter does not record how long it takes for you to answer. By pausing before you answer the question, it gives me time to object to the question, if necessary.

Listen Carefully to the Question: Make sure you understand the question. If you do not understand a question, ask the defense lawyer, "Can you rephrase your question?" or say "I do not understand your question." Never answer a question that you do not understand.

Answer with "Yes" or "No": If you can answer with a "Yes" or "No," that is always the best answer, and the next best answer is "I don't know." Do not volunteer information or answer in more than a single sentence, if possible.

> **Question**: Were you at the hospital when your daughter arrived?
>
> **Answer**: I was working until six that night and had dinner with my husband after work, so I got to the hospital at 8:15 p.m., about an hour after my daughter was admitted.

No, no, no! This question calls for a "yes" or "no," and the witness should have answered this question, "No." The defense lawyer did not ask whether the witness went to dinner with her husband after work or when she arrived at the hospital.

The witness volunteered a lot of information that will lead to more questions and make the deposition longer. You are not helping yourself by volunteering information.

Question: What color was the traffic light when you went through the intersection?

Answer: Well, as I was approaching I could see that it was red. Then it turned to green, and the cars began to move . . . so it was green.

This is wrong—the answer is simply "Green." When you volunteer information that is not a direct response to the question, you are helping the defense attorney.

The BIGGEST Mistake That You Can Make

The most common mistake made at a deposition is GUESSING. When you are not certain of an answer, you should respond, "I don't know" or "I don't remember."

Question: What time did you arrive at the hospital?

Answer: It was *probably* midnight.

The use of "probably" in the answer indicates that you really don't know. Furthermore, "midnight" is a precise time, and if you are not absolutely certain of the time, you should not testify as to a specific time. Remember, *if you don't know, don't guess.*

The medical records indicate the time that the patient arrived at the hospital, so there is no need to guess. When you are unsure of the answer, it is better to testify, "I am not sure" or give an estimate, such as: "I estimate sometime between approximately 11:00 p.m. and 1:00 a.m."

What Documents to Review to Prepare for Your Deposition

You should only review ONE document for your deposition: the plaintiff's Bill of Particulars. The Bill of Particulars will be provided to you before the deposition for your review.

Question: Did you review any documents to prepare for this deposition?

Answer: Yes.

Question: What documents did you review?

Answer: The Bill of Particulars.

Question: Did you review any other documents?

Answer: No.

It is important for you to review the Bill of Particulars, as it might refresh your memory and you may notice inaccuracies in the list of your injuries or dates of medical treatment. Do *not* review any other documents to prepare for your deposition.

Most Common Questions at a Deposition

At almost every deposition, you can expect the defense lawyer to ask the following questions:

- Did you keep a journal or diary about your medical care?

- Did you review any documents in preparation for the deposition?

- Have you ever been convicted of a crime?

- Have you ever filed for bankruptcy?

- Have you spoken with anyone about your deposition, other than your lawyer?

- Was any doctor critical of the care provided by Dr. Smith?

If you prepared a journal or diary or have been convicted of a crime or filed a bankruptcy petition, please make sure you tell me at our meeting before the deposition.

Confirm that You Will Follow Our Instructions

To confirm that you've read this document, please sign where indicated and initial the lower right corner of every page. I will do the same.

Please bring the signed agreement to our pre-deposition meeting and review it as frequently as you can.

Dated:

_____

Client

_____

John H. Fisher

* * *

How to Avoid Social Media Landmines

Just days away from a huge trial, you're scrambling to prepare for trial and you're convinced that you're on the verge of winning the biggest trial of your career. Then your case implodes. Your trusty paralegal brings up social media posts of your client selling their services as a prostitute. The social media posts are worse than you could ever imagine, and there's no question that defense lawyers can't wait to use the social media posts against your client.

You didn't do your homework, and now you're faced with the consequences of losing your case based on damaging social media posts. You can try to blame your client, but you've got no one to blame but yourself. At least you've learned one lesson: this will never happen again.

Searching for Social Media Landmines

As soon as you are retained, conduct a thorough search of your clients' social media pages. This includes not only a review of your clients' social media pages, but also the public pages of their spouse and friends. Run a social media search of your clients' families and friends, adversaries, and witnesses in every case.

Advise your client about their use of social media and how it can impact their case. Sit at the computer with your client and review the public portions of their social media pages and those of people close to them. The date on which a photograph is taken and the date on which it is posted may be, and often are, different. Clients may post, or repost, old pictures to their page.

Warning Your Clients About the Dangers of Social Media

Advise your client that the internet is forever—nothing is forever deleted. Photographs that have been removed from your clients' page may remain on the public social media pages of friends and family if they were shared. Postings of comments or photographs become part of the permanent record on the internet. To the extent that a post is taken down or deleted, the post still exists.

Have your clients review and sign a document setting forth your advice and rules for social media as soon as you are retained. The following are our rules for social media:

Our Rules for Social Media

Social media posts, photographs, and video can be full of damaging information that the defense lawyers will use against you. As soon as you file your lawsuit, the defense lawyers will be searching through your social media profiles (e.g., Facebook, Twitter, Instagram, etc.) for damaging information about you. Additionally, defense lawyers will be searching the social media profiles of your family, coworkers, and friends.

We strongly recommend that you take the following three steps to prevent the unwanted disclosure of damaging information from your social media profiles:

1.   Set the highest levels of security and privacy to all of your social media sites so that nothing can be viewed by the general public.

2.   Stop posting any photographs, video, or other information on social media until the case has resolved.

3.   When in doubt, remove or take down photographs or postings from social media sites.

All social media content, even if set to private, may become subject to a court order and eventually have to be produced.

Any postings or photographs that are removed should be printed and preserved before they are removed. Even when you delete or remove posts from your social media profile, they will still exist on the timelines of your friends and followers, and you should not assume that your social media posts are unavailable to the defense lawyers.

If you need help following our rules for social media, please call us.

Please sign our rules for social media, where indicated, to acknowledge that you read, understand and will follow our rules for social media.

Dated:

_____

Client

48

HOW TO PREPARE YOUR CLIENT FOR TRIAL

Your clients have no idea what to expect at trial. A trial can be very intimidating and scary for your clients, and many will ask you to settle to avoid a trial. This creates a problem—the defendants' settlement offer is either non-existent or is low and you don't want to settle for a fraction of the case's true value. What do you do?

Explain the process of a trial and gradually ease your clients' fear and anxiety. Show your clients exactly what to expect and what they can do to prepare. A little at a time, your clients will see that a trial is not that bad and with preparation and hard work, they might win.

This is the form,"Our Best Advice for Winning Your Trial," that we use to prepare our clients. Our clients must review and sign this agreement. The education process begins on day one and continues during preparation for their deposition and at the pre-trial meetings.

Our Best Advice for Winning Your Trial

Ms. Jones:

Thank you for the opportunity to represent you at trial.

To help you prepare for your day in court, we offer our best advice for winning your trial. Preparation is everything. We cannot win your trial without your help. If you take the time to prepare for trial, you will have a much better chance.

What to Wear in Court

Wear conservative clothes that you would wear to a funeral. Do not wear sneakers, jeans, or t-shirts, and if you have tattoos, cover them.

Men: Wear dress pants (no jeans), black shoes, and a collared white or blue shirt. It is not necessary to wear a suit and tie. If you have a nose or ear ring, remove them.

Women: Wear a dress pant suit or a dress. Do not wear high heels or an elegant gown. Your clothing should be conservative, but not over-the-top. If you do not have the appropriate clothing, call us and we will make arrangements for you.

Length of the Trial

On average, medical malpractice trials last two weeks.

Court begins at 9:00 a.m. and usually ends at 4:30 p.m. with a one-hour lunch break. You should always arrive early for court. It is never acceptable to arrive late to court, as this is disrespectful to the judge and jury.

How to Behave in Court

Stand for the Judge and Jury: When the judge and jury enter the courtroom, you should always stand and remain standing until they sit. Standing is a sign of respect.

The Jurors are ALWAYS Watching You: The jurors watch everything you do—inside and outside the courtroom. When you are entering the courthouse or walking to lunch, the jurors are watching you and forming opinions of you.

No Goofing Off: Do not goof off, smile, or even act casual inside or around the courthouse. The jurors will think you're not taking the case seriously.

Do NOT Smoke: *Do not smoke outside the courthouse.* If you smoke, the jurors will think that you don't care about your health.

Bring Family and Friends to the Trial

Family members and friends can sit in the spectator gallery in the back of the courtroom. The presence of family and friends is much better than an empty courtroom. The presence of family and friends in the courtroom is important, as it shows the jurors that the outcome of the trial is important to a lot of people.

How to Prepare for Your Testimony

Study your deposition transcript as often as you can. Have a friend/spouse read the questions in the deposition transcript to you and ask them to make sure that the responses that you give are consistent with your deposition testimony.

If there is even a slight inconsistency between your deposition testimony and trial testimony, the defense attorney will accuse you of lying during cross-examination.

How to Testify at Trial

Three Rules for Your Testimony: When you testify, follow these three rules:

- Make eye contact with the jurors.

- Do not look at the floor or ceiling or away from the jurors.

- Keep your hands away from your face and do not fold your arms.

Eye contact is a sign of honesty. You should always have constant eye contact with at least one juror during your testimony. When you look down, up or to the side, this will be perceived by the jurors that you are either lying or being evasive.

When you cover your face with your hands or fold your arms, this is a sign that you are hiding something or taking a defensive posture. Keep your hands on your lap.

Be Yourself: Don't be afraid to smile or tell a small joke during your testimony. This will create a bond with the jurors.

No Whining: Jurors do not like whiners. Do NOT complain about your injuries or losses during your testimony; it is far better to testify about mini-stories that show the things you have done to overcome your disability.

Avoid Drama: Do not be overly dramatic when you testify. Crying and emotion is okay, but only if it is real. Jurors do not like phony displays of emotion.

Tell Stories: Think of sixty-second stories that illustrate how you've overcome your injuries and losses. Jurors LOVE STORIES during your testimony.

Jurors love *positive* stories. For example, testimony from an injury victim that he discovered that his fiancé truly loved him through the care that she provided during his rehabilitation.

Don't Fight with the Defense Lawyer: During cross-examination, do not argue with defense counsel—you'll never win. If you make a mistake, admit the mistake and make no excuses. Do not grimace or scowl at the defendants or defendants' counsel.

Beginning of the Trial: Jury Selection

The first day of the trial is jury selection. During jury selection, the attorneys ask questions of eight prospective jurors who are randomly selected among the forty to sixty prospective jurors seated in the spectator gallery in the courtroom.

Jury selection begins by the plaintiff's lawyer asking questions of the prospective eight jurors and when finished, the defense lawyers question them. The lawyers ask the prospective jurors about their family and employment background, experience with medical malpractice, and their familiarity with the injuries and medical issues that are relevant in the lawsuit.

By the end of the first day, we have usually completed jury selection and accepted eight jurors. The trial begins the next day with the opening statements and the presentation of your witnesses, e.g., doctors, expert witnesses, coworkers, etc.

Challenge for Cause: The goal of jury selection is to identify prospective jurors who have a bias in favor of the defense (e.g., *"My daughter is a doctor"* or *"I hate people who sue"*) and remove them from the jury. For those prospective jurors who have expressed a bias in favor of the defendant, they can be excused from jury service with a "challenge for cause."

A challenge for cause is made outside of the presence of the prospective jurors and the judge will make a decision to accept or reject the challenge for cause. Occasionally, the attorneys agree that certain prospective jurors are so biased or unable to serve that they will not be acceptable jurors and agree to excuse them by stipulation.

Peremptory Challenge: After the attorneys question the prospective jurors, you have the right to excuse up to four of the prospective jurors (known as a "peremptory challenge"). You can excuse a prospective juror *without giving any reason* with a peremptory challenge.

A peremptory challenge is made by the lawyers outside of the presence of the prospective jurors. Before exercising a peremptory challenge, we will ask you if you have a strong feeling against any of the prospective jurors. Your intuition and gut instincts are usually right and we will excuse the prospective juror(s) that you don't want to serve on the jury. We always try to save at least one peremptory challenge.

Alternate Jurors: Two of the jurors will be selected by the Court as "alternate jurors." Occasionally, jurors are excused from jury service during the trial due to health reasons or unexpected emergencies. The alternate jurors serve as substitutes for the other jurors, when that occurs.

First Week of Trial: The Plaintiff's Case in Chief

During the first week of the trial, we will present the testimony of our witnesses (a.k.a. "plantiff's case in chief"). These witnesses consist of a combination of medical witnesses and lay witnesses, such as your coworkers, family, and friends. By the end of the first week, our case in chief is usually completed and we rest our case.

Second Week of Trial: The Defendants' Case in Chief

Usually, the defendants must present the testimony of their witnesses during the second week of trial. This consists of the defendant and their expert witnesses.

Once the defendants are finished presenting the testimony of their witnesses, the judge will excuse the two alternate jurors, and give instructions on the law to the remaining six jurors jury (a.k.a. the "jury charge").

Following the instructions on the law, the jury will then be sent to the jury deliberation room to begin their deliberations and answer the questions on the verdict sheet.

The Verdict

The verdict of the jury does not have to be unanimous—five out of six jurors must agree on the questions on the verdict sheet.

The first two questions on the verdict sheet ask whether the defendant was negligent and if so, whether the negligence was a substantial factor in causing the injuries/losses.

Was the defendant, James Smith, MD, negligent?

___ YES ___ NO

Was the negligence of defendant, James Smith, MD, a substantial factor in causing the injury of the plaintiff?

___ YES ___ NO

Once the jury agrees upon an answer to the questions on the verdict sheet, the foreperson of the jury informs the judge that the jury has reached a verdict. The judge asks the jury to enter the courtroom and announce the answers to the questions on the verdict sheet. This announcement of the jury's verdict concludes the trial.

What You Should Know about Expenses

Trials are very expensive. A medical malpractice trial is a battle of the experts. To give you the best chance of winning, we only hire the best expert witnesses, but they aren't cheap. Each expert's fee for their time in court will typically range from $5,000 to $15,000 and that does not include their fee for preparing for trial.

You have the right to request a list of costs (a.k.a. disbursements) at any time. The disbursement list contains each expense incurred in your case, the date of the expense and the amount of the expense; you even have the right to view each invoice. If you have any questions, we will be happy to meet with you to explain why each cost was incurred.

Our Advice for Easing Your Anxiety

Everyone experiences stress and anxiety during trial. This is perfectly normal and we would be concerned if you weren't having any stress at the time of the trial. If you are feeling stressed out, we can help you.

There are things we can do to help you, including (if necessary) informing the jury during jury selection that you may not be present for the entire trial. Rest assured, we can handle most of the trial without your presence in court, if necessary.

Why We Practice Law

Thank you for joining us in this quest to stop medical injustice. Your lawsuit will help improve the quality of medical care and hopefully avoid the same thing from happening to other patients. We take this responsibility seriously and we are grateful for this opportunity.

But we cannot win your trial without your help and cooperation. We encourage you to keep this document, read it often, and let us know if you have any questions. We are confident that, *with your help*, we can win your trial as part of a team effort.

Read and Sign this Agreement

Please sign this agreement where indicated, in duplicate, keep one original for yourself and provide an original to John H. Fisher, PC, 278 Wall Street, Kingston, New York 12401. This document is protected by the attorney-client privilege and is intended only for you. Please do not share this document with anyone.

Dated:

_____

Client

Part 4

Jury Selection, Trial Skills & Negotiation

49

THE SECRETS TO A POWERFUL JURY SELECTION

Many trial lawyers (and even some judges) are unfamiliar with the law of jury selection. Judges and lawyers think they know what they are doing, but don't take the time to become familiar with their procedural rights for jury selection.

This will give you the law of jury selection for your next trial in New York.

How to Fight for More Time in Jury Selection

Trial judges have discretion to determine the length of time given for jury selection. However, there are constraints to the time limits that can be imposed by a trial judge. At the last pre-trial conference, make sure you ask whether the trial judge will impose time limits for jury selection.

If the trial judge has a time limit for jury selection, gently remind them that the courts must grant the parties "a reasonable time period" for jury selection. If the trial judge tells you that you've got twenty minutes for the next round of jury selection, give the trial judge a memo of law that recites the law of jury selection. The trial judge will know that you know the law, and there are constraints to what they can impose for time limits.

The Best Case in Your Arsenal

The leading case in New York is *Zgrodek v. McInerney*,[1] where the trial judge only allowed fifteen minutes per round of questioning during jury selection. In *Zgrodek*, the Appellate Division, Third Department, set aside the verdict of the lower court and found that the court's allowance of only fifteen minutes per round of voir dire was inadequate as a matter of law.

Citing a publication on voir dire on the court's website, the court in *Zgrodek* stated that "**a reasonable time period to report on the progress of voir dire is after about two or three hours of actual voir dire.**" The court declared that "[w]hile the trial court is accorded discretion in setting time limits for voir dire, the fifteen minutes per round allowed here was insufficient, mandating a new trial for all damages issues."

The court in *Zgrodek* held that:

> "We find merit in plaintiffs' argument that Supreme
> Court placed **unduly restrictive time constraints** on the
> questioning of prospective jurors ... the fifteen minutes

---

1   *Zgrodek v. McInerney*, 61 A.D.3d 1106, 876 N.Y.S.2d 227 (3rd Dep't 2009).

allowed for each round under the circumstances of this case was unreasonably short."

Citing "Implementing New York's Civil Voir Dire Law and Rules,"[2] page six states that "**[i]n a routine case a reasonable time period to report on the progress of voir dire is after about two or three hours of actual voir dire**."

"We cannot conclude from this record that plaintiffs were not prejudiced by the extremely short time permitted for voir dire."[3]

The court in *Zgrodek* referred to the "extremely short time permitted for voir dire" as an "error in voir dire" and ordered a new trial on all issues.[4]

Fighting Back When Pressed for Time

The court's dicta in *Zgrodek* is valuable when you're confronted with a trial judge attempting to impose time limits on jury selection. This Third Department case is controlling law throughout New York, since there are no inconsistent decisions in other departments.

Significantly, the "two or three hours" is not the time limit for completing voir dire, but rather the reasonable time period to "report on the progress of voir dire." By implication, the time period to complete jury selection should be longer than the "two or three hours of actual voir dire."

---

2   Ann Pfau, "Implementing New York's Civil Voir Dire Law and Rules," New York State Unified Court System, January 2009, http://www.nycourts.gov/publications/pdfs/ImplementingVoirDire2009.pdf.

3   *Zgrodek v. McInerney*, 61 A.D.3d 1106, 876 N.Y.S.2d at 228.

4   *Zgrodek v. McInerney*, 61 A.D.3d 1106, 876 N.Y.S.2d at 229.

If the judge tries to limit your time for jury selection, remind them that the two- to three-hour period refers to actual voir dire and should not include the time spent meeting with the judge, waiting for jury selection to begin, or lunch or bathroom breaks.

Have your paralegal keep track of the time you spend in "actual voir dire," and remind the judge that you only spent fifty-two minutes in actual voir dire, even though you are still in the first round of jury selection in the early afternoon.

Your Last Resort ... Just in Case

If the trial judge is not convinced, gently remind them that the court in *Zgrodek* overturned a jury verdict based on the inadequacy of time allowed for jury selection. When confronted with the law and a strong memo of law, the trial judge will be hard-pressed to cut short your questioning during jury selection.

But if the trial judge still disagrees, *make a record*. Kingston, NY injury lawyer, John G. Rusk, Esq., did an excellent job of making a record regarding the inadequacy of time allowed for jury selection in *Zgrodek*.

How to Remove Pro-Defense Jurors for Cause During Jury Selection

During jury selection, the pro-defendant juror admits that he socializes and has dinner with the defendant. However, when questioned by the trial judge, the juror solemnly swears he can be "fair and impartial." The trial judge nods their head and denies your challenge for cause.

During jury selection, trial judges ask prospective jurors whether they can be "fair and impartial," listen to the evidence and set aside their preconceived biases in favor of the defendant (or against the plaintiff). But should the litmus test be whether the prospective jurors can be fair and impartial?

The Statutory Litmus Test for an Acceptable Juror

Under New York's CPLR section 4105, entitled, "Persons who constitute jury," the jury should consist of "The first six persons who appear as their names are drawn and called, and are approved as *indifferent between the parties* ..."

The critical question for a prospective juror is not, "Can you be fair and impartial?" or "Can you set aside your feelings and base your verdict only on the evidence?" If a juror admits that they are leaning toward the defense, they are not "indifferent between the parties," as required by CPLR section 4105, and should be excused by a challenge for cause.

Eliminating Bad Jurors with Four Questions

First, get the pro-defendant juror to admit that they have a leaning or prejudgment in favor of the defendant with a closed-end question:

- "It's fair to say you have a leaning in favor of the defendant, is that right?"

Nod your head as you ask this question. Jurors will mimic your nonverbal communication—if you nod your head, they will too (just as they will smile when you smile at them). Once the pro-defendant juror admits to a leaning or prejudgment, you have to reinforce the strength of their conviction with three questions:

- "It's fair to say you've held these convictions for a long time and they're not likely to change over the course of this trial, is that right?"

- "No matter what the defense lawyer tells you, your convictions aren't likely to change, fair to say?"

- "When you hear the witnesses and listen to the instructions of the law from the judge, you'll still have this strong conviction, is that what I'm hearing you say?"

With three questions, you destroyed the questions that will be posed by the defense lawyer and trial judge to rehabilitate the prospective juror. This pro-defense witness has strongly held convictions in favor of the defense that won't change, even after they hear the evidence and instructions of law. The trial judge has to remove this pro-defense juror for cause.

Never use the words "bias" or "fair and impartial" during jury selection. Few prospective jurors will admit to being biased or unwilling to set aside their convictions to be "fair and impartial"—it makes them sound as if they are not fair-minded.

The Ace Up Your Sleeve

Let's say the trial judge is still hemming and hawing even after you confirm the prospective juror's leaning and prejudgment and isn't quite sure whether the pro-defendant juror should be removed for cause during jury selection. Remind the trial judge that "indifferent between the parties" defines when a prospective juror should be removed for cause. And remind the judge that the prospective juror admitted that

- they have a strongly held leaning or prejudgment in favor of the defense,

- the leaning or prejudgment is a strongly held conviction that is not likely to change over the course of the trial, and

- even after hearing the witnesses and listening to the court's instructions of the law, they will still have this strongly held leaning or prejudgment.

If the trial judge refuses to grant your challenge for cause, *make a record*. Ask for a court reporter, and state on the record that the prospective juror admitted to a leaning or prejudgment in favor of the defense and that this bias is unlikely to change during the course of the trial. Then state on the record that the prospective juror does not meet the statutory criteria for an acceptable juror, pursuant CPLR section 4105.

Building Your Tribe During Jury Selection

Jury selection can be an anxious time for prospective jurors and lawyers alike. Your job, as the plaintiffs' lawyer, is simple: you want to bond with the prospective jurors. That won't happen by spitting out the questions on your legal pad and getting generic responses.

You build empathy through active listening—a process of listening, processing the response and responding without another single thought in your mind. Easy? No. But who said there's anything easy about being a trial lawyer?

Here are a few tips for active listening during jury selection:

Mirroring: Mirroring is essentially imitation. A "mirror" is when you repeat the last three words of what someone has said (or the critical one to three words). You are reinforcing that you listened to the juror and you are building rapport.

Try this—smile at a juror and they will smile back. It's a natural reflex to respond in kind with the same facial expression.

Talk Slowly: Talk slowly and convey one idea. This sends a message that you're in control. Talking too fast is a common mistake made by trial lawyers.

> *"Your most valuable tool in any verbal communication is your voice."*
> —Chris Voss, *Never Split the Difference*

Radiate Warmth: Smile! When you radiate warmth and acceptance, conversations seem to flow. Keep an open posture, e.g., hands out of your pockets and by your side. Do not put your hands on your face or cross your arms.

Focus on One Thing: Do not think about what you are going to say next. Focus only on one thing, what the juror is saying. Nod your head in agreement.

> *"Make your sole and all-encompassing focus the other person and what they have to say."*
> —Chris Voss, *Never Split the Difference*

Active Listening: Your goal is to extract and observe as much information as possible. You will never change a juror's mind, so don't bother trying.

> *"Listening is not a passive activity. It is the most critical thing you can do."*
> —Chris Voss, *Never Split the Difference*

Active listening shows that you care. If you are thinking of anything other than what the juror is saying, you're not listening.

Silence: Silence is powerful. Whenever you pause, you emphasize the words that were spoken. Pause and be completely silent whenever you want to emphasize a point.

Getting More from Jurors: When a prospective juror is done answering a question, say:

- "And ... ?

- What else ... ?

- "Uh huh ..." (while nodding your head)

- "Anything else?"

Each goes another level deeper and gets more information.

Study the Law of Jury Selection

In addition to the statutory grounds for the disqualification of prospective jurors, the case law provides additional grounds. For example, it is an abuse of discretion to deny a challenge for cause where a juror has personal and professional relationships with a witness expected to testify at trial.[5] Be ready with the case law when you're confronted with defense lawyers who are unfamiliar with the law.

Why Your Clients Should Waive Their Right to a Jury Trial

Plaintiffs' lawyers ask for jury trials without any strategic thought, and since it seems everyone does it this way, why should you be different?

---

5   *People v. Furey*, 18 N.Y.3d 284, 938 N.Y.S.2d 277 (2011).

Juries are impossible to predict. Even when you're convinced the jurors are on your side and paying close attention to each witness, you're rolling the dice. Juries can be unpredictable, capricious, and arbitrary, and many prospective jurors arrive to the courtroom with preconceived biases that injury lawsuits are frivolous.

Bench trials are different. Judges tend to be fair, logical, and much more predictable than juries, and you'll face fewer courtroom theatrics from defense counsel in bench trials. Judges can tell a good case from a bad one, and isn't that what you want?

Getting Permission to Waive Your Clients' Right to a Jury Trial

We recommend that our clients waive their right to a jury trial. But you have to make sure you receive your clients' permission to waive their right to a jury trial.

Here is our waiver form:

Your Right to a Jury Trial

After depositions are completed, we will request a trial date, and at that time, you have the right to select a trial by jury or a non-jury trial (also known as a "bench trial"). It is your constitutional right to a jury trial, and we want to make sure you have all of the information that you need to make this decision.

We will explain both options (e.g., jury or non-jury trial) and make our recommendation. However, we are only making a recommendation, and you have complete authority to make the choice that you feel is best.

What is a Trial by Jury?

A jury consists of eight people who are randomly selected to listen to the witnesses and evidence and decide which witnesses and evidence are worthy of belief. At the end of the trial, two of the jurors are excused (known as "alternate jurors") and six of the jurors are sent to the deliberation room to decide upon a verdict.

Once they complete their deliberations, the jurors will render a verdict that determines whether you win or lose your trial. Five of the six jurors must agree upon the verdict.

What is a Non-Jury Trial?

You can waive your right to a jury trial. When all of the parties (e.g., plaintiffs and defendants) waive their right to a jury trial, the facts and evidence will be heard by a judge—this is known as a "bench trial."

During a bench trial, there is no jury, and the judge is the sole finder of fact regarding the credibility of the witnesses and evidence. Instead of six jurors reaching a verdict, there is only one person, the judge, who will render the final decision.

Differences between a Jury Trial and Non-Jury Trial

Juries can be very unpredictable. Even when the facts appear strongly in your favor, juries may disregard the evidence and base their verdict upon facts that are irrelevant.

Juries tend to have biases against personal injury victims due to publicity that inaccurately portrays our civil justice system (e.g., the McDonald's spilled coffee case). Many of the prospective jurors have pre-conceived notions that malpractice lawsuits are frivolous. For these reasons, you may begin the trial with the odds strongly favoring the defense.

On the other hand, judges tend to be rational, logical, and much more predictable than juries. Most judges have presided over many trials during their career, and as a result, they tend to be good at assessing the merit of a case. Judges rarely have the preconceived biases and prejudices against malpractice and personal injury law that jurors often have.

Overall, non-jury trials tend to have fewer courtroom theatrics from defense counsel and result in more rational and predictable outcomes.

Our Recommendation

We believe that non-jury trials are better for your case. For this reason, we recommend that our clients waive the right to a jury trial. Of course, if you want a jury trial, we will respect your decision.

Even when you waive your right to a jury trial, the defense also has the right to a jury trial. It is very likely that the defendants will serve a "demand for a jury trial" within fifteen days of a waiver of your right to a jury trial, and if they request a jury, you will have a jury trial.

Your Decision

Please confirm your choice for a jury or non-jury trial by placing a checkmark next to the appropriate box below, sign and date below your decision, and return this acknowledgment to John H. Fisher, PC, 278 Wall Street, Kingston, New York 12401. Thank you for the opportunity to represent you.

I want a jury trial: ____

I want a non-jury trial: ____

Dated:

_____

Client

How to Educate the Jury about the Burden of Proof before the Trial

For jurors, the burden of proof in a civil action is a mystery. The vast majority of jurors have no idea what the civil burden of proof is, as they are only familiar with the criminal standard (e.g., beyond a reasonable doubt). And by the time the jurors reach the end of the trial, they've filtered through the evidence applying the criminal standard.

Prior to trial, you should send a letter to the court requesting a pre-trial instruction regarding the burden of proof. At the first pre-trial conference, remind the judge of your request, and if the judge is reluctant, you might tactfully remind them that the deputy chief administrative judge of the state of New York for courts outside of New York City always gives a pre-trial instruction regarding the burden of proof, *even if it is not requested by the parties.*

Here's the letter we use when requesting a pre-trial instruction regarding the burden of proof:

Dear Justice Smith:

We respectfully request a pre-trial jury instruction concerning the burden of proof (New York Pattern Jury Instruction 1:23) in the above-referenced action. This letter sets forth the basis for our request.

Most jurors' experience with the law is criminal and its higher burden of proof. As a result, many jurors will see and hear the evidence while applying a burden of proof that does not apply. Many prospective jurors do not know that they will be asked to decide negligence, causation, and damages based on the civil standards for those issues, namely, preponderance of the evidence.

"Most jurors walk into the courtroom thinking the bar for proving medical negligence is higher than it is."

—Jeffrey D. Boyd, Esq., "What's on Jurors' Minds?" May, 2017, *TRIAL*

By the end of the trial, the jurors have heard and seen the evidence *without knowing what the burden of proof is*. Jurors should not sit through a week(s) of trial before they hear—straight from the judge—the correct burden of proof.

Hon. Michael V. Coccoma, Deputy Chief Administrative Judge for courts outside New York City, gives a pre-trial jury instruction regarding the burden of proof in all of his civil trials, even if the charge is not requested by the parties.

While there is no disadvantage to any of the parties by informing the jury of the burden of proof prior to the trial, the failure to give such a charge can be very harmful to the plaintiff.

For these reasons, we respectfully request that the court instruct the jury as to the burden of proof before the trial begins.

Respectfully yours,

John H. Fisher

50

HOW TO WIN YOUR NEXT TRIAL

Many trial lawyers pray for a settlement, but you're not a "settlement lawyer"—you're a trial lawyer. Trials are what you do for a living, and you're proud of it. And settling for a fraction of your case's true value is wrong.

"Politicians should know this: there's no law they can pass to stop trial attorneys from trying cases and working hard for their clients."
—Mike Campbell, Esq., Columbia, Missouri

So, you don't even think of a settlement. You focus on presenting the best possible trial you can, and get ready for trial. But it's easy to get distracted by other "stuff"—an occasional dinner with your spouse and kids, and your other clients.

Streamline your Trial with Five Witnesses or Fewer

There is one basic rule that trumps all others for plaintiffs' lawyers: *the longer the trial takes, the worse it will be for your client.* Jurors have lives too, and they don't want to be sitting around in court.

Your goal is to streamline your case. Begin by avoiding witnesses who are not essential to your case. Even in the most complex cases, if you can't try your case with five witnesses or fewer, you're not streamlining your case, and it's virtually guaranteed that you'll bore the wits out of the jurors (and lose the trial).

Make a game out of paring down the number of witnesses. Your client must testify, and you'll need a treating physician and, in most cases, an economist. If you're thinking about adding some fluff witnesses, just think: *Do you really need them?* If not, get rid of them—jurors hate redundant trial testimony, and ultimately, your client will pay the price.

Get to the Point as Quick as Possible

Keep trial testimony short. The attention span of the average juror is ten seconds—that means you have seconds to get to the point. Forget about the witness's hobbies—determine the two or three points you need to make with the witness, and get right to it.

If your client rambles during their testimony, you have to rein them in. You have to cut off your client during their testimony and keep them on point. Even if you have to be rude with the witness, you have to keep the testimony brief and on point.

The best trial testimony of expert witnesses often takes thirty minutes. What's better than watching a trial lawyer and an expert who know exactly what they're doing? You're showing the jury that you respect their time.

Whatever you do, *never overstate your case.* If your client has medical or psychological conditions that are unrelated to his injury, admit to the jury that, "We're not claiming Joe's memory problems were in any way caused by the crash."

Your Twelve-Week Plan for Trial

Twelve weeks before trial, you should map out a week-by-week plan of things that need to get done to prepare for trial. Sit down with your paralegal and secretary, and set up a plan for what each person must do:

- Serve motion in limine re: client's criminal convictions.

- Edit video depositions of defense employees for trial presentation.

- Conduct a focus group on comparative fault issue.

- Meet with trial consultant.

- Serve proposed jury charge, statement of contentions, and verdict sheet for the submissions to the court.

You review the "twelve-week plan" every week with your staff to make sure everyone's doing what they're supposed to do. Adjust and make changes to the twelve-week plan as necessary, but don't let your other cases get in the way of your trial preparation. With one week before trial, you and your team will be ready for trial.

The exhibits should be pre-marked by the court reporter, admitted into evidence by stipulation with defense counsel, and offered into evidence before your trial begins.

Show Me, Don't Tell Me

Jurors remember little of what they hear and a lot more of what they see.

> *"I hear and I forget. I see and I remember."*
>
> **—Confucius**

Medical illustrations and time-lines are scratching the surface of "show me, don't tell me." Have your client's personal aide show you how they bathe and toilet your disabled client—yes, have them bring the toilet and do a mini-show-and-tell. Now the jurors are getting an inside view to your client's everyday problems.

Most trial lawyers forget the jury after opening statements. You want to include the jurors in every part of the trial and look at the jurors when you cross-examine defense witnesses. Jurors will love you for making them a part of the trial, and they will reward you with eye contact, nods of their heads, and just maybe they won't nod off.

Don't be the Biggest Jerk in the Courtroom

If the defense expert is a humble, mild-mannered octogenarian, you should return the witness's humble, mild disposition with a soft cross-examination. The jurors will hate you for bullying a nice, elderly man, and you never want to come across as a bully with lay witnesses.

Don't object unless you absolutely have to. Jurors think you are hiding something with objections and wonder why they're not allowed to hear all of the evidence. Focus on one day at time, and when you're tired after a long day in court, go to bed. You're useless to your client if you're a zombie in court.

51

A NIGHTMARE ON ELK STREET

If I could have crawled under the counsel's table or magically disappeared, I would have. Unfortunately, neither was an option.

My star expert witness is doing his best to answer questions about his notes and emails during cross-examination. The defense lawyer asks about each note in painfully slow fashion. Mr. Defense Lawyer asks the star expert whether he asked the plaintiff's lawyer (me) the following questions:

- "Should I wink at the jury?"

- "Is it alright to smile at the jurors?"

- "Will you give me cues [prompts] during my testimony?"

- "Remind me, what is this case about?"

- "What do you want me to say?"

Yes, almost tragically, these were statements contained in the handwritten notes of our star expert witness. With each question, the pain became immeasurably worse and it quickly became obvious that the expert was clueless ... and the trial would be lost.

Never Sanitize Your Expert's File

Many defense lawyers (and some plaintiffs' lawyers) sanitize their experts' files before trial. The lawyers scour the expert's file and when they find a note or email that could be damaging to the case, they remove it from the file. When asked whether they brought their entire file, the expert is instructed to answer, "Yes." Make no mistake, the expert is committing perjury.

I always tell expert witnesses that they should NEVER remove anything from their file. All emails, handwritten notes, invoices, and correspondence must be retained in the file and at the time of trial, they will be disclosed to the defense lawyer. Regardless of what others do, this is the right thing.

Three Simple Steps for Avoiding Catastrophe

Truth be told, the expert is not to blame for the Nightmare on Elk Street. I am the only one to blame because I didn't prepare the witness and do my homework. This nightmare would not have happened had I followed these three simple steps.

#1: Warn Your Expert from Day One

Here's the problem: *your experts don't know what you know*—specifically, that every note, email, and letter will be prime material for cross-examination at the time of trial. You must warn your expert of this in the initial retainer letter and repeat the warnings verbally throughout the case.

The initial retainer letter to the expert witness should have a warning about handwritten notes, emails, and reports:

> You are not required to prepare a written report, or summaries of your opinions in notes or emails. We do not want you to prepare a written report, notes or emails of your opinions.

> Your handwritten and electronic notes must be disclosed to the defense counsel at the time of trial and any written notes/reports or emails will be the subject of cross-examination at trial. The defense counsel will attempt to use your notes and emails to challenge your character, integrity, and opinions.

With this letter, your expert is on notice of the possible dangers of note-keeping. But your expert may not even read your letter and even if they do, it will be long forgotten by the time of trial. One written warning is not enough.

#2: Review Every Note and Email

You have to sit down with your expert and review every single note and email that they possess. You have to view each scrap of paper from the vantage point of the defense lawyer, namely, how will the defense lawyer try to use this? Nothing is too small or insignificant. If you don't take the time to review every note with the expert, the defense lawyer will exaggerate and try to mislead the jury.

Once you've reviewed every note, you need to get your expert ready to answer questions about them. Defuse the cross-examination by asking your expert about their notes during direct examination.

> *Question*: Why did you write a note asking whether you should look at the jury?

> *Answer*: It's been fifteen years since I last testified in court and I forgot where I am supposed to look when I testify.

Perfect answer? Perhaps not, but it is much better than letting the defense lawyer exaggerate and mislead the jurors about each note. For every note, have the expert quickly explain why it was written and eliminate the potential cross-examination material for the defense counsel.

#3: Do Your Homework about the Expert

Never assume your expert witness is a saint. Before trial, have your paralegal conduct an exhaustive research about the expert's prior trial testimony and ethical and disciplinary history. If there are any skeletons in your expert's closet, you need to know.

Don't forget to warn your expert that the defense lawyer will know everything about them.

- Are there any issues that tend to come up repeatedly during cross examination when you testify?

- Have you ever had any licensing or ethical issues?

- Is there anything that you think I should know about you?

If there is damaging information about your expert, you need to know before they testify (and hopefully in enough time to retain a different expert).

52

HOW TO SETTLE YOUR CASE FOR TOP DOLLAR

When it comes to mediation or negotiation, most plaintiffs' lawyers wing it. Most have no strategy and simply hope for the best. This is a recipe for failure.

Three Simple Rules for a Successful Mediation

Within moments of arriving at mediation, you can almost instantly know whether the defense is serious about settling the case. You walk into the mediator's office and sitting alone is the defense lawyer. You inquire where the adjuster is, and you're given the news that the adjuster will be available by phone during the mediation. When you hear that the adjuster will not be at the mediation, you might as well go home.

There are no hard and fast rules that can guarantee a settlement at mediation, but there are three rules that will give you the best chance of success.

Rule One: The Adjuster Must Be Physically Present at the Mediation

You should never agree to mediation unless the defense counsel stipulates *in writing* that the adjuster will be physically present at the mediation *with authority for the full policy limits of the insurance.* Even if the mediator does not require the presence of the senior adjuster at the mediation, you should make this a condition of the mediation.

If the defense is not willing to confirm in writing that the adjuster will be present at the mediation, there's a good bet that the defense is simply using mediation to learn more about your trial strategy and as an opportunity to discover your bottom line for settlement. You and your client are taking an entire day of your busy schedules for the mediation (including spending good money for the mediator's fees), and if the adjuster is not willing to do the same, they are not genuinely interested in settlement.

Rule Two: Insist upon the Presence of the Senior Adjuster

You must insist upon the physical presence of the adjuster who has authority for the highest limit of the insurance policy. You do not want a junior adjuster with limited authority at the mediation.

The senior adjuster will have authority to settle the case and will not have to make a phone call to get authority. With the senior adjuster, you're dealing with the decision-maker and not some junior-level adjuster who is having a fun day away from the office. Unless you insist upon the presence of the senior adjuster at the mediation, it's a safe bet that the senior adjuster will be "out of the office" and will not be accessible by phone during the mediation. This will guarantee an unproductive mediation.

You should insist that defendants' counsel sign a stipulation containing this condition prior to agreeing to mediation.

> All insurance carriers involved must have a representative physically present at the mediation who not only has authority to settle but also the ability to negotiate without a superior. This representative shall be the senior most representative who has participated in evaluating this case and who has the "final call" in negotiations.

> The personal appearance of this representative may not be waived except by the written consent of all counsel, and on the affirmance that the representative will be readily available by phone at all times during the mediation.

Rule Three: Money Talks, BS Walks

At mediation, there is always a point when the mediator or defense counsel will ask for your "real bottom line." You should *never* answer this question. The defense counsel or mediator can find out your bottom line only by doing one thing: offering cash.

When the defense lawyer asks for your bottom line, you simply respond that you will only respond to settlement offers and will not discuss the parameters of settlement without an actual offer. You might say to the defense counsel, "Make an offer, and you'll find out what our bottom line is."

If you make the mistake of telling the defense what your bottom line is, the defense will always tell you that your value for the case is unreasonable. Don't make the mistake of disclosing your bottom line to the defense lawyer or the mediator.

How to (Almost) Guarantee the Defense Is Serious About Settling at Mediation

You may want to consider demanding that the defense make an initial settlement offer prior to mediation as a good faith gesture. If the defense refuses or offers a piddling amount as an initial offer, you know they are not serious about settling the case at mediation—and there's a good chance you will be wasting your time.

The Best Way to Break a Deadlock at Mediation

The big day finally arrives for mediation in your biggest case. You have big dollar signs in your head as you wait anxiously in the mediator's conference room. After meeting privately with Mr. Defense Lawyer, the mediator returns to see you with a glum look on their face and shakes their head in frustration at the defendant's initial settlement offer. You're told that the defense lawyer's initial settlement offer is a pittance and that the chances of a settlement are low.

The mediator asks if you want to respond to the low settlement offer, or go home. Before you walk away from the mediation, there are proven methods for breaking a deadlock without compromising your settlement position.

Breaking the Ice with Bracketing

To get things moving at mediation, propose a bracket. A bracket is a proposal to simultaneously reduce the settlement demand in exchange for an increase in the offer.

Let's say your settlement demand is $1.8 million, the defendants' initial settlement offer is $100,000, and you want to settle the case for $850,000. You and Mr. Defense Lawyer are a world apart in the initial settlement demand and offer, and neither side wants to budge. You might propose a bracket of $600,000/$1.3 million (e.g., you will drop the settlement demand by $500,000 on the condition that the defense lawyer increases the settlement offer by $500,000).

It's virtually guaranteed that the defense lawyer will balk at your bracket and propose different terms. Let's say Mr. Defense Lawyer proposes a bracket of $400,000/$800,000. Okay, this bracket won't work for you, but you have a good idea that Mr. Defense Lawyer wants to settle for $600,000 (the middle of his bracket). You can make a counter proposal of $500,000/$1.2 million and keep working until you have an agreement on a bracket.

Bracketing works because it gives you insights into the price the defense lawyer is willing to pay without compromising your position. If you cannot agree upon a bracket, no problem—your settlement demand remains $1.8 million. There is no downside to bracketing as a method to get things moving at mediation.

Breaking the Deadlock with the "Mediator's Proposal"

If the defense lawyer won't agree to bracketing or his proposals are ridiculously low, don't walk away from the mediation table yet. The "mediator's proposal" is a settlement amount chosen by the mediator that is submitted to both sides for a "yes" or "no."

If one (or both) parties say "no" to the mediator's proposal, the mediator does not share either party's response with the other party. The mediator does not disclose the response of either party unless both agree on the amount, in which case they simply say, "We've got a settlement."

With a mediator's proposal, you do not reduce your settlement demand, and the defense has no greater insight into your bottom line. You either have a settlement or you don't.

When All Else Fails, Try This

Before you leave the mediation, propose that each party write their best offer on a scrap of paper, fold it up, and give it to the mediator in confidence. If the offers are within 10 percent of each other, you agree in advance to split the difference, and you have a settlement. If the offers are not within 10 percent of each other, the mediator shreds the scraps of paper and discloses nothing about the other side's offer.

If everything fails, you need to send a message. Slam your books on the table and walk out—there's still a good chance the defense lawyer will come rushing out to the elevator to get you.

It takes chutzpah to go to court, but defense lawyers know there are some plaintiffs' lawyers who go to court and others who settle everything. You are not a *settlement lawyer*—you are a trial lawyer, and going to court to gain justice is what you do.

53

MY LIFETIME OF FAILURE

After a string of defense verdicts, my new law firm's prospects were bleak. Our line of credit was maxed out (as well as my credit cards) and there were no "A" cases on the horizon for trial. Things could not have looked worse, but I was looking for some sign of encouragement at a meeting with our law firm's bookkeeper. When I asked, "Where do you think we'll be in twelve months?", our bookkeeper's response was brutally honest, *"I think you'll be in bankruptcy."*

Hard to believe this could be true, but I knew this was not an unrealistic assessment of our young law firm's prospects. I did what I had to do to survive: I went without income for nine months (and sometimes had no money for lunch) and fought to survive. And, eventually, our law firm's prospects began to change.

Building a Higher Degree of Intimacy

This was not the first time I had faced failure. Just to give you a sample:

- As a young lawyer, I was fired from my first job after only three weeks.

- The senior partners of my former law firm laughed when I told them of my plan to write a book about law firm marketing and management (*The Power of a System*).

- I was labeled as incompetent by the senior partners of my former law firm over the way that I had handled a train-wreck trial.

- I was fired from a job that I loved at a prominent plaintiffs' law firm, after almost fourteen years.

- A family member told me that it would be a waste of time for my wife to run for Supreme Court Justice against long odds.

By sharing your fears, faults, and failures, you build a higher degree of intimacy with your coworkers, friends, jurors, and the fans of your blog. Sharing your failures goes way beyond the common pleasantries exchanged by strangers (e.g., sports and weather), and builds a relationship based upon trust.

Why not begin by doing this with your star paralegal? When your paralegal makes a mistake, tell them that you've done worse and share the details of your mistakes. Your paralegal will know that you're not judging them and with some luck, your relationship might get a little stronger.

* * *

Final Thoughts

When my father was dying, he confided in me that he had no regrets about his life with one exception: he wished he had spent more time with his family. With all of your successful settlements and verdicts, remember there is nothing more important than your spouse and kids. Make them the center of your life and you will be rich.

Thank you, Dad, for the reminder that there is much more to life than the practice of law.

"On the day I die a lot will happen.

A lot will change.

The world will be busy.

On the day I die, all the important appointments I made will be left unattended.

The many plans I had yet to complete will remain forever undone.

The calendar that ruled so many of my days will now be irrelevant to me.

All the material things I so chased and guarded and treasured will be left in the hands of others to care for or to discard.

The words of my critics which so burdened me will cease to sting or capture anyone. They will be unable to touch me.

The arguments I believed I'd won here will not serve me or bring me any satisfaction or solace.

All my noisy incoming notifications and texts and calls will go unanswered. Their great urgency will be quieted.

My many nagging regrets will be resigned to the past, where they should have always been anyway.

Every superficial worry about my body that I ever labored over, about my waistline or hairline or frown lines, will fade away.

My carefully crafted image, the one I worked so hard to shape for others here, will be left to them to complete anyway.

The sterling reputation I once struggled so greatly to maintain will be of little concern for me anymore.

All the small and large anxieties that stole sleep from me each night will be rendered powerless.

The deep and towering mysteries about life and death that so consumed my mind will finally be clarified in a way that they could never be before while I lived.

These things will certainly all be true on the day that I die.

Yet for as much as will happen on that day, one more thing that will happen.

On the day I die, the few people who really know and truly love me will grieve deeply.

They will feel a void.

They will feel cheated.

They will not feel ready.

They will feel as though a part of them has died as well.

And on that day, more than anything in the world they will want more time with me."

—John Pavlovitz, "On the Day I Die"

Conclusion

ACTION IS EVERYTHING

Simply reading this book shows that you are a motivated lawyer who wants a bigger and better life. Reading this book places you in the small percentage of lawyers who put an emphasis on learning and developing their marketing and management skills.

WARNING! Reading this book, without action, will accomplish nothing. Take one or two action items, put them in play, and gradually keep implementing more. You will eventually begin noticing the improvements in your law practice, and in a year, you will be on your way to building the law firm of your dreams.

Immerse Yourself in Knowledge

Read constantly and invest in yourself with seminars and workshops outside of the legal profession. Find others who are doing things bigger and better than you, and absorb their advice.

> *"Life is a learning opportunity and lessons are constantly being taught all around us."*
> —John Wooden, *A Game Plan for Life*

Pick up a self-improvement book and read ten pages every day. Your life will change.

Make the Super Successful Your Mentors

Building the law firm of your dreams is not something that you should do alone. Leveraging the successes and failures of other lawyers is the most important thing you can do—don't make the same mistakes that I've made.

You should put together a mastermind group of the best lawyers in your region. If you don't want to create your own mastermind group, try the Mastermind Experience (www.MastermindExperience.com).

> *"If you are the most successful person in the room, you are in the wrong room."*
>
> —Grant Cardone, *Be Obsessed or Be Average*

Create Your Legacy

What do you want to be remembered for? Write down what you want to accomplish in your life—your "Life Manifesto." You won't achieve your dreams unless you know what they are. Where do you want to be in five to ten years?

> *"Give yourself permission to throw yourself all in on your dreams."*
>
> —Grant Cardone, *Be Obsessed or Be Average*

Create a legacy that will outlast your time on earth. Dream big. Don't live by the limitations imposed by others.

Let Me Know How You're Doing

I want to hear about your success. Call my office (845-802-0047) to schedule a time to chat—I'd love to play a small role in helping you build the law firm of your dreams. If you need a speaker for one of your events, let's talk. I love public speaking and will be happy to help you and your organization. Just give me a call or an email (jfisher@fishermalpracticelaw.com).

Dare To Be Bold

When your back is against the wall and you've got nowhere to go, think of these words by Theodore Roosevelt and keep fighting.

"It is not the critic who counts;

not the man who points out how the strong man stumbles,

or where the doer of deeds could have done them better.

The credit belongs to the man who is actually in the arena,

whose face is marred by dust and sweat and blood;

who strives valiantly; who errs, who comes short again and again,

because there is no effort without error and shortcoming;

but who does actually strive to do the deeds;

who knows great enthusiasms, the great devotions;

who spends himself in a worthy cause;

who at the best knows in the end the triumph of high achievement,

and who at the worst, if he fails,

at least fails while daring greatly,

so that his place shall never be with those cold and timid souls

who neither know victory or defeat."

—Theodore Roosevelt, "*The Man in the Arena*"

Special Gifts for You

I put my best advice for marketing and management in my weekly email newsletter. Subscribe at www.UltimateInjuryLaw.com.

If you want my monthly print newsletter, *Lawyer Alert*, send an email to jfisher@fishermalpracticelaw.com, and I will be happy to add you to the mailing list. This is my small gift to you for reading this book.

If you have not read my first book, *The Power of a System*, send me an email (jfisher@fishermalpracticelaw.com), and I will be happy to send you a copy.

If you'd like a copy of my best legal forms for lawyers, send me an email (jfisher@fishermalpracticelaw.com) and I will send you a link to our forms.

A Small Favor to Ask

Thank you for reading.

If you enjoyed this book, I will be grateful if you'd post a review on Amazon. Your support really does make a difference and I read all the reviews personally so I can receive your feedback and make this book better.

When you have a spare moment to leave a review, go to TheLawFirmofYour Dreams.com and you will be sent to the Amazon review page for this book. Just click the tab, "Write a customer review" and write the review.

Thank you for your support.

Acknowledgments

At the beginning of our firm's "Daily Huddle," each member of our law firm recites a "Positive Focus"—a statement of one thing in their personal or professional lives for which they are grateful. This book would not be complete without a Positive Focus.

My Wife, Lisa

Even in my darkest hours when I had my doubts about opening my own firm, my wife, Lisa, has been a rock of reassurance. I would not be here without Lisa. Thank you, Lisa, for believing in me.

My Dad, James H. Fisher, Esq.

A special thanks to my Dad, James H. Fisher, Esq., for teaching me a crucial lesson: hard work beats talent. Whenever I doubt my ability as a trial lawyer, I think of this lesson, work harder, and most of the time things work out fine. Thanks, Dad, for teaching me the value of hard work. I love you and think of you every day.

Seth Price, Esq.

For making the Mastermind Experience what it is today. Your generosity and commitment to excellence are unmatched. Our tribe is grateful.

Our Tribe at the Mastermind Experience

You know who you are. I would not be who I am without your continual challenges, encouragement and friendship. Thank you for taking a chance with us.

My Final Positive Focus for You

This Positive Focus would not be complete without thanking you for reading this book. Owning and operating your own firm is hard, but at the end of the day, you are the master of your destiny and for most of us, we wouldn't have it any other way. Thank you for taking this journey with me.

About John

John Fisher is the owner and founder of John H. Fisher, PC, where he limits his practice to catastrophic injury law for injury victims.

First and foremost, John is an entrepreneur. John was selected as the National Marketer of the Year by Great Legal Marketing in 2013 and has been called a "master of referral marketing" by Ben Glass, Esq. John is AV-rated by Martindale-Hubbell, has a perfect 10/10 ranking on www.Avvo.com, and is a graduate of the University of Notre Dame and Notre Dame Law School.

John is the author of the best-selling book *The Power of a System*—the first of its kind book with explicit "how-to" steps for the technical, managerial, and entrepreneurial implementation of a multi-million-dollar personal injury law firm.

John has been cited as a legal expert on numerous occasions by *Trial* magazine of the American Association for Justice and by the *New York Law Journal,* and he speaks frequently for the New York State Bar Association, The National Trial Lawyers, PILMMA, Great Legal Marketing, and county and regional bar associations concerning law practice management, internet marketing for lawyers, referral-based marketing, and trial skills.

John believes in sharing and collaborating with other top plaintiffs' lawyers and hanging out with lawyers who are doing things better, bigger, and faster. John is the founder of the Mastermind

Experience (www.MastermindExperience.com), a unique mastermind group where elite lawyers collaborate and share their best practices and challenge each other to take action and create a law practice that serves their ideal lifestyle.

John lives in Ravena, New York, with his wife, Hon. Lisa M. Fisher, three children, Tim, Alek, and Lily, and their fourth "child," Patch (a miniature Australian Labradoodle). John loves Notre Dame and the Chicago Bears, and whenever he can, he enjoys slalom and barefoot waterskiing.

Appendix

OUR RECOMMENDED READING LIST

These books have the power to change your life.

Books About the Power of a Growth Mind-Set

Mindset: The New Psychology of Success, by Carol S. Dweck, PhD

The 7 Habits of Highly Effective People, by Stephen R. Covey

How to Win Friends and Influence People, by Dale Carnegie

How to Stop Worrying and Start Living, by Dale Carnegie

Be Obsessed or Be Average, by Grant Cardone

The ONE Thing, by Gary Keller and Jay Papasan

The Slight Edge, by Jeff Olson

The Go-Giver, by Bob Burg and John David Mann

Never Eat Alone, by Keith Ferrazzi

Feel the Fear and Do It Anyway, by Susan Jeffers, PhD

The 10X Rule, by Grant Cardone

Made to Stick, by Chip Heath and Dan Heath

Switch, by Chip Heath and Dan Heath

The Magic of Thinking Big, by David J. Schwartz, PhD

Secrets of the Millionaire Mind, by T. Harv Eker

Give and Take, by Adam Grant

Drive, by Daniel H. Pink

Take the Stairs, Rory Vaden

The Millionaire Next Door, by Thomas J. Stanley, PhD, and William D. Danko, PhD

Start with Why, by Simon Sinek

Grit, by Angela Duckworth

Books About Time Management

Essentialism, by Greg McKeown

Multipliers, by Liz Wiseman

The 4-Hour Work Week, by Timothy Ferriss

No B.S. Time Management for Entrepreneurs, by Dan Kennedy

Books About Leadership

Shoe Dog, by Phil Knight

Tribal Leadership, by Dave Logan, John King, and Halee Fischer-Wright

Leaders Eat Last, by Simon Sinek

EntreLeadership, by Dave Ramsey

No B.S. Ruthless Management of People and Profits, by Dan Kennedy

A Game Plan for Life, by John Wooden and Don Yaeger

Wooden on Leadership, by John Wooden and Steve Jamison

Wooden, by John Wooden and Steve Jamison

The Four Obsessions of an Extraordinary Executive, by Patrick Lencioni

People Over Profit, by Dale Partridge

Books About Client Communication/Happiness

Delivering Happiness, by Tony Hsieh

Zombie Loyalists, by Peter Shankman

Fish! A Remarkable Way to Boost Morale and Improve Results, by Stephen C. Lundin, PhD, Harry Paul, and John Christensen

The Fred Factor, by Mark Sanborn

Books About Managing for Success

Traction, by Gino Wickman

The 12 Week Year, by Brian P. Moran and Michael Lennington

Mastering the Rockefeller Habits, by Verne Harnish

Profit First, by Mike Michalowicz

Principles, by Ray Dalio

The E-Myth Revisited, by Michael E. Gerber

Good to Great, by Jim Collins

Great by Choice, by Jim Collins and Morten Hansen

Built to Last, by Jim Collins and Jerry I. Porras

Getting Naked, by Patrick Lencioni

The Five Dysfunctions of a Team, by Patrick Lencioni

Death by Meeting, by Patrick Lencioni

The Four Agreements, by Don Miguel Ruiz

Tiger Tactics, by Jay Ruane, Esq., Ryan McKeen, Esq., William "the Law Man" Umansky, Esq.

The Ultimate Guide to Social Media for Business Owners, Professionals, and Entrepreneurs, by Mitch Jackson, Esq.